the SEX course

Trina E. Read
Author of Till Sex Do Us Part

Praise

The Sex Course

"As a long-time supporter of women's sexual pleasure, I look forward to diving into The Sex Course." Cynthia Loyst, TV Host on The Social and author of Find Your Pleasure

Praise for *Till Sex Do Us Part: Make Your Married Sex Irresistible*

A must-read for couples who want to kick start a lacklustre sex life. Dr. Trina's book shows why your sex and intimacy went flat, how to get it back on track, plus what to do to make sex fabulous.
   Marian Keyes, International best-selling author

Who knew sex was so much more than having an orgasm? Or that focusing on having sex once a week could be the reason why women aren't interested. Dr. Trina's intelligent book puts a new spin on an old couple's conundrum.
   Fanny Kiefer—Studio 4 with Fanny Kiefer

Dr. Trina's book has put the yummy back into being a mummy. It has playful ideas, tips and tricks to give married sex back its mojo.
> Erica Ehm, Founder YummyMummyClub.ca

Finally, a down-to-earth, entertaining book that shows busy women how to feel sexy again!
Wendy Sandwith, Host Breakfast Television Edmonton

Dr Trina knows a lot more about sex than I do. Which may not be saying much – but it sure made reading the book illuminating. Till Sex Do Us Part is a great guide for anyone who wants to kick start a lagging sex life.
> Dave Kelly, Host Breakfast Television Calgary

Even single gal needs to learn the pitfalls of sex before she gets into a relationship. Read this book and never get stuck in a sex rut.
Jennifer Parks, Sex Columnist for the Edmonton Journal

A must-read for newlyweds to couples married for over 50 years. This book gives a great perspective on why the sexual dynamics erode and how couples can stay connected over the long term.

  Steve Cooper, CEO of Hitched Magazine

Copyright © 2024 by Trina E. Read

The moral right of the author has been asserted. All rights reserved.

This is a work of fiction. Names, characters, places, and incidents are either the product of the author's imagination or are used fictitiously, and any resemblance to actual persons, living or dead, or to actual events or locales is entirely coincidental.

No portion of this book may be reproduced in any form without written permission from the publisher or author except as permitted by Canadian copyright law.

ISBN: 978-0-97-817957-1

SENSUAL TASTES PUBLISHING
Canada

Sensual Tastes Publishing is a subsidiary of Sensual Tastes Events located in Calgary, Alberta, Canada.

Cover design: Kleera Tullo

For Dennis, Andrew & Evan
You are my everything

The Sex Course is … Jumpy

Thank you, dear reader, for picking up *The Sex Course*.

I sincerely hope you enjoy this story and gain sexual self-esteem and sensual wisdom.

Here's the thing: this was my first attempt at writing a fiction book. Rest assured, I spent thousands of hours and paid four professional editors a lot of money to whip this manuscript into shape.

Ultimately, it reads like a first attempt.

> I believe one reason is: *The Sex Course* jumps back and forth between present and past events.

I didn't have the writing chops to smooth out those jumpy segues. Despite this, the sex ed is legit, and the story arcs are interesting and thought provoking.

Thanks so much for understanding, supporting me, and lifting up women's sexuality.

It makes a huge difference when you share your feedback and leave a review on Amazon or Goodreads.

Happy sex, Dr. Trina Read, Sexologist

Isabella's Assignment

January 4

I CAN'T GET FIRED.

"Jessica, can you hold for one moment?" Isabella's sweaty fingers fumbled to push the mute button, her editor's irritated tsk barely audible in the chaos.

"Mommy! Want down!" Her daughter Rosa's flailing, chubby little arms yanked Isabella's earbud out.

Isabella cupped the sore ear and went down on one knee to put the girl on the floor. Rosa playfully bounced, and her head connected squarely with Isabella's round jaw. Her almond-brown eyes watered, and her tongue throbbed as the adrenaline pumped in her veins, helping her regain a modicum of control.

You need to try a new tactic.

"Mommy has an important phone call. If you go to your room, I'll give you chocolate ice cream." The mom guilt, ever hovering, reared its ugly head. She was bribing her child—again—after promising herself she would never be one of *those* moms.

"Noooo!" Rosa's adorable little face was resolute.

Why does this always happen?!

Isabella inhaled a deep breath, wishing a parenting manual on juggling a bored, demanding two-year-old and a professional career from a home office crammed into a dining room corner would magically appear in her hands. But, of course, it didn't because that was too easy. This was why mommies drank mommy juice. She looked around "her office," a playroom strewn with toys because she didn't have time to tidy.

"Okay, honey, what do you want?"

Rosa pointed her little toddler finger at Mr. Wigglebottom. The bright-yellow stuffed bunny was in a time-out because Rosa fought with her four-year-old brother, Marcus, who was now at playschool. Isabella grabbed the toy and maneuvered it and Rosa into the upstairs bedroom, then closed the door.

Pressing unmute, she said, "Sorry, Jessica," while silently gulping air to calm herself. What she heard on the other end was Top 40 Muzak. Jessica must have put Isabella on hold, but the clock was clicking down.

I have two minutes before Rosa escapes. Isabella hustled back to her office, putting her pitch together on the fly.

"Isabella?" Jessica's clipped voice was back on the line.

"Hi, Jess —"

"Where were we?" Jessica interrupted, letting out an audible sigh.

"My pitch. So I, uh, I want to do a piece on whether women's sexuality has changed for the millennials and Gen-Zers." The silence was not good, but she pressed forward. "A revealing exposé into how women's sexuality has changed since the 1970s. Give *Femme* magazine readers a timeline to track women's sexual emancipation."

Isabella heard Rosa's door open. *Just stay calm.*

"It's lukewarm." Control-freak Jessica was an excellent editor but also exacting and dismissive. "I want it to be fresh. A contrarian viewpoint of young cis females' sexuality. How this generation of women is stepping into their sexual power."

Isabella knew better than to ask Jessica, the perpetual mommy-shamer, what her idea of fresh meant. Asking questions infuriated Jessica. For the umpteenth time, she'd complain about how Isabella was a part-time, remote employee with a full-time family.

"Look, Isabella, get your head in the game. *Femme* readers want juicy how-tos, not history lessons. I'll approve this, but I expect a wow with your next pitch."

"Okay, thanks, Jessica —"

But Jessica hung up before Isabella said goodbye. Steeling herself, she took another deep breath and dialed.

"Hi, sweetie! What do you need?" Her husband, Alex, answered on the second ring.

"Hey, Alex —"

"Daddy, Daddy, Daddy!" Rosa's big, almond-brown eyes popped up behind the stained cushiony chair as she strained for Isabella's cell.

"No, it's Mommy's turn to talk to Daddy." Isabella darted into the kitchen to get some privacy. "I spoke with Jessica, and she accepted my pitch. I'll need you to look after the kids for a few nights this week."

"Sorry, honey. I found out this morning that I have to fly to Toronto."

Again?!

"You know I'm up for a promotion."

"I have a deadline." She closed her eyes, careful to keep her temper in check.

Fighting will complicate things, and we already know the ending to this worn-out discussion: You make more money, and I have all the time in the world to get my work done.

"Hey, we just have to make it through this patch of me working so much." A common refrain for at least three years.

"That doesn't help me right now." Isabella hated the whine in her voice. She wasn't a whiner. She was the one who worked her way up at *Femme* from admin assistant to sex columnist.

How am I going to do this? She put her elbows on the counter to prop up her aching head. *I'll do what I've always done: work late into the evening.*

"Why don't you call my mom or your sister?" He said, as he did every time, believing he was a hero and taking full credit for providing her with the obvious solution.

"I ask them to babysit way too much."

"They don't mind. Listen, I can't talk. Up to my eyeballs. Love you, bye."

"But —" It was the second hang-up silencing her, interrupted by a loud wail.

"Daaaaaaddddy," Rosa sobbed.

Frustrated tears filled Isabella's eyes. As soon as the kids opened their eyes, there was never a moment's peace. Even when they were asleep, she had no peace. Guilt constantly reminded her she was a terrible mother, bribing her kids with way too much screen time. And a horrible employee, only giving half her attention to work. No matter her choice, she felt guilt, especially when she didn't stretch herself too thin.

"Mommy, ice cream," Rosa hiccupped through her sobs.

"You wanted Mr. Wigglebottom, sweetie. It's time for your nap." Isabella's gut clenched, hearing Rosa suck in a breath, winding herself up.

Isabella picked up the tired girl and hugged her as they went to Rosa's bedroom, through the kitchen and the office-turned-playroom, avoiding dolls and balls. She tucked her precious little girl into bed with her soft pink-knit blanket. Closing the bedroom door, Isabella's tired shoulders sagged with the weight of a solid eight hours left in her day and coming up with the next wow pitch.

Claire's Flowers

January 15

CLAIRE SMELLED THE FLOWERS before they walked into the room. The three-foot-tall exotic bouquet marched into her small, urban office and forcefully plunked itself on the edge of her modern sit-to-stand desk.

"You understand people in this office have allergies?" Shauna's sharp face looked through the cascade of large white flowers and greenery. Claire's mind tugged her back into the legal briefs, knowing this was a waste of a conversation. "You'll have to keep your door shut," Shauna announced, hitting her stride as the self-appointed office sheriff.

Giving up, Claire's weary eyes traveled up Shauna's short legs to her pale-as-Dracula face. "Shauna, you know the partners don't like our doors closed when we're not with clients." Claire put on her well-rehearsed, tight, neutral smile while picturing Shauna as a petulant five-year-old on the cusp of a tantrum.

"That's your problem." Shauna walked out, closing Claire's door with a flourish.

Great. Shauna was going straight to the people living with allergies. Claire knew she should act before the flower gate got out of hand, but standing up to Shauna promised at least two weeks of hell. Claire reached for her water bottle, took a long drink, closed her hazel-green eyes, and rolled her long, stiff neck. Her slender shoulders were so tense she could bounce a quarter off them.

Screw it. Claire was too busy to get bogged down in female office politics, but that meant looking at the flowers.

Claire reluctantly rose to admire the bouquet, an exquisite arrangement of trumpet lilies and gardenias. She buried her face in the bouquet and breathed deeply to let its heavy scent envelop her. Nothing. She took a step back to appreciate its beauty fully and willed herself to love the grand romantic gestures. Nothing again. What was wrong with her? But pragmatic Claire wasn't the swooning type, and flowers were never her thing. The over-the-top flowers for every occasion were getting old, and it felt like a cop-out that Carlos had the florist on speed dial.

Boom, right there. This was why she had her "problem." She yanked the little card from the bamboo card stem, determined to appreciate lovely gifts from an attentive boyfriend.

"Happy first anniversary. I'm super excited about your surprise!" The shopkeeper's loopy handwriting had underlined "super" twice.

And there it was: the unpleasant reminder. Claire had kept herself busy to forget about her "surprise," the so-called *Project Up My Sex Game* she and Amy had come up with. Imagining herself in sky-high stilettos with a cropped leather whip caused her stomach to churn. She took a Tums from her desk drawer and slowly chewed it.

Claire mentioned to Amy that their *Project Up My Sex Game* plan, concocted amid laughter and too many beers, was way out of her comfort zone. That, according to a tipsy Amy, was the point. Fortified by the beers, Amy's sexual confidence, and an unyielding determination to change her circumstances, Claire assured herself that the time frame would be enough to buck up her courage. But she was wrong. So very wrong. Carlos had big expectations for tonight, and she was in over her head. She wanted to bail, to tell Carlos she was suddenly sick, and gauging by the state of her churning stomach, it wasn't a complete lie.

She picked up her cell from her perfectly ordered desk and texted Amy.

> Can't do it. Going 2 bail.

Amy sent a text right back.

> Pre-date jitters. It's like riding a bike. After u start u'll be fine.

Claire doubted that, but reminded herself that the only way to see new results is to do things differently. She looked down to see her foot tapping and needed to get on top of this.

She snapped a "surprised" selfie with the bouquet. After inspecting the pic, grateful that her perfect, ash-blond, asymmetrical bobbed hair, ethereal good looks, and the morning light meant she didn't have to do any photo editing, she captioned: *Look what I got! Carlos is taking me to Karma for our first anniversary.* #Grateful #LuckyToHaveHim. She was about to post on Instagram when she remembered to tag Carlos.

She thought about sending Carlos a suggestive message, but she had no idea what to say and no time to think of something clever and flirty. She wanted—no, scratch that—needed to get it right this time. Her mind raced, checking off, for the umpteenth time, that night's *Project Up My Sex Game* checklist. She put her cell phone back on the desk.

A pungent whiff of lilies drew her attention to the huge arrangement, and she asked herself, for the millionth time, what Carlos saw in her. The answer was simple: opposites attract. She was cool and calm to his fiery Latin-ness. The stabilizer in his over-the-top shows of affection. They were an excellent match, and she loved him very much, so she was willing to bend herself into a pretzel to make him happy. If their relationship was to go anywhere, she had to do whatever it took for that night to work. He deserved it.

Her cell vibrated. It was Carlos, wouldn't you know? She wanted to thank him, but the legal brief was due, and she couldn't concentrate with a rolling stomach. Deliberately ignoring his call, Claire opted to focus on her work and not think about *Project Up My Sex Game*.

Somehow, Claire needed to find the courage to get through tonight.

Amy Gets a Phone Call

January 13

SOME PART, ANY PART, of Amy's body struggled to get her attention. In her stifling, cramped office, she sat for too long, hunched over with a stiff neck, grading papers. Her nose finally got through, picking up a funky smell and pulling her out of a deep focus. Sniffing the air, she turned her bright blue hair closer to her armpit.

"Ew!" She flapped her arms like a flightless, sweaty bird, blowing at her damp underarms. The beads of sweat ran down her back onto her multicolored kaftan, making it stick to her body. Annoyed, she opened her messy top desk drawer: a few chocolate bar wrappers, scattered stationery supplies, and something that smelled moldy she needed to deal with one day. There was not a tissue or napkin in sight.

Stomping a seed of frustration, she reminded herself how lucky she was and how she'd vowed never to complain. When the administration had anointed her as assistant professor of women's studies and handed over the key, it had been a hard-won victory, won with her blood, sweat, and tears. Someone would always nip at her heels for this tiny, hot, stuffy office.

As she rolled her neck and shoulders to relieve the tension, her stomach, which had not eaten since breakfast, protested with a gurgle. Standing up after hours in her ancient torture device, the university called a chair, her head swam, and her joints popped and cracked.

There was enough space between the desk and the side wall for sun salutations. Her petite figure hunched forward, and her protruding stomach made a rude, protesting noise. She needed to grade the remaining papers before the next day, but couldn't do it on an empty stomach. Amy threw her favorite bag—a colorful satchel spun by the hands of Peruvian women—over her shoulder and headed for the cafeteria.

Keeping her arms aloft to dry the sweat, Amy looked like a brilliantly feathered bird against the sterile hallways on her way to the corporate-issue, bland cafeteria. She passed a loud group debating the latest government scandal. "You can't accept that —" Listening to them so riotously indignant, there was a sharp sense of pride in the freedom of university debate. Then, a plastic cafeteria chair crashed as a passionate debater jumped up, thrusting her finger to make her case.

Amy grinned. That's how she and Claire must have looked—what was it—ten years ago already? On the first day of Women's Studies 201, they took one look at each other and instantly disliked one another. Intensely. Claire thought Amy was a flake; Amy thought Claire was a wound-too-tight capitalist. They were both a little right. Fierce debaters, they went toe to toe in many classes, simultaneously infuriated yet with grudging respect for the other's moxie and intelligence. And yes, a few crashing chairs between them.

A year after university, they bumped into each other, volunteering at a local soup kitchen. Somehow, they kept ending up on the same shifts, and eventually, they found themselves hanging out afterward. They'd both mellowed after university and could cringe and chuckle at their passionate save-the-world youth. The soup kitchen became their once-a-week meetup. Claire was Amy's longest-lasting grown-up relationship, and although she would never understand their chemistry, they had it in spades.

Amy grabbed the most semi-healthy food in the cafeteria when a gender-neutral colleague wearing androgynous clothes and a blunt haircut sidled up to her.

"Hey, Amy. Did you hear Dr. Gwen Saunders is coming?"

"What! Gwen Saunders! She's coming here?"

"She's here for a year. The faculty debate was lively," they chuckled. "Admin wants her to open the class up to anyone, but she will only teach cis females. Truthfully, I'm surprised the faculty agreed. Obviously, I won't be going, but if you're not busy, you should audit her class. I'm told there's full nudity."

Amy followed Dr. Saunders on social media, a controversial figure who'd gotten bad press because of her approach to sexuality. Dr. Saunders didn't abide by standard academic rules, and Amy saw it as an opportunity to shake up the uptight university.

Her cell vibrated in her bag just as a couple of young, adoring students waved at her from the other side of the cafeteria.

"Hey, Dr. Tam," they giggled as if she were a pop star. She freaking loved her job and was good at it. The hot, stuffy office would not break her.

Scrambling to find her cell in the messy bag, she pulled it out and glanced at the caller ID: Paul Phillips. Paul Phillips? She'd bumped into him working at a political rally the previous week. He must be looking for a donation.

She tried hitting the end button, but hit answer instead. "Hello?"

"Oh, uh, hi. Is this Amy? It's Paul. From the rally. Do you remember me?" His voice was unnaturally high.

"Hey Paul, I'm pretty busy."

"Okay. Well, I won't keep you. I have a quick question."

"Paul, I'll stop you there. I'm not interested." Amy supported the political cause but had to be careful with her money.

"What? That was blunt ..." He trailed off, his voice wounded.

"I'm sorry. Look, I'm tapped out financially. I recently bought a townhouse and did a kitchen renovation."

"No worries. I can pay."

"That's nice of you. But why would you pay? Are you that desperate?"

"I don't date often. It's fine. I understand if you're not interested. Sorry to take up—"

"Wait! Did you say date?" Amy's head spun. "I thought you were looking for a political donation."

"No," he laughed a little too loudly. "I called to see if you wanted to have dinner tomorrow."

"Dinner?!" There was a long pause as Amy's brain scrambled to recalibrate. Paul was smart, nice, cute, and had a good job. The perfect guy and way out of her league. So what was the catch?

The mild panic rising in Amy's chest eased as Claire's stern lawyer voice swooped in, talking Amy down from the ledge. In her practical, Claire way, she said that Paul was a fresh start, a perfect opportunity for Amy to move forward and stop the questionable dating.

Paul cleared his throat discreetly, bringing Amy out of her musing. Still, she didn't have an answer, and the uncomfortable silence stretched out. Claire's impatient voice interrupted again, acknowledging Amy's fear but urging her to leap.

Just do it.

"Yes! Sure." Pushing the dread aside, Amy attempted to sound enthusiastic. "That sounds good."

"Oh! Great." He exhaled anxiously. "Your choice. Where would you like to go?"

"Well, there's an authentic little Thai place I love. I'll text you the name." Amy's fingers sent the text robotically.

"Great! Got it. Oh, that is great! Does seven work? Can I pick you up?"

"Seven is perfect. I'll meet you there. So I'll see you then?" Paul agreed, and they disconnected.

Amy stood in the cafeteria, stunned, saying aloud to no one, "What happened?"

She wanted to tell Claire, even with a quick text, but couldn't because of Claire's stupid dating ultimatum.

Jeanette Chats with Pierre

January 16

"Mom, your face isn't on the screen. Move your phone to the left," Pierre explained patiently in French—or as patient as any Gen-Zer instructing their parent on new technology can be. Jeanette knew perfectly well how to use FaceTime, but she didn't like how her aging face looked in the little window on her screen.

Over a year ago, Jeanette's older son, Pierre, had moved into his first apartment, paying for it with his first grown-up job. He was always busy, and his calls were infrequent. So when she saw his name on her caller ID, she automatically answered, even though she was without makeup, with messy hair, and wearing casual clothes.

She shifted her gaze from herself to Pierre's attractive face, with his captivating blue eyes and abundant curly auburn hair. She saw his frustration and fatigue, enough perhaps to hang up. Her ever-present loneliness loomed heavy, and she was desperate to keep him on the line.

"Tell me again what to do," she said, relenting. Her Quebecois French still perfect after years of speaking English. Pierre explained, and her long, slender arm moved upward so the phone looked down on her freshly scrubbed face. Ignoring the dark circles under her eyes, Jeanette settled into her favorite soft, pillowed armchair with a cup of herbal tea and her Jack Russell terrier, Max.

"Okay, tell me how your job is going." She was eager to have a much-needed talk with her firstborn. She missed him very much.

Pierre sucked in his breath through his teeth, a nervous tell. She took a long sip of tea, then another. It was her turn to wait patiently, as he didn't like being pushed into talking.

"So, I met someone."

Jeanette wrapped her hand tight around the hot teacup and kept her face neutral. This child won the gene pool jackpot, getting the best of Jeanette and Andre's good looks, smarts, and charisma. They had given him the best of everything, and he led a charmed life with many friends, fun adventures, and a great job. He was only twenty-five years old—a kid. He was much too young to settle down with a serious girlfriend, and she would not tolerate him making the same mistake as her.

Keeping her voice composed, Jeanette asked, "Does she have a name?"

"How do you know it's a she?" Pierre kept a straight face for a moment before bursting out laughing at Jeanette's ashen face. "Kidding." And gave her the briefest description of Amber.

Who names their child Amber?

"Is she Christian?" It needed to be asked. Jeanette held her breath at the disappointed look on his face.

"Mom, I've already told you not to ask that anymore. It's not okay. But, ya, she's Christian." Then he casually threw in, "You might know her parents."

Were they a family from her church? She wondered, but asked the more pressing question.

"When can your dad and I meet her?" She bristled with a bright flash of anger at the thought of her husband, Andre. He was MIA again, although she knew where he was. He would be back soon enough. Jeanette pushed the anger into the pit where 28 years of unresolved fighting lived.

Ignoring her question, he said, "The reason for my call, Mommy—" He only called her Mommy when he wanted something big. She narrowed her eyes, and he giggled. They both knew he was working her, and she needed to set better boundaries. But her boys were the chink in her thick armor, the only people she ever exposed her soft underbelly to. She would live and die for them, so naturally she listened to what he wanted, happy to do whatever he asked.

"Can you set up a nice date night for me? I want it to be special, but I don't know how, and you're so good at it." He was persuasive, like Andre. Her body cringed, and she locked the anger down tight again.

"I need more details." She was about to ask why he wanted a special date night when he cut her off.

"Mom, my buddies are here, and we're off to the hockey game. So I'll text you the details, okay?" He nodded to his friends to let them know he was wrapping up the call. "I love you so much! Thanks for doing this. Oh, it's for next Friday. Bye, I love you." Like when he was young, he sang the last part, and Jeanette's heart melted. Her cell screen went black, and he was gone.

She looked around the superbly decorated room and drew Max closer; his warm little body was her only comfort these days. As ticked off as she was, at least she had something to occupy her long days.

She had done an excellent job raising her two boys, Pierre and Jacques. They were happy, healthy, and completely independent. As thrilled as she was to watch them make their way in the world, it was still a tough transition from being a full-time mom, involved in their many activities, to absolutely nothing.

She looked at her watch to ensure she had enough time before her next gym class. Then, she grabbed her tablet from the side table and opened Facebook to search for Amber and her parents.

Claire

Class One, February 10

Late again!?

Her last nerve frazzled, Claire drove around the unnecessarily complicated university campus and cursed like a sailor as someone nabbed the parking spot she'd been angling for. On her third go-around, Claire rammed her accelerator and slid into a tiny spot, almost hitting the car beside her.

Her cell rang, and, no surprise, it was work. She wanted to ignore the ongoing work drama, but had to take the call.

"Look, the research needs to be done tonight. The client changed the deadline," she explained to the student-at-law while squeezing out of her car.

Claire received fifteen texts during the drive and regretted leaving the new intern with such an enormous responsibility. "No. I can't come in tonight. I gave you detailed instructions and walked you through it step by step. Sorry, but I'm turning off my phone."

Disconnecting, the low throb of a tension headache started as she remembered how Amy had begged her to try one class. In a rare moment of weakness, right after the *Project Up My Sex Game* disaster, Claire reluctantly agreed. She was now lost, trying to find the classroom and seriously questioning whether this was worth the hassle.

Looking for any excuse never to return, she found it the instant she barged into the classroom. The lecture room was hot, sparsely populated, and smelled like damp feet.

"Women love sex. But the way we're having sex is broken. As such, the majority of women in long-term relationships grow bored with a framework that sets her up for failure, and she loses interest —"

Every female head snapped in Claire's direction, including the professor, who filled the room with her dominating presence.

Nope, not worth it. Claire was about to turn and do a runner when the professor addressed her.

"Thank you for joining us, Ms."

Claire's pale cheeks flushed crimson, and her throat instantly dried, but she managed, "Claire. My name is Claire, Claire Skalmar."

"Well, Claire, Claire Skalmar." The tall, substantial African-Canadian professor assessed Claire through her chunky square eyeglasses. "In the future, I expect promptness. You do not need to be in my classroom if you cannot be on time. Do I make myself clear?"

"Yes, understood." Mortified and wanting the ground to swallow her, Claire sat beside Amy. A gorgeous older woman, a row down, gave her a bitchy smirk, then tossed her long, dark hair to face the front.

What the hell was that?

Claire read the digital whiteboard: "Welcome. I am Professor Gwen Saunders. Please address me as Dr. Gwen," Claire's already numb butt squirmed to find comfort on the too-small, hard, black plastic seat.

"As I was saying, this is a trial program for women only, and I will not teach it in a regular academic fashion. Sexuality is neither linear nor analytical and, therefore, impossible to teach as such. The best way to learn about sexuality is experientially."

An attractive but tired-looking woman with black curly hair, sitting two seats over from Claire, raised her hand. "Can you explain what you mean by experiential? Do you expect us to perform sex acts in the classroom?"

A loud giggle erupted from Amy, and the professor's ample bosom turned her way as she smirked back. Leave it to Amy to be inappropriate and get away with it.

"Part of the class will be theoretical and part experiential." Dr. Gwen scanned the class with her stern, dark eyes. "You will not be performing sexual acts, per se, unless you request it in advance. I must approve everything if you want the class to watch. There are permission slips to sign, bureaucratic paperwork to fill out, etc."

"What the actual f?" a young lady who exuded trouble muttered loudly while holding her phone.

Thank goodness someone is standing up to this weirdness, Claire thought, sitting back in the uncomfortable chair to watch the spectacle.

Without missing a beat, Dr. Gwen turned to the disruption as her cascade of long micro-braids swayed over her shoulder.

"No cell phones or other recording devices permitted in this classroom. Please turn off all your devices or put them in airplane mode. May I remind you that even though you signed a release form, there are laws against videotaping someone without their consent. This is a safe space, and I will not tolerate any nonsense to the contrary. Failure to comply with this request will result in immediate removal from the class."

Dr. Gwen's impassive face did not blink as she looked at the disruptor. "Do I make myself clear?"

The young lady gave an incredulous, "No one ever talks to me that way" stare, with a hint of, "The dean will be hearing about this," as she put her phone away.

"You will form groups to help with your class homework and out-of-class group work. No group work, no grade." Dr. Gwen paced the front with panther-like grace. "Each group will go on one field trip to a sexuality event."

The tired-looking woman two seats down said, "I don't know of any sexuality events. How are we supposed to go on field trips when we don't know where to go?"

"There is a list of events being held over the next month in your syllabus. Or you can create an event; however, it will need to be pre-approved by me." More than one set of eyebrows flew to their hairlines. "You will now form groups of four. As forty people enrolled, there will be ten groups. No more, no less."

A palpable panic hit the windowless, stuffy room as everyone looked around, a wild free-for-all of weary and annoyed people. Claire hated group work and now had less than thirty seconds to find two other people who would be in her sex group for the next six weeks?

She was done.

"Do you want to go together?" asked the beautiful, bitchy lady.

"Absolutely," Claire couldn't believe the woman's audacity, but didn't care who was in her group. She wasn't returning, and this Real Housewives wannabe wasn't her problem.

Amy wrangled the tired lady two seats down, and the four women moved their seats together. After the flurry of forming their group, they sat silent, staring and appraising each other.

The Cartier watch caught Claire's attention as it glinted off the Real Housewife's delicate wrist, her fingers too long and slim for the massive diamond wedding ring. A bored, wealthy trophy wife here to add some spice to her marriage? Claire's eyes moved to the tired woman as she pulled a cheap-looking jacket over a big stain down the front of a dress that had seen better days. She looked like a mom taking a university course to find meaning in her dull, only ever-cooking-and-cleaning life. Claire's gaze shifted to Amy, who was authentically herself. She wore her black hair in a blunt pageboy with magenta streaks, matching her magenta feather earrings, which complemented her quirky outfit. Amy wasn't attractive in a conventional way but stood out in a crowd.

Claire's bored gaze scanned the all-female class of mostly university-age young women, then returned to the front, where Dr. Gwen stood, waiting to speak. Claire shushed and then had to shush again before the room quieted down.

"I will give you fifteen minutes to introduce yourselves." Dr. Gwen grabbed a clicker off the table and added a new slide. "The two things you will cover in your introduction are: (1) Why are you taking this class? And (2) What are your masturbation habits?"

Claire's stomach dropped. She threw a death stare at Amy, who practically jumped out of her seat, saying, "Yes!"

Amy

Class One

"Isn't this amazing?" Amy turned to her new group as if it were Christmas morning, but stopped short. They stared slack-jawed at the whiteboard as if rereading the instructions enough times would transform them.

The beautiful older woman looked apoplectic. The curly black-haired lady looked around as if she were in the wrong class. And, as always, Claire was wound tighter than a Swiss watch. Amy figured she screeched in from work, stressed out after taking on too much on her fast track to partner. Amy had explained to Claire a million times that if she wanted to have good sex, she needed to slow down. But Claire wasn't ready to listen, which is why Amy had strong-armed her into this class.

"Let's dive right in, shall we?" Amy encouraged the group.

"What the hell, Amy?" Claire turned a ferocious glare on her friend, which Amy ignored. Claire took time to warm up to new things.

Still, Claire was uncomfortable, and the other two looked equally green. Amy glanced over at the larger-than-life presence of Dr. Gwen. Her posture was calm, but her wise, large brown eyes were alert, shrewdly observing the class's response and processing the room's temperature. Through Dr. Gwen's lens, Amy watched in fascination as the low grumbling in the room grew into a swell of protest.

"Did she say masturbation? That can't be right."

"I'm not talking about that."

"Uh-uh. No way I'm doing this."

"I don't even share this with my girlfriend."

Amy's dark, hooded eyes scanned the room for an ally, someone who wasn't freaking out, and found no one. What's the big deal, people? Sure, talking about masturbation was uncomfortable, but so was talking about menstruation. Women needed to gather in groups and, as a united force, tear down patriarchal social constructs and claim their rightful sexual happiness.

Amy clocked Claire's miserable, obstinate, I-don't-want-to-be-here scowl. She loved her friend like a sister, but why wasn't Claire even trying?

And then Amy heard the thud of the penny drop.

She needed to be the directional compass for Claire, this group, and even the class. Magnanimously, she switched into professor mode to support and be there when her group needed a nudge.

"Okay. Let's start by introducing ourselves. My name is Amy Tam," she gave a small wave. "I'm cis-female and prefer the pronouns she/her. I enrolled in this course because I admire Dr. Gwen and heard it led to powerful sexual breakthroughs. I'm proud to call myself sex-positive and excited to learn new things." Amy smiled brightly to indicate it was someone else's turn.

"I'm not sure how to respond." The curly-haired lady looked at everyone apologetically, a blotchy rash forming on her chest.

"Are you comfortable sharing your name?"

"It's Isabella. Castello." Her words and back were stiff as a board, and her scared almond-brown eyes darted about the room, unable to look at her group.

Amy gave a welcoming gesture. "Hi, Isabella. It's nice to meet you —"

"It's just that the first question blindsided me, and I'm not ready to share private information with strangers."

"That's fair. Are you comfortable telling us why you are in this class —"

"My name is Jeanette Michaels, and I'm certainly not going to discuss my private habits." The beautiful, mature woman's slight French lilt did nothing to soften her impenetrable face. Her arms and long legs crossed, folding her svelte body into an origami shape that shouted, "Stay away!"

Amy took a wild guess that Jeanette was the repressed one of the group.

"We'll come back to you, Jeanette, when you're ready. How about you, Claire?"

Claire shot back a sarcastic, fake smile.

"I'm also uncomfortable talking about this. I need a couple of minutes." Years as a lawyer had helped her sound confident, but Amy saw the slight tremor in Claire's hand as she smoothed her impeccably coiffed, angular blond bob.

"Sure, take your time, Claire. But, uh, this is an important question." Amy, dumbfounded, scrambled to navigate this impasse. "Can I ask why we're uncomfortable?"

"Are you from Mars? Look around this room. Everyone is uncomfortable." Jeanette gestured to the rest of the class.

Why was this woman even here? Amy frowned, but then reminded herself that her job was to meet Jeanette where she was at. And sure enough, when Amy looked around, every woman in the room was as miserable as her group.

"Thanks for pointing that out." Amy's neutral voice belied the difficulty of staying in non-judgmental professor mode. "Are you comfortable saying why you're taking this course?"

"No!" Jeanette bristled, but Amy caught the anguish pass over her delicate face.

"Okay? Well, Jeanette, I'm comfortable talking about my masturbation habits, so let's start there." Amy was about to share her masturbatory session from that afternoon when Dr. Gwen stood up and cleared her throat.

"From your protests, there seems to be confusion. Is there a problem understanding my instructions?"

A few people muttered, "No."

"Alright then. If you don't like my curriculum or how I teach it, 60 people on the wait list will be ecstatic to take your place. If you don't want to be here, now is the time to leave."

There was a shuffle at the back of the room. Everyone turned to see a curtain of silky black hair, wearing a T-shirt that read, *"She's Sweet But A Psycho."* The one who'd taken the video. "I'm going to the dean about you and this pathetic class."

"Entirely your prerogative." Dr. Gwen leaned back on the table with an amiable nod as if agreeing to leave was the most logical thing. The click of the young lady's boot heels echoed around the room as she threw the door open to leave.

"Anyone else?" Dr. Gwen took a beat and then strode to the middle of the room. "No? You have less than ten minutes to cover these two questions. And in case you want to avoid your first assignment, I will choose one person to share their answers."

Holy f—. Did that really happen? Like the rest of the class, Amy sat stunned, admiring this professor and how she handled herself.

She turned back to her group. "Okay, where were we?" Amy was even more inspired to be the group's sex-positive mentor. "I have an awesome sex life."

"You do, but —" Claire interrupted, her scowl replaced with exasperation.

"But what?" Amy turned to see Claire throw her eyes and hands to the ceiling. What was Claire going on about, and why was she being so weird?

Claire opened her mouth to speak, then looked at the other two women, pursed her lips, and said, "Never mind," her words trailing into a long sigh. "Let's move on. We have less than ten minutes."

Amy shrugged it off. Claire didn't want to be here, so Amy had less than an hour to get her friend on board with the class.

Isabella

Class One

ISABELLA WATCHED THE YOUNG lady stomp out of the classroom and saw her opportunity to grab her stuff and go. Her eyes darted around the stuffy, windowless classroom with its harsh fluorescent lighting as she reached for her knapsack.

When Dr. Gwen asked, "Anyone else?" Isabella's body refused to move. The intimidating professor looked around the classroom. "No? You have less than ten minutes to cover these two questions."

Isabella zoned out as she watched her chance slip away. Being in a group was her worst nightmare. She needed to be invisible, to come and go from class unnoticed, and write her sex columns undercover. Resigned to being stuck, Isabella studied Amy, Claire, and Jeanette to get a read on them. She needed to blend in.

It was a relief that Amy took charge. Isabella had interviewed many of Amy's type: bold, free-spirited, zealously spreading the sex-positive gospel, and effortlessly loving their bodies and sex. Claire was a young urban professional who seemed to have her life together. What was she doing here? The impeccably dressed Jeanette looked as if she'd walked off a reality TV set. Isabella would totally watch a reality show about this uptight woman taking a sex course. Her eyes darted around the room for any tiny cameras.

"It's important to masturbate at least once a day." Amy's patronizing tone was akin to that of the other sex-positive people Isabella had interviewed. "How I masturbate depends on the day. The vibrator I use depends on whether I want a quick or slow orgasm. Occasionally, I like an old-fashioned hand job. Rarely, when I'm sad, I like to return to my childhood and hump the edge of my bed."

The way Isabella's sex column read, you'd think Amy was the norm. As the three women stared, appalled at Amy, Isabella wondered if this was how her readers felt.

"Are you for real?" spat the perfectly coiffed Jeanette.

Isabella hated any confrontation, but unable to stop this argument, she tugged her too-small jacket over her generous belly.

"Masturbation is a normal part of my day," Amy pressed on, ignoring Jeanette. "Something is missing if I don't have time to channel my sexual energy."

Did Claire just roll her eyes? She looked like a corporate exec in her understated, expensive suit. Someone so naturally good-looking, she never needed her looks to define her. Isabella had mommy friends like Claire: intelligent, driven, and confident, whose careers defined who they were.

"Jeanette, why don't you tell us why you took this class?" Amy asked patiently as she sat back in her chair.

"I've been married for twenty-eight years, and I'm doing this for my marriage." Jeanette looked as if she wanted to say more, but stopped herself.

"Is there anything else?"

"No," Jeanette inspected her perfectly manicured, blood-red nails. Amy shrugged, then turned to Isabella.

Please don't ask me. Please don't ask me. Please —

"Okay, Isabella, are you ready?" Amy gave a reassuring smile.

With three sets of expectant eyes on her, she hesitated. Was this where she admitted she was doing a series for *Femme*? Would the group self-edit what they shared and never get what they needed out of this class? That wasn't fair to them. Or her readers. Losing her nerve, Isabella made something up.

"I'm a working mom of two toddlers and disconnected from my husband." Isabella looked down at her hands; her jagged nails needed clipping. "We, well, we can't seem to make sex happen regularly. I took this course to help us get our marriage back on track."

"That's tough," Jeanette said under her breath.

"What?!" Claire leaned over and got into Jeanette's face. "Can we at least be civil?"

"I am being civil." Jeanette was obviously used to being the female alpha. Still, there were two other alphas in this group, and Isabella was stuck in the crosshairs.

Amy jumped in. "If you don't want to be in this group, Jeanette, Dr. Gwen can switch you."

"That's the point. I don't want to be in this group. Or any group. I don't want to be in this class."

Claire sat back and crossed her arms. "Nothing is stopping you from leaving."

"Yes, there is." Jeanette's words caught in her throat. Before she looked down, Isabella glimpsed Jeanette's teary eyes, her rigid body deflating, and her chest taking silent, deep gulps of air.

Luckily, Amy knew how to manage this high-maintenance and awkward situation. "We don't know each other, Jeanette, but this is a safe space."

Jeanette waved her hand before picking up her purse, aimlessly rummaging around.

After a long pause, Amy moved the focus to Claire. "Claire, tell us why you're taking this course."

Claire glared at Amy, but then spoke.

"Well, Amy, I'm in my first serious relationship," her voice dripped with sarcasm. "And I took this course so we don't break up."

"Awesome." Amy looked like she wanted to pull her hair out. "So, let's do our best to answer the second question: What are your masturbation habits? Who wants to go first?"

"I'll go," Isabella jumped in. She and her mom-friends had complained about this on the playground. "Because I have two small children, finding time to, uh, you know, do that is impossible. It's difficult enough to find time to shower." Isabella waited for the laughter, but a wave of shame and nausea hit when she looked up. Amy gaped, horrified, while Claire discreetly kicked her.

"Go on." Amy made an encouraging motion with her hands.

"That's it." But as the group stared, the peer pressure broke her, and a truth surfaced. "It's so far down the list. This is the first time I've thought about it in months, maybe years!" Her armpits began to sweat.

Mercifully, Claire tapped Amy's arm, who shifted the focus. "What about you, Jeanette?"

"I don't."

"What do you mean you don't? Like, never?"

"No, like, never," Jeanette mimicked. If judgmental looks could burn, Amy would be a pile of ashes.

"My bad," Amy laughed, throwing her hands up in mock resignation. "Okay, moving along. Are you ready, Claire?"

Claire arched one eyebrow, but her face took on a determined look. "I've masturbated, but without success. At least it never ends in an orgasm. It's just soreness and frustration down there. Ultimately, it's never worth my time."

"You're using a vibrator?" Amy looked confused.

"I haven't." Claire gave Amy a warning look. "And no, we're not going to a sex store after class."

"Technically, the sex stores will be closed. But we can go online. I can't believe we've been friends this long and never discussed this."

"Hey, that can be our field trip." Isabella was grateful to change the subject. "I'll look at the syllabus."

"I won't go," Jeanette announced.

"Do you have a vibrator, Isabella?" Amy asked, ignoring Jeanette.

Blindsided, Isabella froze at the blunt question. Only twenty minutes in, and she, the sex columnist, was already in over her head.

Flaying, she remembered what a bold playground mom had said and replied, "Yes, but it sits at the back of my closet collecting dust." Again, no laughs, only the group staring blankly at her. "I never have private time, and I'm paranoid my husband will catch me." The admission made her gut clench.

Why is this so hard?

Because this wasn't some joke out on the playground. Isabella was in a sex class talking about her sex life. And her sex life was a mess.

Her friend Allison was right.

Isabella's Play Date
January 3

THAT FATEFUL MORNING — many weeks before the sex course — it had started like every other. Isabella was getting nowhere with her pitch idea when she heard the muffled thumps of the kids getting out of bed. After wake-up hugs and kisses, she created a breakfast tailored to each child's liking. Then there was the daily battle with four-year-old Marcus over his filthy Spiderman T-shirt, which he pulled from the dirty clothes pile. And two-year-old Rosa insisted she couldn't live without her ragged tutu. Dressed and bored, the two kids ran around the house, throwing Legos at each other's heads.

It wasn't even nine, and Isabella was losing her mind, so she grabbed her cell off the kitchen counter and dialed. "Hey, Allison. We're restless and need to blow off some stink." Allison, also a mommy at her wits' end, agreed to meet at the kiddie play center.

Two more hours passed as Isabella cleaned breakfast, got the kids and herself ready, and packed everything in the SUV. When they arrived, the kids were bursting out of their car seats. Like a Sherpa, Isabella traversed the icy parking lot carrying Rosa while loaded with the snack bag, diaper bag, and a bag of clean, dry clothes. She stepped inside and set her screaming kids loose to tackle the massive jungle gym.

Breathing in the aroma of strong coffee brewed especially for tired moms, Isabella relaxed a fraction as she found a seat. She spotted Allison, who had arrived, letting her minions loose.

"Oh, Lord! I need a cup of coffee and to put my feet up!" Allison flopped onto the green, cushy, stained chair. She had a no-fuss short haircut and wore standard-issue black leggings and a long dark T-shirt with an unidentifiable stain streaked down the front.

Without so much as a "Hey there," Isabella pounced. "Can I bounce an idea off you? I need to submit a pitch to my editor, pronto."

"You can ask. I'm not sure I'll have any answers." Allison's makeup-free face shot back a "do we have to do this now?" look while keeping one eye on her kids.

"Great," Isabella spoke slowly. "I read this article about how, as women enter into her sexual power, it emasculates men. Because of this power imbalance, it's difficult for both men and women to find pleasure in the sexual experience. Until we can course correct, women can't step into her true sexual potential."

"Uh-huh," Allison sipped her coffee, half-listening.

Isabella swallowed a frustrated sigh. If Allison didn't find this interesting, chances were her readers wouldn't either. She flopped back into the faded chair and scanned the jungle gym for her kids.

"Wait! What?" Catching up to the conversation, Allison bolted forward. "This article said women have come into her sexual power. You're joking, right? This was a satirical article, like from *The Onion*?"

"No, of course not." Her friend's response dialed Isabella's journalistic instincts. "You don't think women own her sexual power."

"How can they? Women aren't sexually equal." Allison snorted at the absurdity. "None of my friends enjoy sex. They have it only when it's absolutely necessary and avoid it if possible. I have more than one friend who's never orgasmed. How is that sexually equal?" At this, she raked her hand through her lank brown hair, making it stand on end, and sipped her coffee. "Oh! And I know one couple with an actual signed contract where she has to have anal sex at least twice a year. Sexually empowered and equal? As if!"

Beside them, a mom popped her head up, glared, and muttered, "Not appropriate conversation," then went back to scrolling her phone.

In a subdued voice, Allison continued. "Have you ever spoken to an average woman in an average relationship about her average sexual happiness?"

"Of course I have!" But as the words came out, Isabella wasn't sure she had.

"I'm no expert, but women have not — what was your expression? — stepped into her sexual power." Allison gave an ironic chuckle, as if the very thought were a conspiracy theory.

Isabella crossed her legs and looked down at her ratty socks. *Stay calm.* She was tapped out of ideas and couldn't afford to miss her pitch deadline.

"Sorry if I came across as harsh." Allison avoided eye contact. "My husband and I are having issues. You struck a nerve. I'm exhausted, yadda, yadda."

"Me too." Isabella gave a shaky smile as Marcus bolted over, and their conversation screeched to a halt.

They watched as he took a sip from his juice box, tossed a few fish crackers in his mouth, wiped chubby hands on his already dirty Spiderman T-shirt (Isabella had lost the battle), and went screaming back into the fray.

"Everyone says kids do a number on your sex life, but I thought it would be different for us." Isabella's admission felt scary but good.

"To answer your original question, as an average woman in an average relationship," Allison winked at her. "It's still a man's world. I highly doubt that women being sexually equal will happen in my lifetime. At least not for me." She took a sip of her coffee.

"That's depressing." The truth of Allison's words settled hard.

"It is depressing. The thing I don't understand is why women still put up with this BS." Allison gave a resigned, what-can-you-do shrug, but then snapped her fingers. "Here's an idea for your article. One of my friends works at the university and told me they're offering a new sex course. It's taught by this controversial professor who's made ripples in the media. If you're looking for answers to these questions, you might find them in that course."

Allison abruptly launched out of her chair to tend to her wailing son.

It was a good idea, but there was no way Isabella had time for a university class. Or the money to cover the course. Or a babysitter.

Women aren't sexually equal.

Allison was so matter-of-fact about it, as if it were a foregone conclusion.

I'm not equal.

It was a hard truth to admit.

Isabella looked around at the bored moms, and it hit her: None of these women were equal. None of them were having good sex, if they were having sex at all. They were stuck in a mommy hell where intelligent, strong women like Isabella and Allison accepted that this was how sex would be for the rest of their lives.

There's nothing we can do about it. Women just have to put up with this BS.

No, they didn't. At least, not on her watch.

Isabella picked up her cell and typed an email to her editor requesting that *Femme* magazine cover the costs for the sex course and, fingers crossed, a babysitter.

Claire

Back In Class One

What kind of sadist does that?

Claire watched as Isabella's body folded into itself, making her as small as possible. Her face was a mishmash of anger and humiliation. Claire had had enough of this professor and her exercise, with its shock value, humiliating people and their sexual inadequacies.

Claire raised an angry hand, ready to give Dr. Gwen a piece of her mind.

Claire's hand was up for over a minute when Amy said, "I don't think she's going to answer you."

Claire snatched her hand down, even more enraged.

Turning to Isabella, she said in solidarity, "It never occurred to me that someone would masturbate after she's married. I assumed it was a single thing." Isabella's mouth gaped, then she looked down, a cascade of bushy hair covering her face. "But, duh, why would you stop?" Claire backtracked. "I barely have time being single. It must be so complicated if you live with someone."

Amy's hand jerked in a slashing motion at her neck for Claire to stop.

"Time's up." Dr. Gwen stood up from her chair, smoothed her navy suit jacket with its crisp white button-down shirt, and walked around the cheap university-issued desk. "Does anyone want to volunteer and tell us how you masturbate?"

Amy's enthusiastic pick-me hand went up in a room full of downcast eyes. Claire noted that the contrarian professor ignored Amy and ran a long, pointer finger down the class roster.

Why would you ask for a volunteer if you don't choose the volunteer? Claire seethed.

"Claire Skalmar. What did you have to say?" Dr. Gwen's eyes searched for Claire.

What the?! Is the professor targeting me because I put up my hand? Was this meant as intimidation?

Claire was about to tell this professor precisely what she thought of this exercise when she glanced at Amy, who was practically bursting out of her skin.

"Perhaps you can ask Amy, who volunteered and wants to share," Claire stared back at Dr. Gwen, mirroring her benign expression.

"Ms. Skalmar, please don't tell me how to run my class. I will ask you again: What are your masturbation habits?" Dr. Gwen stood her ground as if she had all the time in the world.

Unbeknownst to the professor, intimidation would not work; stressful situations brought out Claire's cool intellect. She had two choices: gather her things and leave, or answer the question. Leaving would show weakness, so that wasn't an option. The room stared and held its breath, hoping she would fold into herself with shame like Isabella. The years of being an overachiever refused to let that happen.

"When I, uh, you know —"

"Masturbate," Dr. Gwen prompted.

"Yes, when I do that —" Her voice came out strained and halted; a flush crept up her neck and onto her face.

"When I masturbate," Dr. Gwen gently corrected.

"Sure. When I masturbate," Claire forced a calm demeanor, determined to show this professor. "I don't always. I mean, I find it hard to, you know, uh, climax. So, it's never been worth it." She looked at the other students judging her, and the cool intellect vanished, her brain scrambling in an emotional free fall. "But Amy said she would help me buy a vibrator to help with my ... situation."

Her body burned with humiliation, made worse by Amy's I'm-proud-of-you smile.

The adrenaline pulsed so hard in a tight band around her head that it took a moment for Claire to register a small clap, then another, and soon the entire class was clapping. For her?! Claire's face turned crimson, and she looked to the front to see that Dr. Gwen was clapping, too!

What was happening?

"Well done, and welcome to this class, Ms. Skalmar." Claire barely registered Dr. Gwen's smiling praise, her logical brain working hard to catch up. Dr. Gwen turned to the class. "As for the rest of you, this is only the first question."

"Can't wait." Claire's words were flippant, but as much as she tried to ignore them, something momentous had just happened. Her mind changed in the blink of an eye, and she committed herself fully to Dr. Gwen and her course. In true Claire fashion, she decided that if she took the time out of her hectic life for a class that was so out of her depth, she would give 110 percent.

And there would be no turning back.

Claire ignored Amy's excited hug. She was still angry at Amy for talking her into the disastrous *Project Up My Sex Game*.

Claire's Project Up My Sex Game

Many Weeks Before & Why Claire Ended Up In The Sex Course

I'M NO BASIC BITCH. Claire Skalmar is one sexy badass.

Yeah, right! Claire wasn't kidding anyone, certainly not herself. Her fingers drummed the steering wheel as her dazed hazel-green eyes flitted to the rearview mirror, catching the terrified look on her face.

I'm driving to my doom. She was going to kill Amy.

If Claire were a basic bitch, then she was also one badass planner. The advantage of being overly prepared was that very little could go wrong, and she had enough time on the drive to her place to review Amy's insane *Project Up My Sex Game*.

She'd appear in her bedroom doorway, snapping the crop whip on her palm. Then she'd Beyoncé-walk toward Carlos in the stupidly high black stilettos and teal blue Agent Provocateur bustier. (That, of course, Amy picked out when they were online shopping.) Claire chose a black, intricate lace mask that gave her a mysterious aura.

You need all the help you can get. Came the mocking voice.

Claire didn't have time for her insecurities, so she promptly went back to her to-do list.

"Do you like what you see?" Claire's voice would be seductive and husky as she performed a slow, teasing pirouette.

When Carlos reached for her, the crop would slap his hand away because — why would she slap his hand away? — because she enjoyed making him beg? Oh dear Lord, begging wasn't her thing, but it was the best she had, and she needed to move this along.

"You can look, but you cannot touch." The tone of her voice would make it clear she was in charge. "Now undress," she would command, expertly slapping the crop on his stomach. Claire would watch, hands on her hips in a Wonder Woman pose.

Oh, Wonder Woman pose, that's good. Keep that part.

Pointing the crop's tip to the floor, "On your knees." She would then tie the newly purchased black, silky *Fifty Shades of Grey* blindfold around his dark, pleading eyes. Amy had used the word pleading and then told Claire to say with authority, "Now pleasure me!" Claire would let her panties slip to the floor in a silky teal blue puddle as she pulled his head toward her—.

Claire's foot slammed on the brakes, her tires screeching her fantasy back to reality.

"Come on!" She shouted at the steering wheel as Carlos's cherry-red Tesla ran the yellow light. He couldn't get into her house without her, so why didn't he wait for her? Guilt answered that he wanted to pick her up for dinner. Still, she'd worked until the very last second, arriving late and agitated at the restaurant. An undercurrent of tension sparked a whispered fight over the exquisite appetizers, only to drop when the entrées arrived.

Claire made a left turn after the light finally changed. Their fight stubbornly looped in her brain, opening a space for her real problem to rear its ugly head.

Stop it! Ignore the problem.

But it was no use. No matter how hard Claire tried, sex with Carlos was always one step below meh. Her orgasms were only ever a blip, like some intermittent Doppler radar. It might predict a storm, but it rarely showed any signs of a lightning strike. It defied all logic. Mr. Tongue, with his swirly, sucking expertise, was happy to spend as much time as needed to get her off. And that finger thing he did while down there. Her orgasms should be nothing short of mind-blowing.

But they weren't. Not even close. Claire rarely orgasmed.

"You need to channel your inner sex goddess and tell Carlos what you want," Amy assured Claire that taking charge would help her stop faking.

Faking?! Claire spat the word out.

Every time she and Carlos walked into the bedroom, her sexual inadequacies hovered. Taunting Claire that if Carlos found out she couldn't orgasm, he would be gone faster than a 75 percent off pair of Jimmy Choos. So, she did what she thought she needed to do. She put on a show. But tonight, that was going to change. Lightning was going to strike!

Not likely. Came the mocking voice, winding itself up for a big anxiety dump.

Stop it! You need to focus.

A spicy whiff of lilies floated to the front seat, and their fragrance niggled something in her brain. Did she remember to thank Carlos for the flowers? Was that why he was upset at the restaurant? She'd thanked him on Instagram. The post had gotten over a hundred likes.

She slowed her car to a crawl, putting off the inevitable as she pulled up to her house. Thank God Carlos was on his cell.

"I need 5 minutes! xoxo"

Claire texted, and Carlos gave her a thumbs-up from his car.

Stepping out of her warm car into the chilly winter evening, she had to use both hands to carry the massive bouquet. She fumbled to put the key in the lock and then turned on her hallway light. Carelessly plunking the flowers down on her hallway entrance table, she kicked off her work pumps and ran to her bedroom.

The complicated Agent Provocateur teal underwear was spread out neatly on the perfectly made queen-sized bed. Mocking her. Only someone with a sliver of confidence should wear something so erotic. The stress vice around Claire's head tightened as she shed her work clothes.

Are you kidding me? Her fingers, slick from nervous sweat, fumbled with the straps and tiny snaps.

I need an extra pair of hands and a step-by-step manual to maneuver into this bustier.

The stretchy lace mask fit snugly over her eyes, and her feet slipped into the four-inch heels. Running out of the bedroom door, Claire caught her reflection in the mirror. The mask was hot. But the rest? Online articles promising sexy underwear would spark her sexual senses had lied. She looked foolish, but the alternative was her go-to T-shirt and shorts. Her eyes flitted to her dresser, where her comfy shorts were. She nearly caved.

Brace yourself. You're not a quitter. Limping to the front door, phase one of *Project Up My Sex Game* running in her head, Claire froze mid-stride. She'd forgotten the crop. She jumped out of the stilettos and ran to her bedroom to find the crop on the floor by her bed. Running back, she shoved her slightly swollen feet into the heels that now pinched.

I forgot to shower?! Her right leg shook uncontrollably. She took a deep breath. There was no time for showers.

The front door opened. Claire's ankles wobbled as she struck her best Wonder Woman-ish pose, convincing herself it was okay that things weren't fresh down there.

Amy

Back In Class One

MIND BLOWN.

Amy's jaw dropped as she stared in disbelief at Claire and then at Dr. Gwen. Less than thirty minutes in, Claire told a room full of strangers about masturbating. Claire even looked different; the grim line of her mouth, the hardness in her intelligent eyes softened, and her posture relaxed.

Imagine where she'll be in five weeks when the course is over.

As if things couldn't get any better, Dr. Gwen asked, "Who is comfortable saying the words 'I masturbate' in everyday conversation?"

Amy joyfully raised her hand. But when she looked around, hers was the only hand up.

"For those who didn't raise your hands, the shame stops here. Talking about your masturbation habits should be as comfortable as discussing the weather. Shame is a societal construct that, over centuries, effectively repressed the gift Mother Nature gave to you. Today, the world has billions of masturbators who feel pleasure from the experience but shame immediately after. Have a deep-seated shame from talking about it. If we truly are modern, sexually emancipated women, then why is masturbating still a dark, shameful secret? Yes?"

"I read that promoting masturbation was a feminist conspiracy to stop women from having sex with men. Is that true?" A sulky, emo-looking young lady asked.

A troubled look passed over Dr. Gwen's stern face as she shook her head.

"Society's goal has always been to suppress women's sexual pleasure. We frame a woman who owns her sexual power as the ultimate threat, which sounds over the top, but is the sad truth. We are so used to the absence of female sexual power that our first instinct is to tamp it down rather than rev it up."

"Can you give an example?" Asked a fresh-faced young woman with a halo of blond curls.

"Sure," Dr. Gwen nodded. "We label women a whore or slut for having too much sex or too many sex partners. A woman choosing to make money from selling sex is villainized to the point where it is a criminal offense. Have you ever wondered why we cannot support and celebrate a woman who enjoys making a lot of money from having a lot of sex?"

A few of Amy's colleagues had secretly worked as escorts to pay for grad school. They claimed it was an easy, well-paid gig and kept their best clients to subsidize their meager university wages. Amy had considered it and wasn't ruling it out.

"Outside influences are directing and manipulating your sexual pleasure at a micro-level." Dr. Gwen wandered to the middle of the room. "When sex is initiated, thousands of tiny negative messages loop in your subconscious, preventing you from being fully present and fulfilled."

The class looked confused, so Dr. Gwen asked. "What are sex-related words that elicit a negative reaction?"

Someone shouted, "Cunt."

Dr. Gwen nodded. "Yes, cunt is an excellent example."

"Whore."

"Bleeder."

"French abortion."

"All fine words. Thank you." Dr. Gwen put her hands in the pockets of her pleated navy pants. "If a single word can create a visceral reaction, imagine what the daily onslaught of negative messaging has done."

Amy glanced at her group's reaction. Isabella was madly scribbling. Was it strange that she took extensive notes? Jeanette sat immobile as a stone. She didn't want to be here, and Amy was still working out why she was in this class. As usual, Claire dissected every word that came out of the professor's mouth.

"What should surprise us is that women have sex despite the obstacles she faces. Feminist conspiracy theories notwithstanding." The professor caught herself mid-rant and softened her tone. "Thank you, and I encourage your questions. The only way to dismantle the many myths holding women's sexuality down is to share and talk about them."

Dr. Gwen put up a new slide. "This course is about you creating a new, healthy sexual mindset. To stop listening to a society that wants to keep you repressed. To no longer put your sexual needs second and become an equal in the bedroom."

"Isn't that a dated concept?" Claire loved being the contrarian.

"What do you mean?" Dr. Gwen's half-smile implied she knew precisely what Claire meant.

"The feminist movement started in the 1960s," Claire said. "The pill was invented. Women advocated for their sexual rights, and now women expect to orgasm."

Dr. Gwen raised her chin, ready to debate with Claire.

"Is it expected? Or do women go through the motions while the point of sex is to ensure her partner's orgasm? "

Claire didn't answer, so Dr. Gwen kept going.

"A woman's sexual needs still rank a distant second. And in fact, expecting women to 'cum first' has had a devastating effect on her sexual self-esteem. As you will learn, orgasm is only one piece of a woman's overall sexual satisfaction. True sexual equality is whether you can confidently tell your partner what you want, or don't want, out of your sexual experience." Dr. Gwen pushed a few micro-braids over her shoulder.

"With that in mind, please ask yourself, why do you have sex? Is it for you or your partner?" Dr. Gwen ignored the confused murmurs. "This course will teach you how to be an equal partner in your sexual experiences. How to tap into your pleasure spectrum, and how to ask your partner for what you want or do not want. Then to relax and receive the pleasure you asked for."

That sounded pretty freaking awesome to Amy.

"To answer your question," Dr. Gwen turned back to Claire. "No, I don't think women's sexual equality is a dated concept. Little has changed over the last century, and women stepping into their sexual equality is long overdue."

It's long overdue because being sexually equal is too much for men.

The bile rose in her throat. Amy's mood suddenly shifted when memories of her date with Paul came rushing back.

Amy Gets Ready For Her Date

Many Weeks Before On January 14

"I agree. First dates are the worst." Amy said to her cat, Orgasm, who yowled at the overly vigorous head rub.

Indignantly, he hopped off the university couch that had seen better days, and Amy feebly threw a small cushion at his departing calico butthole.

"Why are you leaving me?" Her mind was awhirl with so many unanswered questions.

Should she bring Paul back to her hip townhouse after the date? Foolishly, she promised Claire no sex. What else were they supposed to do? Talking sounded b-o-r-i-n-g. Amy tugged awkwardly on the completely date-worthy black slacks with a short-sleeved, cowl-necked white top Claire picked out. Amy hated it.

Right on cue, first-date jitters swooped in, begging Amy not to get her hopes up. Telling her not to think this date was any different from the others. Warning not to throw herself at Paul, only to never hear from him again.

This was why she preferred hookups, which were fast and straightforward, with no messy complications. But then a tiny, tentative smile crossed her lips, remembering how nervous Paul was on their call. It was a beacon of light amid the storm of emotions raging within her.

Amy put her head in her hands, trying to focus on what was going right in her life instead of what was going wrong. But it didn't work. It never worked. The self-help gurus who insisted Amy would meet her best match when she did the reflective work were mistaken. Her reward, so far, was a series of dreadful dates. Or, as Claire called it, her dating shit show.

I should text Paul and cancel.

It was pointless to put them through this just for it to be a dating failure. Amy picked up her phone but then stopped because, and this was weird and scary, she sensed a genuine connection with Paul.

I need to go on this date.

But since Amy was a bundle of nerves, it was time to bring in Mother Universe.

Amy headed to her quirky bedroom, which she created using her creative eye, a lot of time, and a few dumpster treasures. She sat at her womyn's shrine, with its marble bust of a naked woman, two half-burned candles, five small, framed photos of female heroes, her favorite, Betty Dodson, and an incense burner.

Lighting both candles, Amy closed her eyes, slowed her breathing, and did a body check. With every inhale and exhale, she traced her energy from her toes to her head. She asked Mother Universe for guidance to make this date successful. Its purpose was to get to know Paul and to flourish in a relationship. She slowly opened her eyes, expecting her emotions to reset, but her stomach somersaulted instead.

Frustrated, she reached into her pocket to text Claire, then let go of the phone. Damn that stupid dating ultimatum.

Amy remembered Claire's voice, strained as she'd issued her New Year's edict:

Do not tell me about any guy, gal, nonbinary, etc., or sexual adventure until you've been on over three successful dates. With the same person. Getting together only to have sex, no matter how amazing, is not a successful date.

Amy had argued that sixty-nine-ing wasn't technically sex, as Claire stared back, not blinking. She was tired of Amy not giving people a chance, not letting them in, and then running to Claire when it didn't work.

Bah humbug! Claire completely dismissed Amy's considerable ability to abstain. There would be no thinking of a hot, sweaty, naked Paul between her thighs tonight.

"Stop it," she warned herself. She needed to corral her sexual urges. But how?

As she stood up from the womyn's shrine, her intuition told her to look around the higgledy-piggledy room, which stopped at the open closet. Thanking Mother Universe for the straightforward answer, she moved to the closet and pulled out her vast vibrator collection. Opening the treasure chest filled with thirty vibes, all shapes and sizes, was a soothing balm for her frazzled nerves. One vibe was for taking her time while smoking weed. One for her G-spot. One for her A-spot. Some were for male partners, others for female partners. She even had a complicated vibe for non-binary partners.

She moved a few vibes to the side and found the perfect one.

The Wand by We-vibe was like Goldilocks' preferred porridge: her orgasm wouldn't be too fast or too slow. It would be just right. She'd be on time for her date and less likely to jump Paul's bones.

Mother Universe was such a practical badass.

Laying the Wand on the edge of her bed, Amy went to the full-length mirror to watch herself undress. She looked terrible in the conventional date-worthy outfit and couldn't take it off fast enough. Throwing them in a crumpled pile, she looked at her naked reflection, turning this way and that to admire her glorious Rubenesque curves. She saw her shoulders move away from her ears as more tension drifted away.

She thought about Paul's comment at the political rally, where he said he found her confidence attractive, and she found that attractive about him.

With the sweet anticipation of Jilling off, Amy sighed as she spread a dollop of water-based lubricant around her labia. She turned the Wand to the lowest setting for a slow buildup. As she rested the vibe against her slippery clit, the familiar thrum of pleasure pulsated through her body. Sinking into the sensation, her low, throaty groan told her this was exactly what she needed. She traced the vibe's tip up and down from her clit and over her labia, the deep, rumbly vibrations building her excitement.

Pulling the vibe off her clit, not wanting to orgasm just yet, Amy moved the Wand up to her breasts rhythmically, moving the tip of the vibrator around her dark nipples. Her arousal deepened as she watched them grow hard in response.

I wonder if Paul is into pegging. Her thoughts drifted to what a turn-on it had been with past partners who let her put a dildo up their ass, which led to the next super turned-on Paul fantasy, and then the next.

Many years of daily masturbation told her she was in the good-orgasm zone and to savor the body buzz. Inspired, she knelt on the bed and watched herself in her full-length mirror. Her bedroom eyes pleased with her body's sex flush, the heaviness of her breasts, and every curve of her bodacious body.

"You are a goddess and deserve this pleasure," she told her reflection, who couldn't agree more.

Placing the vibrator on the most sensitive spot of her clit, her back arched, and her body clenched, moving her to the first blissful peak of an intense orgasm. Taking the vibrator off her now sensitive clit, she placed her wet, lubey fingers and stroked her labia to prolong the sweet orgasmic pulses.

Blissed out, she rode the multiple-orgasm wave until the intensity slowed. As the last wave of orgasm passed, she flopped back onto her bed with a satisfied sigh. She thanked Mother Universe again — you could never be too thankful, grateful, or amazed — at how her body brought her so much pleasure.

Slowly rolling off the bed, her vulva tingling from the fantastic orgasms, she was certain this was a sign for her to be her authentic self.

Amy tossed the period panties, specifically chosen to ensure she didn't have sex with Paul, on top of the crumpled clothes pile. She opened her immaculate lingerie drawer, its military order at odds with the eclectic bedroom. Gently moving the lavender sachets aside, Amy breathed in their scent and pulled out the high-cut, hot-pink lace thong. She then locked and loaded her breasts into the matching bra.

Paul is going to love this. She admired her reflection, the hot pink glowing against her olive-tatted skin.

Dressed in her regular clothes, she took one last look at her fresh, makeup-free skin and went out into the cold January evening to conquer her first-date jitters. And then, hopefully, Paul.

Isabella

Back In Class One

AFTER HER PLAYDATE WITH Allison, Isabella pitched the idea of representing her readers as the everywoman taking a university sex course. She assured her editor, Jessica, that there would be silly and unbelievable situations. Her mom's work-in-progress sex life on display for everyone to see and judge. Jessica liked the idea, especially the part where *Femme* readers got to dive into Isabella's messy sex life.

Isabella knew the university course wouldn't be a fun gals' night out, downing Fuzzy Navel shots and, while slightly intoxicated, learning hand-job techniques on cucumbers. But never in her wildest dreams did she think a class on sex would be so academic and dry. While listening to Dr. Gwen drone on, she scanned her notes for something she could use in her first column.

"The way society talks about sex is very different from the sex you have, and even less related to the sex you want." Dr. Gwen's fingers moved from her ample hips up to her temple. "We are told good sex happens to our bodies when, in fact, it starts in our minds. Your relationship to sex is what we will call your mindset, which is how you respond to and make sense of sex."

They were learning about mindset? Isabella stifled a big, tired yawn. The long day that started at five a.m. was catching up, and the initial buzz of excitement was gone.

"Mindset is the magic bullet." Dr. Gwen let the words sink in. "Having satisfying sex over a lifetime can only happen with a positive mindset. Not that you believe sex will forever be amazing, because it will not be. Rather, a positive mindset shifts your perspective. It empowers you to see what is going right with your sex life instead of focusing on what is going wrong." Dr. Gwen looked out at a sea of blank faces.

Nope, no cucumbers or Fuzzy Navels here.

Isabella made a colossal mistake. There was no way to spin this into an exciting *Femme* sex column. An invisible band around her chest tightened as she remembered Jessica clearly stating *that Femme* was "taking a big chance" by paying for the tuition and the babysitter. Jessica would certainly not understand if Isabella abruptly pulled out of the class.

Dr. Gwen pushed her point. "What is the core problem that stops women from having a positive mindset and owning her sexuality?"

"Not being able to communicate?" Isabella threw out the standard sex therapist's answer for every single sex question.

"An inability to communicate sits under the umbrella of the core problem." Dr. Gwen nodded and went on. "A woman's inability to communicate even the most basic sexual wants is a big reason she is not satisfied; however, it is not the core problem. Why is it that she cannot communicate?"

"Not being able to communicate is a self-esteem issue." Claire's eyes narrowed as if solving a riddle.

"Exactly. The sex life you currently have is the sex life you are asking for."

"What the —?!" Claire whispered loud enough for the class to hear.

"Your sexual self-esteem is how worthy and deserving you feel to demand that your sexual desires be met. It takes courage to change your beliefs and make new choices. The only way to make this change happen is to choose you." A confused silence dropped like a final curtain over the room. "Although you have sex with another person, this journey is about you and you alone. It is not up to your partner to fulfill you sexually; rather, it is up to you to understand what you want from the sexual experience and then ask for it."

Isabella threw her eyes to the ceiling. First, she had to have a positive mindset and then ask for what she wanted. Both sounded complicated and horrible. Half hysterical, she imagined submitting her first column titled: "Robotic Sex," and Jessica promptly demanding Isabella's resignation.

"I will teach you the theory, but it is up to you to implement it with homework and group work." Dr. Gwen pushed herself off the edge of her desk. "To start your sexual journey, you will need to look back. For this week's homework, you will write a full account of your sex history. I've included a sex history worksheet in your online handouts to help you get started. Please push yourself to go to your vulnerable place. Explore what is buried deep, difficult to dredge up, and write it down. Pay attention to your body and any emotional reactions, and write them down. The more you write, the simpler your journey will be." Dr. Gwen took a beat as if hesitating to say the next part.

"Fair warning: While you work through your past, you will feel the opposite of sexy and sexual."

It was official: the sex course was a bust. Why would anyone take a sex course to feel the opposite of sexual? Isabella closed her notebook with jittery hands. She had kids and a mortgage payment and couldn't afford to lose this job.

What am I going to do?

"Think of sorting through your negative emotions as the pot of gold at the end of a rainbow: Once you acknowledge and clear out these negative emotions, your brain has space to welcome new and proactive thoughts. You will find, as you build your positive mindset, your sexuality will instinctively open up." Dr. Gwen smiled at the weary class. "You have five minutes to set up your first group meeting."

Isabella slowly turned toward her new group, unsure how to proceed.

"What are we going to do for the group meeting?" Claire pulled out her cell phone calendar, her body language screaming that a group meeting was the greatest imposition on her life.

Isabella needed to call the registrar's office tomorrow and drop the class. She couldn't do this.

"We could FaceTime, Skype, or Zoom," Amy suggested.

They agreed on Zoom, and Isabella hesitated, hating confrontation, so she gave her email and cell number.

Dr. Gwen's voice boomed over the class chatter.

"Thank you for attending. If you have questions, I will be here for fifteen minutes."

"I've got to run," Isabella said as she scooped up her belongings. "A babysitter is looking after the kids."

Isabella ignored Jeanette as she sat fixed in her chair, eyes slit, face like thunder. The other two said goodbye, also ignored Jeanette, and followed Isabella, who couldn't get out of there fast enough.

Jeanette

Class One

JEANETTE SAT PERFECTLY STILL. A lioness stalking its prey.

Only a few students waited in line to ask Dr. Gwen a question after class. Soon enough, it would be her turn, but it took every fiber of self-control for her to wait. When the room finally emptied, she stood to find her knees stiff from the morning's spin class, where she had taken out her extensive anger.

"Yes? How can I help you?" Dr. Gwen didn't look up as she packed her things, signaling she was ready to leave.

Jeanette didn't care if the professor wanted to go. She expected the professor's full attention. Jeanette tapped her foot to show her impatience, but Dr. Gwen didn't seem to notice or care, taking her sweet time to put her laptop cords in her bag.

"Now, what was it you wanted to discuss?" Dr. Gwen looked up, her wise brown eyes locked with Jeanette's steely navy-blue gaze. Jeannette dismissed the unfamiliar flutter in her nether regions.

"I'm Christian, and your course doesn't align with my faith." Jcanette's voice was crisp and businesslike. The last thing she wanted was for this professor to interfere. Jeanette could manage this on her own.

"Why did you take this course if you object to the curriculum?" Dr. Gwen didn't bat an eyelash at Jeanette's open hostility. Rather, she seemed amused and leaned into the line of fire.

"Why is anyone here? My husband and I are having difficulties." Jeanette was used to women cowering when she was in a mood.

Dr. Gwen waited for more of an explanation, but getting none, she advised, "Perhaps what you need is a sex therapist or counselor. I do neither." Jeanette was about to reply when Dr. Gwen cut her off. "I find that in these situations, your relationship challenges intertwine with your sexual challenges. Like DNA. As interwoven and tangled for however long you have been in the relationship."

"You have no idea what's happening in my relationship." Jeanette's sore, spin-class legs trembled as she held her ground.

Dr. Gwen grabbed her bag and started walking. "You will need to compartmentalize and work separately on your relationship issues. Until you and your husband have worked through what is going on in your relationship, you cannot have a meaningful sex life."

"That's not helpful." Jeanette sniffed at Dr. Gwen, with her strange ideas and eccentric attitude.

Dr. Gwen continued as if she hadn't heard, let alone felt, Jeanette's barb. "It is about working on one challenge and then, with your relationship strengthened, working on the next issue. The curriculum will help and guide you." Dr. Gwen gave Jeanette an appraising look. "But it does not seem like you want to be here. If so, please drop the course. And if you so choose, I have a list of excellent therapists." Dr. Gwen strode to the door.

Jeanette trailed the professor; a scowl contorted her symmetrical, Botoxed face. Dr. Gwen held the door open, and Jeanette looked into the professor's eyes. Every angry emotion screeched to a halt, and she stopped short, breathless, as if she'd caught herself just before running off the edge of a cliff. As the professor stood, holding the doorknob and looking into—not at—Jeanette, her eyes had no mockery or scorn, only compassion and kindness.

Jeanette recognized the moment of grace. Somehow, this stranger wanted the best for her. Jeanette's instincts advised her to stay.

"I'll come back next week," Jeanette announced. Without so much as a goodbye, she turned on her high heel and pushed past Dr. Gwen, who was still holding the door open.

As she stalked away, she heard Dr. Gwen murmur, "That was unexpected."

Isabella's Me-Time

February 12

TWO DAYS AFTER THE first sex class, Isabella tiptoed out of her son's room after their nighttime cuddle.

Her bladder ready to explode, Isabella dashed down the hall, stifling a yelp as her socked foot stepped on a rogue Lego. She barely made it to her en suite, doing a pee dance while fiddling with the unyielding button on her stretchy jeans. Forget exercise; this was why moms wore yoga pants.

Yanking the button free, she pictured Alex peacefully watching TV downstairs, winding down before bed, "feeling bad he wasn't helping." Still, his job was "too important to miss a full night's sleep."

Like her day was a walk in the park. She got up before the kids to work, switched to mommy mode, made dinner, kept the house clean, did some more work, and got the kids to bed. Isabella's days were predictable, tedious, and mind-numbing, keeping her in constant motion but never letting her catch up. Moaning about it only made things worse, so she tried not to. But come on. Four years of waking up several times a night and running on three to four hours of sleep made her day feel like she was tripping on acid, and the world around her was melting.

Pulling up her jeans, Isabella noticed the fluorescent-pink sticky note hastily attached to the bathroom mirror. A note she had the foresight to put on said mirror, knowing she would forget by the time she put the kids to bed. Careful not to look directly at her reflection, she peeled the note off the mirror and stared at its one word.

While cooking supper, she listened to a podcast about "The Importance of Self-Care." The two mom podcasters were authentic, vulnerable, and unapologetically frank about their challenges. They made many good points, but Isabella heard the old chestnut, "Put your mask on before helping others," one too many times. She was about to skip to the next podcast when they said something that sent a chill down her spine.

They called out the social media moms who projected elegant, organized, glamorous, and sexy lives in a tightly contained, smoke-and-mirrors Instagram-fake world. The social media message was clear: the average woman could either keep up or be an epic failure. The podcasters claimed that for Isabella to aspire to maintain this illusion was "completely toxic for her self-esteem."

Their words triggered something—she wasn't sure what—but her brain connected the dots. First, her friend Allison said it was a man's world, and women would never be equal. Then Dr. Gwen said that Isabella needed to feel worthy and choose herself. And now, these podcasters were talking about moms' lack of self-care. Three's a charm.

As she stirred the pasta sauce, an outline of a story formed in her head just as her son's shriek pierced the air. The thread of her aha moment got lost in the manic mix of making supper and the newest kiddie drama. She ignored the background wails, marched to her desk, wrote "Bath" on the fluorescent-pink sticky note, ran upstairs, and stuck it to her bathroom mirror.

Now, hours later, sitting on the edge of her bed, Isabella stared at the sticky note as exhaustion chipped away at her commitment. She wanted to bail, but had a deadline.

The podcasters declared she should make a mental list of everything she'd done that day, then ask herself how she could feel guilty about taking care of herself. They were right. She was as hollow as a chocolate Easter bunny, one with a bite taken every day. Soon, there would be nothing left of her.

She saw Alex's daily morning mess from the corner of her eye. The clothes and towel on the floor, the dark hairs in the sink, the dollop of dried shaving cream on the counter, the white drops below his toothbrush, the comb, gel, and deodorant strewn haphazardly. Every day, she asked herself why he didn't clean it himself. The answer was always the same. Because she cleaned it for him. She let out a controlled, angry breath and then another as she folded his crumpled pajamas.

"It's your turn." The podcasters affirmed. "And do NOT, under any circumstances, let the mess in the corner change your mind. Leave the mess. Take care of yourself."

Screw it. Isabella dropped Alex's pajamas back on the floor. Her guilt swooped in, asking why she dropped folded clothes back on the floor, but she forced herself to step over them.

"How will you take care of yourself?" The podcasters asked. She had dismissed their pedestrian list of self-care strategies until they landed on a hot, scented bath. Goosebumps had slid down her arm; she could finally use the bath bomb a friend had given her last year. Finding it was another matter. She rummaged through her bathroom counter before going into the bedroom closet. Voilà! She spotted the bath bomb on the top shelf of her clothes closet and triumphantly held it in the air for no one to see.

A long-forgotten flutter of excitement settled in Isabella's tummy as she tugged off the stretchy jeans and inspected them for any significant stains. There were several Play-Doh splatters over the bum. Did she go out in public like this!? She tossed her dirty clothes into the laundry basket—like a civilized human—and accidentally glanced at her naked reflection while padding to the en suite. The gentle flutter turned into a nasty somersault.

The mirror was her enemy. Never mind looking at herself with clothes on, but looking at herself naked put her into a tailspin. Since having kids, she didn't recognize this unattractive stranger in a lumpy body. Her eyes automatically zoned in on her stretch-marked stomach and the generous, cellulite-dimpled thighs.

Isabella only had to wait for a second—and bam—self-loathing hit her. She needed more self-control to stop eating the leftovers on the kids' plates and inhaling junk food when no one was looking. She needed to exercise more. Isabella hated her body and everything she was or wasn't doing to maintain it.

"Love yourself." The podcasters had fiercely proclaimed. "And you will love your kids, family, and job better. Love yourself, and everyone wins." Loving herself wasn't in the cards, but at least she could work on being less ashamed. Her readers would love that insight.

She turned the bath taps on and ran the hottest water possible. After dropping the bath bomb into the hot water, the steam mixed with the citrus and lavender scent. Isabella twisted her thick, dark, curly hair, the one thing she liked about herself, into a large clip. The warm, steamy bathroom with its gorgeous scent worked its magic, and as Isabella inhaled, her body relaxed.

"It's the least you can do for yourself." The podcasters trumpeted. She leaned over the tub to test the silky water temperature and willed herself to believe it.

Tentatively, Isabella put her leg into the water. The welcome heat moved up her leg and into her body. She put in the other leg, lowered herself down, and took a moment to relish the luxurious water before sliding in low. She closed her eyes and smoothed the water onto her tired body, blissfully reveling in the foreign sensations. Tears pricked the back of her eyes as she breathed in the warm, scented steam.

Why had she given up caring for herself?

Smoothing more water over her breasts, Isabella smiled in pure delight and made a pact to love herself more often.

"Can I join you?" Isabella's heart stopped as her eyes flew open. Alex stood at the bathroom door.

He was naked.

Jeanette at the Gym

January 22

MANY WEEKS BEFORE THE sex course started, Jeanette wiped the sweat from her neck and shoulders, satisfied after the grueling spin class.

At fifty-three, she worked harder and looked better than most of the twenty-somethings prancing around the gym. Walking into the changing room, she got a satisfying glimpse of her glistening, light-olive skin, which showed off her toned, lean muscles. She was in the best shape of her life and, more importantly, looked fifteen years younger.

"Can you believe that instructor?" Her friend Karyn asked that same question after every workout.

"We've done this class every week for the last year. We should be used to it by now." Jeanette's slight French accent made the haughty tone exotic, even alluring. She opened the locker, releasing its tantalizing scents of expensive shower products as she hauled out the designer bag.

"Are you coming for coffee with the ladies?" Karyn's cheerful face, stuck-in-the-'90s blond hair, and slightly too-close-together bright blue eyes looked hopeful.

"No, not today. I have a ton of errands. My son, Pierre, wants to impress his girlfriend and asked me to help. I need to shop, then decorate his condo." Jeanette gave Karyn a mock pouty face.

"Hey, you could buy twice as much and make it a two'fer." Karyn chuckled at her cleverness. "Make a romantic surprise for you and your hubby."

"No!" it came out as a bark. Jeanette had to force a laugh and gave a dismissive wave. "We've been married far too long for that."

"It seems like a waste to help your son and not have fun yourself. Eric and I are going out with friends tonight." Karyn paused and waited.

Jeanette knew she was supposed to reciprocate and ask about Karyn's night out. But she was too busy trying to take off her sports bra and panties while wrapped in an extra-large towel.

"I bought a new dress and divine heels. I even bought new lingerie. Eric's going to be one happy boy." Karyn gave a lewd smile and waggled eyebrows, oblivious to Jeanette's struggles. Like the other pampered mommies who went to the gym, Karyn was too self-absorbed to notice anything outside her orbit.

"Good for him. And you," Jeanette managed, tugging the sports bra over her head with one hand.

"I haven't bought lingerie for a while, so this will be a nice surprise." Karyn pushed the tummy-toning yoga pants over her ample bum and stomach.

"Sounds lovely." Jeanette was done with this conversation. Grabbing her shower kit, she slipped on her flip-flops. "See you tomorrow?"

Karyn grunted as she tugged off her sports bra, freeing her enormous breasts. Jeanette stared in disgust at Karyn's huge nipples, then averted her gaze to her flip-flops. Unable to stay civil, she turned and left.

"Probably not. I'm going to the early HIIT class," Karyn said to Jeanette's back as it bolted to the shower.

Stepping into the hot water was a welcome relief for Jeanette's sore body. Taking her time, she wanted to wash away the shocking nipple image that looped in her head. How many other women were uncomfortable with Karyn brazenly traipsing her naked body around? There must be other women who wanted to say something but were too polite. Yes, it was a changing room where people undressed, but she needed to tell Karyn to be more discreet. For everyone's sake.

Jeanette redirected her attention to finishing her shower and getting ready. Her je ne sais quoi chic of a classic French-Canadian woman didn't happen by accident. Her long hair—dark, thick, and glossy—came from weekly salon visits. Then there was the expertly applied, understated makeup and the expensive clothes tailored to fit her shapely body.

Taking one last lingering look in the mirror, Jeanette walked through the gym. Women stopped chatting to look at her. She drank in their envy, especially the jealous looks. This triumphant moment meant everything because it was all that she had.

"Bye, Jeanette." A few women waved in awe as she walked by.

"See you tomorrow." Jeanette smiled cheerfully to prove she was both beautiful and friendly. The gym-goers watched through the windows as she nimbly climbed into her Range Rover.

Satisfied with her exit, she marveled at how going to the gym had turned her life around. Somewhere over the years, she'd lost her mojo, and going to the gym helped her find it again. She'd been a gym-goer in her early twenties, but her motivation had dipped and become sporadic once the kids were born. But then, a few years ago, a group photo started circulating on Facebook, revealing Jeanette's robust muffin top. She wasn't having any of it and went to the gym the next day. Regaining her confidence showed up everywhere else in her life, except in her marriage.

She was sure it was God who gave her a helpful push. God, as always, had her back and answered her prayers. Which meant she had to endure the minor inconvenience of schooling Karyn and her large nipples.

Jeanette turned out of the parking lot toward her favorite gourmet store to prepare for Pierre's special night.

Amy's Date with Paul

Many Weeks Before On January 14

AMY RESTED HER FINGERS on the twitchy eye and took an unsteady breath to calm her nerves. If Paul bailed on their date, Amy didn't want to be the sad person waiting alone in the Thai restaurant. She had planned to arrive fashionably late. Naturally, she made every green light and eased her beat-up university car into a parking spot ten minutes early.

Her jumpy nerves made it impossible to wait on the lookout. Cranking on the hard-to-open driver's side door latch, Amy got out and walked to the side of the restaurant building. Leaning against the brick wall, her cheek joined the twitching party.

Visions of her sitting across from Paul as her eye and cheek twitched up a storm. *He plays it cool, but regrets asking her out.*

Digging her phone out of her coat pocket, she had enough time to text Paul and cancel. Her jittery fingers typed out a cryptic message when Amy heard a laugh and looked up. A couple strolled by, hand-in-hand, big puffs of cold following their intimate conversation, contented in their own little world.

It's a sign. What Amy asked for every morning during her meditation. Standing in the snow, Amy centered herself, focused on her breath, and mentally repeated: *I create my blissful relationship reality.* Within seconds, the mantra sent a calming ripple through her, soothing her mind and body.

A cold shiver ran through her body, and her toes complained that they were numb. Amy turned and spotted a warm convenience store and crossed the street. Tucked inside the store, she peered out the window, watching for Paul's arrival, pretending to read a magazine. It took five minutes for her to see Paul stroll down the sidewalk and enter the restaurant.

He was precisely on time.

"Pay for the magazine and go." Behind the counter was an older Asian woman with chunky silver streaks in a blunt haircut. Her eyes sparkled keenly with interest as she watched the scene unfold. Amy obediently took out her credit card to buy the magazine.

The woman asked in Mandarin, "Is he nice?"

"Pardon me?" Amy answered in English.

"Is he a nice man?" The older woman patiently repeated in Mandarin.

"I hardly know him, but he seems nice." Amy stammered, ready to spill her guts to this stranger but not wanting to keep Paul waiting.

"So, why are you waiting in here?"

"I wasn't sure he would show up."

"The right person will come to you only when your soul is strong enough to receive them." The woman's wise eyes scrutinized Amy. "If this is your man, you don't have to try so hard. Be yourself and see how it shows up in him." But the woman's sage words bounced off Amy as she wrapped her scarf around her insecurities, left the store, and crossed the street.

I create my blissful relationship reality. The restaurant door jingled, and Paul looked up expectantly from the menu. His long, narrow Ichabod Crane face lit up like a jack-o'-lantern.

"Amy, hi. You made it!" Paul sounded a tad too relieved as he stood up, and Amy smiled back.

Bending his tall frame to give her a peck on the cheek, he jostled the rickety table, sloshing liquid out of the tiny teacups. His lips missed Amy's cheek and kissed her ear instead.

"Oh, uh, sorry." He tried again, and this time his lips landed on the corner of her mouth. The chaste kiss sent a lightning bolt straight down to her nether regions.

"No sex!" she heard Claire's strident reminder that this would not be a skip-dinner-and-go-straight-to-sex date. Then again, what Claire didn't know wouldn't hurt her. Claire responded to Amy's weak will with a fire extinguisher. "This is a date. Not a hookup."

"I looked through the menu before you got here." Paul fidgeted with the water-spotted cutlery. "You said you traveled to Thailand, so I wanted to hear what you recommend. But I got us tea. I hope that was okay. If you don't drink tea, no worries. You're not obligated to drink it —"

"The Pad Thai is excellent." Amy interrupted just as a loud rumble came from her worn, brown vinyl chair. Her eye twitched as she explained the farting noise wasn't hers but the chair.

"Great," Paul continued, as if he hadn't heard the noise. "Why don't you choose the best dishes? It's my treat."

"Ready to order?" The gangly server appeared, memorized Amy's order while wiping the spilled tea from the plastic tablecloth, then silently left.

"You look terrific!" Paul's adoring gaze swept over her red, off-the-shoulder peasant blouse and a black skirt with red flowers. She glowed under his appreciation, and the twitch left. Good riddance.

Paul commented on the tiny restaurant's elegant watercolor scrolls beside the funny Thai beer poster ads. This led to a delightful conversation about the places they both traveled. Paul, a mountain climber, shared amazing adventures. Amy told him about her love of the Asia-Pacific region. They jovially enjoyed one-upping each other's misadventures when the server set down a steaming bowl of fragrant Tom Kha Gai soup. He unhooked the ladle from the side of the bowl, half-filled their small soup bowls, and left.

"This smells delicious." Paul breathed in the fragrant soup as they kept talking about everything and nothing. The time flew by, and too soon, the meal was over. Paul paid the bill, and they left the warm restaurant to a blast of arctic wind. Amy drew her plush, electric-blue coat collar closer, and Paul put a protective arm around her shoulder.

This is too good to be true. There has to be a catch. Amy steeled herself for the inevitable letdown.

"This is me," Amy stated the obvious when they reached her car, not knowing how a no-sex date ended. Her eye twitched.

They both lingered, not wanting the date to end. Paul looked up, cleared his throat, shuffled from foot to foot, and then looked down at Amy.

"Can I kiss you?" He asked, and she nodded.

Tentatively and sweetly, he softly kissed her lips. The full-body rush flooded back in with full force. She stepped closer, grabbed his coat collar, pulled his head down, and kissed him deeply.

"Gross. Get a room!" A teenager yelled across the road.

Amy reasoned that she'd done this date differently. She made it through to supper, which was progress. But now she needed to have sex. With Paul. Hopefully, a few times.

"I have dessert waiting at my apartment." Amy gave Paul a wicked grin.

"What kind of dessert?" Paul asked, sounding uncertain whether she was serving chocolate cake or a sexual romp.

"Me!" she giggled at his shocked face. "Follow me home."

Amy got in, started her car, and glanced across the street. The lady in the convenience store stared back, her arms crossed and shaking her head.

Isabella's Femme Column

Sex Betrayed Me

How did I end up here?

At the start of my relationship, sex made me feel good and connected to my partner. Somewhere after the honeymoon phase, sex went from something I anticipated to something I avoided. Now I'm stuck in this weird place where there are still many years with my partner, but sex isn't fun. Just the opposite. The constant resentment and obligation around sex disconnects us.

I don't want this, but I don't know how to fix it.

Too many women go through the motions of sex but would rather read a book. Slotting sex in as a choir or one more thing on her to-do list.

Recently, a friend mentioned that women aren't sexually equal and never will be. Then she shrugged as if it was easier to put her sexual needs second than to fight the inevitable. Resign ourselves to being powerless and bitter as a foregone conclusion. To keep sexually calm and carry on.

We deserve better. We should expect sex to feel good and bring us closer to our partner.

I'm on a quest to find out how. I signed up for a five-week sex course through my university. Each week, I'll discuss how the sex course theory bumps up against real life.

On This Week's Sex Menu

> **Class One:** Why did I take the sex course? Why do I have sex?
> **Answer:** I want to reconnect with my partner and have more intimacy.
> **Problem:** Sex is a chore and a quota that needs to be filled, or there will be fights. It's tough to be intimate when I have nothing left at the end of the day. I want to zone out rather than lean into the relationship.

Let's put my answer to the real-life test.

Sexless Soccer Mom?

Last spring, an email from our community association landed in my inbox, announcing we could enroll our four-year-old son in soccer. In my mind, I saw a happy, exhausted child learning how to be part of a team. My husband's decision to become a coach was the cherry on top.

Or so I thought.

"He plays twice a week?!" It was the highly anticipated first night of soccer. I looked at my husband in panic as we scrambled to get to the soccer pitch on time. He gave me a holy crap, what-did-we-get-ourselves-into look back. We made it, but the next two hours were pandemonium. By the end of the first evening, we put the kids to bed and literally collapsed onto the sofa.

Sex? Not a chance. We both needed to zone out and decompress on our devices.

I Needed Help

I called my sister the next day to get her expert advice. She has three kids in after-school activities.

"Soccer is twice a week! How am I supposed to manage?" I vented.

There was a long pause before my sister answered. "Just wait until both of your kids are in activities."

Mic drop.

I will have to schlep my kids to activities four nights a week, on top of everything else that needs to get done. My sexless future flashed before my eyes, and I muttered words I'm not allowed to write in this column.

I went to a second authority, a quote from Ellen Kreidman's book, *How Can We Light A Fire When the Kids Are Driving Us Crazy?*

"Since you are parents, you must be more flexible, creative, and focused in meeting your needs. The older your children, the more flexible, creative, and focused you have to become. By learning to be creative, you'll be forced to find new and exciting ways to be lovers."

Let me get this straight. On top of being hyper-responsible and following rigid helicopter parenting protocols, I then need to switch gears, compartmentalize, and be *more* flexible. And *more* creative. Meaning when I want to zone out, I need to lean in.

Right.

Yet Another Fork in the Sex Road

Since having children, there have been a series of events that brought me to a metaphorical 'fork in the sex road.' At first, it was sleepless nights. Next, I was constantly sick because our first child was in daycare. Then, I had a newborn and a toddler. Now, I'm moving into the our-kids-are-in-activities phase.

My sex life is in constant flux. When I finally get into a sexual rhythm, there's another disruption. The goalposts are constantly moving, which makes creating a space for intimacy an endless work in progress.

I thought sex was supposed to be spontaneous, fun, and effortless, but the reality is it's work to be "more flexible and creative." No wonder parents are so frustrated and discouraged.

Here's the thing: it's not about a lack of time. It's about your intention.

Don't Let Your Relationship Slide

Small shifts over time cause the most extensive cracks in our relationship's intimacy. When you get back from chaotic four-year-old soccer practice. Get a promotion at work. Have a significant loss or upset. Or are fighting an illness. Even though you have little or nothing to give, you must be kind to your partner. And for them to reciprocate that kindness.

Kindness, compassion, and grace are your talismans to help you weather even the toughest of disruptions.

To do nothing and let your relationship coast will create a big and complicated mess. It's better to figure this out now and get intimacy and your sex life back on track. A stitch in time, and all that.

Looking back, when we only had one child, I had oodles of time to make sex happen. With the second child, it's complicated to have sex, but still doable. However, I need to intentionally prioritize my relationships.

There will be many opportunities in your future (said with sarcasm) to be *more* creative and flexible. To learn how to have meaningful intimacy with your partner. Your efforts (said with sincerity) will be worth it.

Guard your couple's connectedness and intimacy as one of your most precious commodities. Because it is.

I don't want to be a sexless soccer mom. So, if you'll excuse me, my husband left a mess in the bathroom, and I must practice being kind, compassionate, and graceful.

Claire

Group Meeting, February 15

"Who's leading the discussion?" Claire stifled a yawn. Her long day was already a treadmill of mind-numbing meetings.

It was three days after the first sex class, and she wanted to be anywhere but on this group call.

"Do we need someone to lead the discussion?" Isabella sounded annoyed.

"Sorry, I'm still in work mode." Claire softened her tone as she tucked a stray strand of blond hair behind her ear. "When someone isn't in charge, meetings go off track and take extra time. I have at least three hours of work after this call."

She frowned at the stacks of work on her desk, lamenting her decision to stay in the course. Writing her sex history took two unbillable hours and hadn't led to any significant aha moments. If she were going to spend this much time on any project, she expected tangible results. Her irritated gaze moved back to her computer screen filled with strangers with whom she was supposed to share her sex homework.

What could possibly go wrong?

A loud scratching noise pierced Claire's earbuds as Amy's purple-and-black hair appeared on her screen. "Oh, that's the unmute button!? Cool." Amy was one of the most intelligent people Claire knew, but a complete mess with technology.

"Hey, Amy," Claire started her computer timer for one hour.

"Did anyone get their sex history written?" Before anyone could answer, Amy continued. "I was too busy, but I went through the questions on the homework sheet, so I'm set for this meeting."

"I didn't get mine done either." Isabella faltered, her face unreadable on the dark screen. "I wasn't procrastinating. I didn't know how or where to start with my sex history and wanted to find out what the rest of you did."

"Why are you so dark?" Claire squinted at her screen.

"I'm in my bedroom closet. It's the only place where there's peace in my house." Isabella's voice answered.

"I didn't find the worksheet questions or writing out my sex history helpful," Jeanette said, superbly coiffed in a slate gray business jacket for their informal meeting.

"Really? I thought there were helpful questions." Claire could tell from Amy's tone that she was provoking Jeanette.

"I've only had sex with one man." Jeanette made it clear that it was none of their business.

"Yes, but so much can happen in one relationship. A lifetime of two people's sexual evolution," Amy tried, but Jeanette sat back and rolled her eyes.

Between her long day and this woman's nonsense, Claire snapped. "Why are you taking this course? You don't want to be here. If you refuse to participate and waste my time, I will ask Dr. Gwen to remove you from our group."

"Fair enough," Jeanette replied reasonably, giving Claire whiplash. "I'm uncomfortable. I've never talked about sex."

"I've never talked about sex either." Claire refused to let this pampered Real Housewife off the hook. "If you refuse to do the homework, kindly get off this call."

"Understood. To be clear, I'm here to learn." Jeanette replied calmly, as if Claire were the unreasonable one. "I promise to do my best and support this group. I won't be perfect, but I will try my best."

Claire couldn't decide if this woman was a narcissist, a psychopath, or both.

"Super. We never expect perfection, do we, ladies?" Amy's tone signaled it was time to move on. "Everyone good with that? Claire?"

"All good." Claire didn't believe Jeanette, but her timer showed they had already wasted five minutes.

"How do we want to do this?" Isabella spoke up.

"Each of us can pick one question from the worksheet," Amy suggested.

The Zoom call went silent, with everyone waiting for someone else to pick their sex history question. After what felt like an eternity, Claire's analytical brain locked in, telling her it was just information and that she could do it now or in five minutes, but either way, she needed to say it.

"Fine. I picked question four. 'Have you reached a satisfying orgasm with yourself or with a partner?'" Claire pulled up her homework assignment and was about to answer when the words caught in her throat. Her analytical brain reminded her that she was skilled at navigating challenging conversations. This was no different.

"I can reach orgasm, but I've never had an intense orgasm. When I do orgasm, it's muted. And I never orgasm during intercourse." She sounded robotic, but whatever; she'd said it. Out loud.

Surprisingly, she felt lighter, as if a bit of steam had been released from a pressure cooker.

"The good news is you can orgasm," Amy reasoned, as if that was helpful. It wasn't.

"I suppose. But it's a blip, and then it's done. Aren't orgasms supposed to be intense?" Again, the pressure lessened, and her stress level eased. Finally, someone besides Amy responded.

"I'm not sure they are," said Isabella. "I've read up on this, and every woman's orgasm is different. Maybe this is how your body orgasms."

"Well, that would suck. I took this course to have better orgasms. What's the point of sex if that's all there is?" A lifetime of mediocre sex flashed before Claire's eyes, bringing back the tense shoulders.

"Babe, the course only started," Amy interjected. "Don't get your panties in a twist just yet."

As much as Claire loved Amy, she didn't get it. How could she?

"I've been trying so hard to get in the mood to make sex enjoyable. But I can never relax." Claire gently scratched her itchy throat.

"Me too!" Isabella, still silhouetted in shadows, answered excitedly. "I can't stop my mind from whirling. I'm always too keyed up. And then, when the sex is over, my body is finally relaxed. When I'm ready, it's too late."

"Not to diminish your experience," Amy shifted, and there was an off-screen yowl from her nasty cat, "but that is the way for most women."

"That doesn't make sense. If most women experience this, why isn't there more information about how to fix it?" Claire asked, frustrated. Whether at herself, the women, or the entire world, she didn't know.

"There is a lot of information on it. Today, I read an article about how stress impacts your sexual response. You, Claire, are constantly under stress."

"Yes, my job's stressful, but how does that impact my ability to have a stronger orgasm?" Amy didn't make any sense, but Claire knew better than to encourage another one of Amy's "great" ideas.

Claire frowned, remembering Amy's great idea, *Project Up My Sex Game*.

Claire's Project Up My Sex Game

Many Weeks Before On January 15

"Wow!" Carlos looked up from his phone after closing the door and rewarded Claire with a low wolf whistle.

Claire's body stood rigid, locked in her Wonder Woman pose. She looked ridiculous in the uncomfortable teal-blue bustier, absurd four-inch black stilettos, a lacy mask, and a leather crop dangling from one hand. Then again, was there a sexy pose that wouldn't look silly?

Her confidence vanished under Carlos's intense stare. Frozen on the spot, the whip's fronds shook, giving away her shaky hand as her analytical brain scrambled to remember the *Project Up My Sex Game* list. She was about to ask, "Do you like what you see?" when Carlos's eyes caught his gift, the massive flower bouquet hastily abandoned on the side table.

"Claire! They're going to fall!" Carlos stretched out his long arms and lunged at the flowers as if they were, in fact, on the verge of falling. Claire opened her mouth to tell him they weren't, that he was overreacting, but closed it.

He was mad because she'd forgotten to thank him.

Like an on-off switch, the moment was gone. Maybe Claire wanted an excuse to let it go. Someone needed to be the grown-up in the room.

Taking great pains to stifle a passive-aggressive sigh, she put the whip down and, teetering on her torturous heels, took the flowers from him and carried them over to the coffee table.

"The flowers are lovely. Getting them at work was a wonderful surprise." She soothed him as the last wisps of any sexy mood vanished. Her workday hit her with a bone-tiredness, and she was ready for bed, but sleeping wasn't on the night's sex menu. Claire buried her face in the bouquet, inhaling its potent scents before gently placing it down. "Thank you so much."

"You're welcome." Pacified, Carlos returned his attention to her sky-high heels and complicated Agent Provocateur teal underwear.

Claire's analytical brain abandoned her, and the *Project Up My Sex Game* list vanished. She didn't have a Plan B, and to say she wasn't good with spontaneity was an understatement. So she stood there, wishing the floor would swallow her up.

Why did she let Amy talk her into this?!

"You haven't given me your present." Carlos took Claire's long fingers and led them to the bulging erection in his tailored black dress pants. "Does it have something to do with this?"

She wanted to snatch her hand away, but that would make things weird.

"Yes," she squeezed her hand unhappily around the bulge. She swallowed a grimace as "I don't want sex" looped in her brain. That Carlos didn't notice, too focused on his needs and his erection, deepened her resentment.

"Give me two minutes." Claire went on her tiptoes and kissed his cheek.

Dashing up the stairs and into the bedroom, adrenaline pumping, she needed to regroup. Fast. Picking up her workout clothes from the floor, she wiped her vag before throwing them in the laundry. She lit a set of four-tiered white candles, then pushed an app on her phone that connected to the built-in sound system. The music helped calm her.

"Come upstairs," she yelled, but he was already there, lurking outside her door, making her guts clench. Did he see her wipe her vag?

"Are you going to show me my surprise?" He stood expectantly.

A promise was a promise.

In free fall, with no idea what to do, Claire defaulted to what they always did. Sex on repeat. Kissing Carlos, she reached to unzip his pants as she led him to the bed. Carlos greedily massaged her breasts, then moved a hand down to her clit. He laid her down on the bed and kissed his way down her belly.

Slipping a hand under the lingerie, he murmured, "I love this," as he slid the panties off.

He kissed the inside of her thighs, teasing what would come next. The thing was, she knew what was coming next: Carlos would kiss and lick the outside and inside of her lips, building her up, making her want and need him to get to her clit. When he got to his signature move of sucking on her clit, she barely felt it.

Can he tell I haven't showered?

Even though she wasn't going to orgasm, Carlos was a man on a mission and wouldn't stop until he got her there. Obligation tapped her on the shoulder, telling her she was tired, on the verge of cranky, and needed to wrap this up. She closed her eyes and moaned, gyrating her hips, then put her hands on his head and gently tugged on his dark, curly hair. Claire stiffened, arched her back, and gave a loud, throaty groan.

Carlos rolled over onto his back for his turn, satisfied with his work. Claire climbed on top and kissed her way down his chest. She licked the head of his very erect penis, then took the whole thing in her mouth, vigorously moving her hand up and down while gently playing with his balls. He let out a groan to indicate he was close, and she stopped, knowing he preferred to orgasm during intercourse.

Shifting around, she lay back on the bed, he mounted her, and she stopped herself from mouthing the words with him.

"You're so beautiful."

Carlos moaned as he put his penis into her not-very-wet vagina. He slowly entered, teasing her with the tip before thrusting deep inside. In response, she put on an Academy Award-winning performance. With breathless arousal, she thrust her hips, writhing and moaning.

"Oh, do that," she sighed. Knowing that the more she got into it, the quicker Carlos would cum.

The telltale groans told her he was close. His thrusting became jerky, faster, harder, more purposeful. His face and neck were flushed, his eyes screwed shut, his face contorted as if in the middle of taking a crap. Claire counted down the seconds until he thrust deeply, let out a groan, and collapsed on top of her.

Thank God it's over.

As he kissed Claire tenderly, her body responded, wanting more of the soft kisses. But as always, she was a beat too late. He was done. Session over.

Less than a minute later, Carlos rolled off her and went to the bathroom. When she heard the toilet flush and the shower come on, she pressed her knees together and went to the bathroom. Carlos had stunk it up and didn't even bother to put the toilet seat down. Covering her nose with one hand and fumbling to put down the toilet seat with the other, she was too late. A long stream of semen ran down her legs. She wanted to jump in the shower but didn't want to risk an encore.

By the time Carlos returned to bed, Claire had washed as best she could, untangled herself from the bustier, and blown out the candles.

Carlos, smelling fresh, moved in close to nestle her manky-smelling body in the crook of his arm. Ten minutes later, he lightly snored. Carlos put out heat like a furnace, so Claire inched away, threw off the blankets, and stared at the ceiling.

Silent tears soaked her pillowcase.

Isabella

Back At The Group Meeting

"My family's going to my mom's for supper, so I have to leave the meeting early."

Isabella eyed the time, unsure she could get her kids' grandma ready and finish this meeting before she had to go. This call was one more burden, wasting her precious time.

"My mom's a typical Spanish matriarch, and we can't be late."

Why isn't Alex getting the kids ready?

The unyielding pressure and stress of being the only one able to get the kids ready — while working — filled her with bitterness.

"That's so nice your mom makes Sunday supper. I'm close to my mom, too." Amy wanted to chat? "What's a typical Spanish meal? I don't know that I've ever eaten Spanish cuisine. Aren't tapas Spanish?"

"Amy, she needs us to stay focused." Claire reined her friend in.

I should have dropped the class. Isabella massaged her temples. But while she worked up the nerve to tell her editor, the days passed, and she missed the penalty-free deadline to withdraw from the course. *And now I'm stuck telling strangers about my sex life.*

Isabella heard a bang at the bedroom door and huddled in the dark corner of the closet, hoping her kids wouldn't find her.

"Isabella, tell me about your mom's delicious meal after the meeting," Amy said sweetly while giving Claire the finger.

Where is Alex? Why isn't he looking after the kids? The resentment in her chest grew.

"Go ahead then, Isabella," Claire instructed. "Which question did you pick?"

Isabella's eyes squinted in the dark, reading the sparse bullet points she had hastily written minutes before the call. "Okay, I picked number eight: Do you want a deeper sexual connection with yourself and/or your partner? What is your connection now?" She paused and looked up at the waiting faces on her screen. "Do I jump into the answer?" Isabella hedged.

Tell the truth. The truth will set you free. Or at least give you a good story. Isabella pictured her editor's delighted face getting the copy of how she confessed her sex life to this group. A loud bang from the hallway made her jump, putting her stressed nerves on edge.

"Since our second child, my husband and I can't connect. We love each other and want to have sex, but it's so difficult." She didn't want to admit the next part. Images of the hot, sweaty, amazingly satisfying sex when they first got together filled her head — replaced with their current barren wasteland of obligation sex. How did that happen? "My sex life is a cliché. I'm a married woman who doesn't want sex."

"It's a tricky phase, but it will pass." Jeanette's kind words came out of nowhere, shocking everyone.

Isabella softly said, "It's not about the sex," struggling with each word. "We're being pulled in opposite directions, and it's so hard to have a civil relationship. Right now, we're roommates, and it feels like we'll never get our connection back."

"What about holiday sex?" Amy asked. "When you and your husband have a night away from the kids. Is your sex still good?"

Isabella jotted down "Holiday sex!!!" That would make a great story.

"We went for a night away five months ago, to a friend's wedding —" Isabella trailed off as warm memories flooded her head.

"And," Amy encouraged.

And it's none of your business, Isabella thought. Yet, dishing on her sex life would make for a better article.

"And when we got to the hotel, we were exhausted and took a two-hour nap, which was amazing. When we woke up, we, uh," Isabella faltered, "I hope my husband doesn't mind me telling you this. I never thought to ask whether I could talk about him."

"This course is as much for his benefit as yours. I'm sure he'd understand." Again, Jeannette was suspiciously supportive. What was her deal?

"This is so hard to say." Isabella's head spun, forcing out the uncomfortable words. "We had lazy sex, which was exactly what we both needed. Afterward, we showered and had some, uh, more fun. We went to the wedding energized and joked we'd discovered the fail-proof elixir for parents with small kids: NBS. Nap Before Sex," Isabella wrote NBS.

"I'm not Dr. Gwen, but if you're having holiday sex, your relationship is okay," Amy assured Isabella.

Yeah, and then we came home, and everything returned to normal.

"Were you able to do a second question?" Claire tapped her fingernails on her desk.

I don't want to discuss this.

Isabella looked at the question mark beside the question she had chosen.

"Is that a yes or no?" Claire's voice had an impatient edge.

Isabella might as well have been under oath on the witness stand, cracking under pressure.

"Yes, I chose number six: Do you love and accept your body exactly as it is? How does your relationship with your body affect your sexual pleasure?" Isabella thought of her answer on the fly. "I apologize for constantly blaming my kids for how I —"

"Never apologize for being a mom!" Jeanette interrupted. "I'm so sick of moms apologizing and making themselves small. Moms need to unite and let everyone know what a demanding job it is. You're doing a magnificent job; don't let anyone tell you otherwise."

"Right, thanks. But I was going to say that after my first son was born, I eventually returned to my original weight, but my body had changed. It's been two years since having my daughter, and I'm not back to my original weight." Isabella flushed, as flashes of her soft body underwater during the me-time bath filled her memory. "When I look in the mirror, I see my face with someone else's body. So, I never look at myself in a full-length mirror. I've tried dieting and going to the gym, but I can never stick with them. My kids suck up my time and energy, but I don't want to use them as an excuse."

"It's not an excuse," Jeanette said firmly.

"My husband says he loves me and my body, just as I am, but he's only saying that. There are a ton of love-your-body articles, websites, and Facebook groups. The frustrating thing is, I get the theory, but once I look at my body, the theory flies out the window."

"I hoped someone would bring this up." Amy smiled at her computer screen, pleased to give Isabella the unwanted advice. "Women's body issues are a topic close to my heart because, as you can see, I'm a big girl and understand what you're going through."

"I don't think you do understand what I'm going through," Isabella bristled. "You don't have a spouse or children. No offense," she backtracked, unsure where the bluntness came from.

Amy pulled a yowling calico cat off her computer, unperturbed by Isabella's disagreement.

"Every person has a lifelong core issue they can never fully come to terms with. For some people, it's never having enough money; for others, it's never finding a suitable partner. With some, like you, it's never being at your ideal weight. Sex could also fit under this umbrella. Even though everyone's challenge is different, the reason they think this way is the same. They lack self-worth and don't feel like they deserve something better. Which means they don't have the internal motivation to change their situation."

Women aren't equal because they don't believe they deserve it! Isabella's friend Allison's words came back to her.

"Amy, maybe —" Claire spoke, but Amy was just warming up.

"Your weight isn't the problem. So, it wouldn't matter how many diets you went on or how often you worked out. You need to believe that you deserve to be fit and healthy. It's okay to prioritize your health and happiness. The moment you understand you're worthy and deserving, you will permanently lose the weight."

Women put up with this BS because they don't believe they are worthy or deserving. Isabella had known this, but doing something about it was beyond her control. Or was it?

"Once you identify your core challenge and dig down to why you lack self-worth, you can conquer it."

"Okay, that means —" Isabella tried, but Amy cut her off.

"To get to your core issues —"

But then Claire cut Amy off. "So, who's next? We're almost out of time."

Isabella wrote "core issue," not sure how it played into her present sex life. Still, her journalistic instincts told her she was onto something. If she could figure this out for herself, she could help her readers. Then she could ask for a raise.

She put her head in her hands. Core issues were way above her pay grade. Especially figuring out how to stop the images of her plump naked body and the disastrous sex from the me-time bath.

Back to Isabella's Me-Time

February 12

ALEX STOOD IN THE bathroom doorway, wearing only an enormous smile.

Isabella's body jerked up, sloshing water over the tub's sides. How did she not hear him come up the stairs and get undressed?

"What are you doing?" He asked playfully. His dark eyes twinkled like once upon a time when they had flirtatious sex banter.

"Relaxing," she tried to match his easy repartee, giving a tight smile. "I thought you were watching football." She didn't invite him in, wishing he'd take the hint.

He didn't. As he squeezed his lean, medium frame into the one-person tub, Isabella shifted to one side, trapped with no escape, dreading the inevitable.

I don't want sex. Now is not a good time.

"It's nice that you surprised me." The pure delight of being "surprised" tugged at her heart as he kissed her hand. They looked at each other, and for a moment, their responsibilities vanished. It was just them in the bathtub, remembering who each other was.

She wanted to ask, *When did this become so difficult?* Instead, she agreed, "This is cozy."

They needed quality time, and it had been weeks since they last had sex.

"It is, and you're so beautiful." Alex sighed, relaxing into the hot, fragrant water, not noticing her flinch. He only complimented her these days when he wanted sex. An awkward silence hung between them, neither knowing what to say next.

"Marcus had an excellent day at playschool." Isabella glowered at her fleshy tummy and thighs. "The moms brought goodies for the party, so we have at least ten cupcakes left over. Did you see them in the kitchen?"

Everything about her body looked worse underwater—the stretch marks, the extra flab, and the loose skin.

"Mmm." Alex wasn't interested. His head fell back, and he looked relaxed enough to fall asleep.

"Jack's mom had another baby, so she's asked me to help her take Jack to playschool for the next month." Isabella's eyes landed on Alex's flaccid penis, bobbing up and down under the water, then looked away. "Of course, I said it would be no problem. They live up the street, and picking him up and dropping him off is no big deal."

Alex shot her a pointed, pained look, tired of this topic, but she couldn't stop the ramble. "Rosa was so disappointed when she didn't get to talk to you today."

"Can we not discuss the kids while enjoying a bath? It's been forever since we've done anything like this."

Who's enjoying the bath? Not me. She wanted to say. *You're forever telling me about your day. Why isn't my day as important?* Instead, she pursed her mouth in silence.

Sensing her upset, Alex sat up. "Let me lather your back." He reached for the pink puff and the grapefruit-scented body scrub.

This bath was supposed to be about me. Somehow, Alex made it about himself.

"I can't turn around in this tub." Her voice was sulky, and she hated how she sounded like Rosa being obstinate.

"Well, then let me lather your front." Alex mischievously waggled his eyebrows. Again, her heart tugged. They used to be open and spent hours experimenting. Somehow, somewhere, it had faded, and now all they ever had was bland, predictable, meat-and-potatoes sex.

He dipped the puff and let the silky, warm water trickle down her shoulders, back, and front. "How's that?" He asked, taking his time to suds her neck, shoulders, and arms. Alex's TLC, the grapefruit scent, and the warm water worked their magic, and her body relaxed.

"Mmm, that's nice," she said truthfully, her body waking up and happily leaning into the sensations.

"Good," Alex said, and then stopped.

What the?! She wanted to say, *Hey, I was just getting into it*. Instead, to put off the inevitable sex, Isabella offered, "Can I do your back now?"

"I'm good. The water's cooling off."

It wasn't. Isabella wanted him to notice that she wasn't ready to leave the bath. He didn't and reached out to help her get out. This wasn't how her me-time evening was supposed to go.

She wanted to say, *I feel guilty when I inconvenience you, but you don't give inconveniencing me a second thought*. Instead, Isabella tried to convey how much she didn't want sex with her sullen silence. He didn't notice.

"Let me dry you off." Alex grabbed a towel and gently rubbed her neck and shoulders as he worked his way down. When he affectionately rubbed the towel between her toes, he looked up at her and winked. Back in the day, it was their secret joke. Isabella returned a flat smile and dried him off. She hated how he treated sex like a quid pro quo: you give me sex, and I'll make an effort with our relationship.

It was time for Alex to make his move. Her body braced. She wanted to tell him not tonight, but heard echoes of what happened when she refused sex after a long break. It turned into an exhausting, days-long silent feud. His disappointment at being sold a bad bill of goods, with a thinly veiled 'What happened to the sex fiend I married?' It took weeks to restore the relationship's equilibrium.

Let's get this over with.

She didn't want sex, but she wanted to fight even less. As always, she reasoned that it was ten minutes of her life, and a fight would last much longer. Sometimes, a wife had to have mercy sex.

But why am I the only one sacrificing for our relationship?

She didn't like Alex's hands groping her body. Then he started French-kissing her, his zealous tongue an unwelcome intruder. The touch, the tongue, was too much too soon. Predictably, her brain churned out a million thoughts. *Will the kids hear us and wake up? Did I put the dishwasher on? I hate how his mouth is so wet! I need to replace the soap in the downstairs bathroom.*

Alex rested his hand on her stretch-marked, bloated stomach. Then he massaged her droopy breasts with one hand while rubbing her dry clit with the other. She shifted her body to show him it was uncomfortable, but he didn't notice and kept stroking.

Alex, my clit is not a remote control. Orgasm is not on the menu tonight, so you can skip the preliminaries, is what she wanted to say. Instead, she pushed him onto the toilet and got on her knees to stop the uncomfortable rubbing.

Taking his penis into her mouth while holding the shaft, she rhythmically moved her mouth up and down in unison with her hand. She learned this technique from researching an oral sex article, and it was a literal godsend for nights like this. His eyes closed, and his hands played with her damp hair. She tugged at his balls with one hand and pulled a stray pube out of her teeth with the other.

His legs tensed up, a tell that he was close to cumming. Thank God. Isabella put more oomph into stroking and licking, relieved she'd be reading her book in less than ten minutes. But Alex took her by the shoulders and gently pushed her away. He went to stand, but she grunted to indicate she wanted to stay down there. He grunted back and pushed at her shoulders to say he didn't want to cum yet.

He led her to the unmade bed and, without preliminaries, turned Isabella so she was on all fours, doggy-style. After the hot bath, her vag was as dry as a British comedy. Improvising, Alex spat on his fingers and spread it over her vulva and the tip of his penis.

Why can't he use the lube? It's in the bedside table's drawer. Her body shuddered as he put his spit-laden penis in her spitty vagina.

Alex gave a few hearty thrusts into her still-dry vag. Isabella's breasts and stomach rippled and jiggled as he reached around her to play with her clit. She wished she could tell him that intercourse did nothing for her. Instead, she responded to each thrust with a pleased groan, knowing he got off faster when she was excited. Isabella glanced at the bedside clock and silently prayed for this to end.

Alex took his time—and she did her best not to enjoy it—but after a few minutes of him rubbing her clit and his rhythmic thrusting, her body got into it. The first inkling of an orgasm bloomed, and Isabella exhaled a real groan of pleasure to let him know she was so close and he needed to keep at it. Three big thrusts later, she heard his familiar finishing moan and felt him slump over her body. She wanted to yell, "Keep going!" as he took his finger off her ready-to-orgasm clit. Instead, she said nothing.

He pulled out his penis, pulled back her hair to kiss her neck, then shifted in the bed to pull her body close. She snuggled into his chest, welcoming the much-earned after-sex cuddles. The warmth and smell of his body were so familiar and comforting that she let herself relax. Happy to let the frustration and resentment drift away. Alex kissed her forehead, squeezed her body, then let go and got out of bed.

Are you kidding me? She rolled over to see him putting on his pajama bottoms.

"Where are you going?" Isabella kept the hurt out of her voice, patting the bed. "Come and cuddle."

"I have a ton of work." He leaned in, kissing her mouth and breasts tenderly. "That's exactly what I needed," he whispered into her hair and left.

She felt the ooze dribbling out of her vagina and ran to the bathroom. When she returned to bed with the uncomfortable sensation of blue balls—or was it a blue vagina?—she was alone and lonely. She wanted to finish herself off with her vibe, but Alex might catch her. Instead, she reached for her book. Minutes later, frustrated, she put the book down and switched off the light.

Dr. Gwen's words, "choose yourself," the podcaster's self-care, and Allison's words about equality were looping in her head.

Why am I putting up with this BS?

Jeanette

Back At The Group Meeting

The natural light from Jeanette's sunroom warmed her light olive skin and made her navy-blue eyes sparkle. She spent the day staging the background for this group Zoom call, and everything looked perfect on the screen. Her gray suit jacket, her wicker chair with its plush white pillows, and the lush green ficus and rubber trees in the background. It took forever to get her laptop positioned so her face would look up at the camera.

This group is lucky to have me, she thought smugly. No one wanted to be in charge of the group meetings, and coordinating the schedules of four busy women became a complicated Venn diagram. It was her mommy-organizing skills that had saved this group call.

"Claire's right," Isabella's voice was strained. That poor woman. "It's better to have someone in charge. We're almost out of time."

Jeanette approved of Isabella's choice to be a full-time mom. The other two, well, she gave their screens a grim look. She would have to tolerate them.

But I don't want to tolerate them. The reality cut through the day's frenetic distractions, spotlighting the truth. She was in this group meeting against her will, and still wrapping her head around God's message from the prayer group. God wanted her to take this course for reasons yet to be revealed. And it was putting her faith to the test.

Writing her sex history had been like pulling a layer of skin off her body. She did the homework questions, including the suggested reading, but she didn't understand some of it because French was her first language. Jeanette printed out her prepared list of answers in an extra-large font so she wouldn't have to wear her reading glasses. She didn't want to share or tolerate, but would do her best.

"Okay, I'll go next and make it short." This Amy was a piece of work, and a professor, no less. Was Jeanette paying the university those exorbitant fees to teach her younger son this woke agenda?

Amy's finger moved down the list. "I'll go with number nine: Have your masturbation habits changed and/or evolved over the years? Or I can do number ten: Have your masturbation habits been positively or negatively influenced by having sex with others? So, when I was married —"

"You were married? You never told us that," Isabella exclaimed.

Jeanette couldn't understand why Isabella sounded delightfully surprised. Divorce was something to be ashamed of and to be avoided at all costs.

"It never came up." Amy brushed the question away with a swat of her hand. "So, when I was married, my husband didn't want me to masturbate without him."

"Wait, you'd do it in front of him?" Isabella sounded as flabbergasted as Jeanette felt.

"Sure. It turned us both on when I would Jill off in front of him," Amy answered with no hint of shame. "But the flip side was, he said, I was cheating on him if I did it in private. So after we split, I thought, fuck him. He didn't control my body and had no right to tell me how to masturbate. To celebrate, I became a masturbating queen."

No wonder she's divorced, Jeanette thought.

"You are the masturbating queen," Claire smirked, as if she condoned such a thing.

Jeanette knew Claire's type. They acted superior, thumbing their noses at the wisdom of a lowly, unambitious full-time mom. Claire's identity was so wrapped up in her job that leaving her career to raise a family would be an epic life failure. Jeanette saw Claire soaring to great heights, overly committed and forever busy, chasing the illusion of having it all but never having the anchor of a family. Fifteen years from now, her moneyed life would show that having it all meant having nothing of true importance.

Amy continued, "Even though my marriage was tough, I learned from the experience and turned at least one lemon into lemonade." Amy sounded like a flaky New Ager who believed in a Universal force instead of God. No wonder she was so messed up.

Amy bent her head to scan the list of homework questions. "Okay, question thirteen is: 'Do you have a low, medium, or high curiosity about alternative sexual relationships and lifestyles? Is this something you would be willing to try?' I have a high curiosity to try BDSM. I just never got around to it."

Jeanette did not know what BDSM was, but she didn't want to ask and look stupid.

"I've had partners spank me and enjoyed it. The pain and pleasure thing. So many endorphins being released, etc." Amy saluted. "Is that short enough for you, Claire?"

"Yes, good. Jeanette, you're next." This Claire was so bossy.

Bristling with umbrage, Jeanette picked up her notes, flashing them on the screen to prove she'd completed her homework.

"I chose number two," Jeanette's voice came out croaky, so she discreetly cleared her throat. "'What were some of the sexual values you were raised with?' I was raised in a strict Christian household. My parents and my church told me to save myself for marriage."

"Did you save yourself for marriage?" Amy blurted. Before Jeanette could answer, Amy added, "To be clear, I'm doing my best to listen with an open mind."

Jeanette snorted. "What's not to understand? I was naïve as a teenager and belonged to Christian youth groups, and we had a great time. A few in our group were messing around, but I wanted to save myself for marriage."

"Can I ask you a question, not because I want to judge you, but because I am interested in your answer?" Isabella tentatively asked.

"You can ask," Jeanette countered. Irritated, they hedged their questions. She wasn't delicate china that would break at the slightest mishandling.

"Are you happy you made that decision?"

"Yes, I'm very proud I saved myself for marriage and have been faithful to my husband." Jeanette got no further before a crash came through her earbuds. As her hearing returned, she heard Isabella apologize, explaining her husband was supposed to watch the kids. Then, there was a long moment of confused chaos as two adorable kids made themselves comfortable on her lap.

"Sorry, Jeanette, for interrupting. I've got to go," Isabella's octopus arms were failing to contain the wriggling children. "Can I email if I get stuck?" Isabella asked as the little girl pulled out an earbud to listen in. Isabella abruptly disconnected.

"My timer shows one hour. Jeanette, are you okay with stopping there? I've got to go too." Claire looked relieved.

"Before we get off the call, I saw that the Taboo Sex Show is coming in a couple of months. It's a trade show that has everything to do with sex.

Even though the course will be over, let's consider going. And ..." Amy did a little drumroll on her desk. "Let's do sex magic for our field trip!"

Taboo Sex Show? Sex magic? Jeanette gave her laptop screen a furious look while barking. "I want nothing to do with witchcraft."

"It isn't witchcraft. It's about energy. You have an intention or goal and use your orgasm to achieve that intention. I'm curious to see if manifesting and harnessing the sexual energy of my orgasm does create results."

"There's no way." Jeanette's head spun.

"Amy, too much too soon," Claire said gently. "How about you take it down about a thousand percent and let the rest of us catch up?"

"Sure. I'll bring it up at the next meeting."

"Hey, I've got to run." Claire's eyes were now focused on her desk.

The three said a hasty goodbye and disconnected from the Zoom call.

Jeanette's rigid posture slumped, and she stared blankly at the computer screen as adrenaline surged through her, making her shake. She had almost confessed everything to this motley group. But God had intervened, and she thanked Him for His impeccable timing.

Isabella

Class Two — February 17

SHE WAS BY HERSELF!

For a few blissful minutes, Isabella sat in her car, eyes closed, her ears filled with silence, the stress of the ever-looming deadline put aside. Driving to the university, she put on the music *she* wanted to hear and found a prime parking spot. A rare giggle erupted as she dodged two guys in shorts playing hacky sack in the snow. As she strode into the classroom with a bounce in her step, the excellent juju faltered when she saw Jeanette sitting alone.

"Hey, Jeanette. Thanks for saving the seats." Isabella said, staying upbeat to keep the positive vibes flowing.

"That's fine. I'm compulsively early." Jeanette uncrossed her arms to reveal a tailored tan jacket, dark jeans, and matching tan boots. She gave Isabella's outfit a swift once-over and subtly winced. "Did you get your homework done? It's so hard with little ones to do anything."

"It is challenging with kids. There are so many hoops to jump through to get here and finish the homework. But you don't want to listen to me complain." Isabella frowned as she waved goodbye to her juju as it drifted away.

"I don't mind listening." Jeanette leaned forward on the desk. Her navy eyes were alert as they focused on Isabella. "Mom challenges are invisible to everyone but other mothers."

"Okay," Isabella paused, confused about why Jeanette was being so friendly. "My daughter, Rosa, had a major meltdown when I left. My husband, Alex, was on an 'important call' in another room and couldn't help. As usual. I had to peel her off me and felt so guilty leaving her while she was crying. It bugs me that my husband can see what's happening but does nothing about it. I always have to ask him for help."

Jeanette pursed her plum-colored lips and nodded to show she had gone through this experience herself. "You need to set boundaries."

"Yeah, like that's going to happen," Isabella snorted.

Jeanette sat patiently, doing the Barbara Walters thing. Isabella fidgeted in her seat and, unsuccessfully, covered her ample chest with her tight yoga jacket before making a joke. "Who are these mythical women who skate through parenthood, marriage, work, and life and still have time for hot sex? Not me!"

"There's no perfect way to make any marriage work." Jeanette gave a sympathetic smile. "But it sounds like you need to stick up for yourself more, or your marriage will end up being about your resentments. Trust me, I should know." Jeanette's voice was matter-of-fact, but her rigid body told another story.

Of course, Isabella needed to set boundaries and stick up for herself, but it was a big hassle and too much work. She slumped back in her chair, exhausted before the class began.

Jeanette's eyes flicked over Isabella's shoulder. "We'll talk about this later."

"Hey, ladies, talk about what?" Amy interrupted with her big, infectious smile. Claire, still on her phone, waved.

"The sex history. It was cathartic," Isabella improvised. Not wanting to get into this with Amy, who would tell her to go home and masturbate to get her libido back or some such nonsense.

"I found it adequate but not life-changing," Claire said, now off her call.

"It makes sense to tackle the tough stuff first." Amy guessed and was about to add more when the classroom darkened.

The white screen at the front showed a close-up picture of something that filled the entire screen. Isabella looked, then looked again, her eyes adjusting and readjusting.

What is that?

"That's a vulva!" Amy whispered excitedly.

The class sat transfixed at the slideshow of ten individual, close-up vulvas.

"OMG, that clit is pierced! Doesn't that hurt?"

"She dyed her pubic hair to look like a butterfly? That's a lot of maintenance."

"I never knew they could look so different."

"Good evening, class." Dr. Gwen turned on the lights while speaking over the class chatter. "The majority of women go through her entire lives without seeing what her vulva or what other real vulvas look like."

Unless you live under a rock and have never watched online porn. Isabella had to call Dr. Gwen on this.

"But so many people, especially young people, watch porn."

"It's true, you can see millions of vulvas on the internet, but what are you looking at?" Dr. Gwen picked up the clicker in a shiny navy blue suit and brought up a new slide. "According to data from the International Society of Aesthetic Plastic Surgery, labiaplasty surgeries increased by 45 percent worldwide between 2015 and 2016. Girls as young as nine have reportedly asked for this surgery. It should concern every woman in this room that millions of women are so insecure about how her vulva looks she resorts to plastic surgery."

It horrified Isabella to think her daughter Rosa might want labiaplasty at nine years old.

"In 2016, Eve Appeal, a UK gynecological cancer charity, asked a thousand women to identify their anatomy in a medical illustration. Forty-four percent of women could not identify their vagina. Sixty percent of them were not able to label their vulva."

"But that's a small sample size," said someone in the back.

"Perhaps, but it is indicative of most women." Dr. Gwen walked over and shut off the lights, clicked her remote, and the slideshow of vulvas turned into individual, close-up photos of penises. "What do you see in these photos?"

"Not another dick pic!" the class giggled.

"I've never noticed that a guy can have one ball that hangs lower than the other."

"Do most penises hang to one side? I thought they hung in the middle."

"It's the opposite of sexual or turned on. But when I watch porn, I like it."

The images stopped, the lights returned, and Dr. Gwen had to speak over the crowd. "Can anyone guess why I showed you ten photos of vulvas and ten photos of penises?"

"Does it have to do with how women view their vulva versus how men view their penis?" Amy guessed.

"Yes, very good. When a man is born, the connection with his penis becomes fundamental and significant. When a woman is born, she cannot see her vulva, and rarely is she encouraged to look at or touch it. Throughout history, men have viewed their erections and ejaculations as vital markers of masculinity. The opposite is true for women."

Dr. Gwen put up a new slide. "This is a picture of Dr. Mary Calderone, born in 1904. She was an American physician and public health advocate for sex education. She taught how women have a 'doughnut hole' sensibility with her vulva. This means many women have so much shame about her vulva that it is easier to ignore it. Like it doesn't exist. Remarkably, in our modern day, most women still have a doughnut hole sensibility. We have a negative relationship with our bodies and especially our vulvas."

Isabella wrote "doughnut hole sensibility" with several question marks, not convinced that such an old idea still had merit.

"This negative messaging starts at birth." Dr. Gwen continued. "By the time most women are ready to have sex, she has internalized countless unconscious negative messages. What this means is that at an unconscious level, shame, guilt, anxiety, and resentment hold your sexuality hostage and control your sexual experience."

Isabella stopped taking notes and looked up, making sense of what she had heard.

"Tonight, you will learn how to identify and then sort through your negative baggage —"

"I don't understand the point?" Came a skeptical voice.

"Once you eliminate these unwanted beliefs, thoughts, and emotions, it will create a vacuum. There will be a vacant space to welcome healthy beliefs and thoughts. This new space is where you create a positive mindset."

Anger, resentment, and anxiety Isabella had plenty of those. That she could turn them around to "happy thoughts" was news to her.

A column idea popped into Isabella's head when Dr. Gwen asked, "I appreciate this is a tough topic, but does anyone have an example of how their negative emotions affect their sexuality?"

In Isabella's column, she envisioned herself as the sacrificial lamb. Her hesitant hand went up.

"I do."

"Go ahead." Dr. Gwen turned to her.

With all eyes on her, the heat rose up onto Isabella's face.

"So when my husband initiates sex —" She blew out a ragged breath, but then pictured Jessica smiling while reading her column and launched. "Okay, as soon as he touches my body, I think now? You want sex now? Can't you see I'm tired? I've spent all day with the kids. Worked. Made supper. Put them to bed. And now you want a piece of me, too?"

Isabella replayed the scene in her head as the familiar resentments grew.

"But the thing is, when he sees I'm tired, he rubs my back and asks how my day was. I want to tell him, but he's not interested in my day. There's an ulterior motive to his kindness. And I'm touched out by my kids. I want him to appreciate that I have nothing left to give." Her voice could no longer hide the anger.

Dr. Gwen opened her mouth, but Isabella cut her off.

"He touches me affectionately only when he wants sex."

"Can you remember how your body reacts when he touches you?" Dr. Gwen managed to get in.

Isabella didn't have to think. "My body stiffens, and I fight the urge to pull away. Because if I pull away, he takes it personally. I want him to respect how tired I am. But of course, his needs are always more important than mine. I know I need to set boundaries, but I'm so busy I don't have the time or energy to deal with it."

Jeanette leaned forward and patted Isabella on the arm.

Isabella expected admiration from Dr. Gwen after her heartfelt confession. Why were her lips pursed?

"There are always different choices, and you always have time. Hopefully, you will find your way through this class. That was an excellent example, thank you," Dr. Gwen looked at her watch. "There is a lot to unpack here, but I need to keep this response short. You feel pounced upon by your husband. You expect your husband to notice and are disappointed that he does not acknowledge your discomfort. You want him to treat you with the same respect that you show him. You are both stuck in a sex rut. And all of this non-communication to avoid confrontation slowly erodes your intimate connection. Is that correct?"

Isabella sat stunned at Dr. Gwen's blunt assessment. But then Dr. Gwen pivoted.

"It so happens that a few years ago, a study showed that when men helped with the housework, his partner would be more sexual. Unfortunately, this idea backfired because women saw this as another obligation. In that when she saw her partner cleaning the bathroom or making the bed, it was a quid pro quo in exchange for sex."

What does that have to do with my *sex life?* Isabella sat stone-faced.

"Most women choose to stay silent and fester in her resentments, taking the anger out on her relationship. Where do those resentments start?" Dr. Gwen looked at Isabella, who shrugged. "It centers around women not believing she is worthy enough to communicate her equality in the relationship. Most women are terrified that a fight will reveal her deepest sexual shames. These beliefs, emotions, and experiences control her self-esteem and, therefore, her ability to speak."

Isabella didn't think she had any shame waiting in the wings, ready to do a gotcha moment when she disagreed with her husband. She put more question marks in her notes.

"What could your sex life be if you were no longer afraid?" Dr. Gwen turned back to Isabella. "You need to do the inner work to feel safe and confident to facilitate an open conversation with your husband. Ultimately, communicating your unhappiness is a much easier and healthier solution than letting it fester inside you for the life of this relationship. Does that help your situation?"

"Not really," Isabella shifted in her chair. "Maybe if I were single and had more time."

"Are you busy, or are you scared?" Dr. Gwen's mild delivery was a one-two punch to Isabella's gut.

She stared back, dumbfounded at this offside professor.

She wrote in her notebook: *Is this why I can't set boundaries? Is this why I put up with the BS?*

Claire

Class Two

CLAIRE GLANCED AT ISABELLA, who looked like she'd just been run over, tapped Amy's arm, and gestured towards Isabella.

"Let's check on her after class." Amy nodded and turned back to Dr. Gwen.

"What is your internal conversation about sex? Is it positive, negative, or neutral?" Dr. Gwen leaned over the table, looking at the class with an intensity that mesmerized Claire. "What you believe about your sexual experience becomes your sexual experience."

Dr. Gwen did not come here to play.

"When a couple first gets together, their body's natural love drugs help to make sex fun, effortless, and highly experimental. A woman can rely on her libido to wake up her sexual desire. However, after a year, those love drugs dissipate, and her libido becomes sporadic. Research shows that the majority of women in long-term relationships will not experience spontaneous sexual desire. Rather, when sex is initiated, she will not feel like having sex and, in fact, it will take time before she can move from her head and into her body's desire."

Wait, that's me! Claire's body snapped to attention.

She and Carlos had been together for a year, and she had noticed the shift in their sex life but didn't have the words to describe what was happening.

"As the relationship progresses, couples become less experimental, and sex becomes a comfortable, predictable routine of giving each other an orgasm. It is at this juncture that many couples fall into an unsatisfying orgasm-as-the-goal sex rut. Even though the sex has not changed, because the sex is routine and boring, a woman's satisfaction and ability to orgasm can diminish."

Holy hell! Claire and Carlos were falling into an orgasm sex rut.

Her orgasms weren't great, and now her ability to orgasm would diminish? She tried not to freak out and snatch Isabella's pen and notebook to jot everything down.

"Why is that?" Dr. Gwen looked hopeful, but only received silence in return. "In 2001, sex researcher Rosemary Basson wrote *The Female Sexual Response*. Basson found that when sex is initiated, men tend to be in sexual concordance. This means that as his body becomes aroused, his thoughts and feelings align, increasing in tandem. His buildup to orgasm and resolution takes, on average, fifteen minutes."

Carlos' orgasms were textbook? Claire was stunned.

If this research was from 2001, why was it the first she'd heard of it? Claire leaned forward, hanging on Dr. Gwen's every word, needing to upload and process.

"Basson found women tend to be in discordance and have a misalignment between her mind and body. This creates a delayed sexual response. Meaning she doesn't want sex when it is initiated, and, in fact, it will take her time to warm up to the idea. Basson found climbing to the peak of her arousal was usually a bumpy ascent, taking up to forty-five minutes to reach orgasm."

I am not broken. I have a delayed sexual response! The relief made Claire want to get up in front of the class and do a happy dance.

"Here's the clincher." Dr. Gwen gave a wry smile. "It is during this delayed response that negative emotions surface. Your negative thoughts and emotions can derail your already delayed sexual response. Making it impossible for your body to reach sexual arousal." The class started talking excitedly, and Dr. Gwen had to quiet the class. "We will call these negative thoughts and emotions your sex speed bumps. Their only job is to slow down, interfere with, or prevent your mind and body from becoming sexually aroused."

Do I have any sex speed bumps? Claire couldn't think of any but kept listening.

"Each sex speed bump on its own is small. Your partner did not clean up their mess. Or, they did not notice that you had a stressful day. Or, something went sideways at work. Or, the kids are awake in the next room."

But isn't that normal? Claire wondered. Everyone thought about the things that annoyed them during sex. Claire's body tensed, and she gently moved her head from side to side to stretch her neck.

"This is where your mindset and responsive desire become your biggest sexual allies. Think of responsive desire like muscle memory, where you put your body into the motions of sex to wake up your body's desire and arousal. Where responsive desire starts your engine, the right mindset takes you to the finish line."

Delayed response, forty-five minutes to orgasm, responsive desire, and mindset. The separate pieces of Claire's sex life clicked into place like a jigsaw puzzle. The albatross around her neck became lighter.

"There's a lot of information here. Can you give an example?" Isabella's flushed face asked, with her pen poised, ready to take more notes.

"Sure. Let's pretend sex was initiated. You utilize your responsive desire and put your body into motion when — BAM — a rogue thought pops into your head. 'Why does my husband only touch me when he wants sex?'" Dr. Gwen winked at Isabella. "Or, 'Why does my partner only make the bed when they want sex?' And instead of being aroused, this negative thought loops in your head and is often joined by its negative thought friends." Dr. Gwen adjusted her glasses. "This is why some women want to talk before sex. It allows her to decompress and let go of the tiny distractions."

It's like Dr. Gwen's a psychic. Claire recently started having these thoughts. *But how do I stop them?*

"You are upset, but it is such a small thing. It is not worth bringing up because it will start a fight." Dr. Gwen took a long sip from her water bottle. "Here is the thing. When you do not address a small sex speed bump, each will fester. Over time, many small sex speed bumps accumulate and snowball into a mishmash of resentments."

The class started talking, and Dr. Gwen raised her hand to stop them. "For the record, this is not the sex's fault. Sex is a neutral state. Do not fall into the trap of associating sex being initiated with your sex speed bumps."

Sex was neutral? What did that even mean? Claire's brain was at capacity, but she forced herself to focus.

"The good news is each sex speed bump is a bump, not a block, and won't disable your arousal." Dr. Gwen moved behind the table.

Claire sat back in the unforgiving plastic chair, her head spinning with the watershed moment. In the space of ten minutes, Dr. Gwen had explained Claire's current sex life. It was a relief to know her sex life was normal.

Now, she needed to get to work and fix it.

Amy

Class Two

AMY SAW CLAIRE PRACTICALLY levitate out of her chair with a big aha moment and sat back with a smug smile. Vindicated, she had dragged Claire, kicking and screaming, to the class.

"When you wrote your sex history," Dr. Gwen continued her provocative lecture. "I hope you identified a few memories that made you embarrassed or squeamish. These are important memories and the starting place for you to reclaim your sexual self-esteem."

Claire tapped Amy's hand and then pointed to Dr. Gwen.

Confused, Amy gave her the "What?" look and shrugged. She never felt ashamed about sex. Amy tapped Claire's hand and pointed, and she looked back disappointed.

"At the core of each of those memories is micro-shame. Think of micro-shames as a highly effective, multipurpose tool that prevents your sexual satisfaction. Micro-shames are the reason you cannot let go and fully experience your pleasure. Micro-shames also paralyze you from communicating."

As if Claire had summoned it, a long-forgotten memory from when she was married surfaced, vying for Amy's attention. She didn't need that drama (or Claire being right), so she shut it down.

"Micro-shames are too small to register consciously but big enough to internalize and compound in the background. The daily barrage of micro-shames silences you by making you insecure, never good enough, and never letting your guard down. You cannot count the infinite ways you have internalized being sexually wrong, broken, or bad throughout your life."

"Your negative emotions are hard to identify, admit, and discuss." Dr. Gwen went over to her laptop and clicked a few keys. "I created a short video with past participants telling their most embarrassing and cringe-worthy sex stories. Can someone turn on the lights?"

On the whiteboard, a poorly shot video cut to a young lady with apple cheeks and long red hair. "This guy went down on me once, and I was super sleepy, so I fell asleep and farted in his face. He jerked back and screamed, 'Oh my God, I felt the wind.'"

The class stifled a laugh, unsure whether this was supposed to be a funny or a serious video.

Next was a petite, dark-haired woman with a squeaky voice. "When I was supposed to have lost my virginity, he didn't even get his penis inside me. He was having sex with my bed and didn't even realize it. I wasn't turned on, but I liked him, so I let him continue having sex on my bed and never told him."

Amy let out a chuckle. Claire snorted. Did she hear Isabella laugh?

Then came a jolly-looking woman. "Once, a guy fingered me after doing a food challenge with hot wings. He didn't wash his hands and got triple atomic hot sauce in my vagina. I've never felt such pain down there."

Groans of empathy echoed through the dark room.

A woman with a full afro and glowing ebony skin admitted, "I grabbed hand sanitizer instead of lube and generously applied it in the dark."

The next woman: "This guy took his pants off, and I said, 'Oh, you're not circumcised,' and he looked down at his penis, confused, and said, 'Yes, I am.'"

Another woman: "I once knocked out my ex switching positions. Straight up, roundhouse kicked him in the face."

Another: "It would be the time I said my name by accident right as we both climaxed."

Been there, done that, Amy thought.

Then another: "I butt-dialed my mom during sex. When I saw her again, she looked me in the eye and asked, 'So, how was it?'"

Everyone groaned and giggled at that one—even Jeanette.

The last woman said, "I didn't realize I got my period during sex. During penetration, he goes, 'Are you bleeding?' And I'm like, 'Nah, just super wet.' We continued, and after five seconds, he stopped. 'Yeah, you're definitely bleeding.' I looked down, and his sweater was all red along the bottom. Then he said, 'So that's why you tasted like iron.'"

There were more than a few retching noises. The video ended abruptly, and the lights came on.

"Did you notice that when you listen to someone else's embarrassing story, it is not a big deal, funny even, but when it is your own, it is unbearable? The best way to get over your embarrassing moments is to share because sharing diminishes the emotional charge." Dr. Gwen looked at the class, which was filled with mixed reactions. "Is anyone brave enough to share their embarrassing story?"

Amy's hand shot up. "Vaginal farts." As the words came out, she was surprised at her discomfort.

When Amy said nothing more, Dr. Gwen asked, "What about vaginal farts?"

Amy was uncomfortable and defensive at hearing the class titter. But that was the point, and she launched. "Okay. So, I was doing it doggy style with this guy, and my bum was high in the air, and my chest was resting on the bed." Amy stood from her chair and contorted her body so the class could get a better visual. "I'm not sure what the angle of my hips was, but after he came and pulled out, it was like all the trapped air went with him. My vagina made a massive farting sound, and he gave me this disgusted look. As I explained, I wasn't farting, more farting noises came out of my vagina."

Claire's shoulders shook as a loud snort escaped, making Amy laugh. Isabella bit her lip, unsuccessfully trying to stop herself from laughing. Jeanette stared wide-eyed at Amy as if she were an alien.

"I can laugh about it now." Amy shared the lesson, "But it wasn't funny then. It took a while not to be paranoid about queefing, and I avoided doggy-style for the longest time."

"Would you like to add your story to my video collection?" Dr. Gwen asked.

"It would be my honor." Amy's cheeks flushed, and her chest puffed with pride.

Claire's face changed from laughing to a pained, frustrated look. Why was Claire frustrated when she'd just shown the class how to slay their shame? Claire should be proud of herself.

"It is time for you to face the memories that lurk in the dark corners of your mind," Amy noticed Dr. Gwen tugging at her suit jacket when she was about to make an important point. "Shame, guilt, anxiety, and resentment will show you no mercy. They are in control, holding your sexual experience hostage and doing everything they can to stop you from enjoying sex."

Amy looked at Isabella, eager for her to have an aha moment. As usual, Isabella madly took notes. There was something about her, like she wasn't completely honest with the group, but Amy couldn't put her finger on it.

"Dealing with your shame is straightforward and doesn't require a lot of time. It does, however, require your awareness." Dr. Gwen put up a new slide. "When you recognize a shameful memory, immediately write it down. Nothing is too small or insignificant. If it bubbled to the surface, the memory is worth sorting through. If you put off journaling until a convenient time, you will forget and lose the powerful feelings."

Amy looked over at Jeanette, whose face was unreadable as she sat as still as a granite statue. Amy sensed that Jeanette was in pain, but could only support her if she wanted help. It didn't seem like she did.

"Managing these emotions will be cathartic and healing, like lancing a boil that lets out the poison that has rotted away for however long. Each time you face and conquer a memory, you get stronger, and the more times you go through the process, the easier it becomes."

It never gets easier, Amy thought bitterly.

Triggered, her mood took a nosedive. The memory shoved its way back up, bringing with it the acute pain of completely screwing up her marriage. Like a fool who hadn't learned her lesson, she opened up to Paul, only to have her heart trampled on.

The waves of pain were always hovering and waiting to roll through her body. She wouldn't allow them to push her over the edge. Again.

Amy looked at her group and plastered a bright smile on her face.

Back to Amy and Paul's Date

January 14

AMY DROVE HOME FROM the Thai restaurant with Paul's headlights following close behind. Her brain lit up like a pinball machine, switching between thoughts of their fantastic chemistry and how effortlessly they got along.

She wanted to fuck Paul's brains out, but needed to do this date differently. Were they supposed to chat while constantly thinking about having sex? That didn't make sense. As she turned onto her street, the devil on her shoulder scoffed, telling her she was a grown-ass woman. That dating rules were the patriarchy controlling her sexuality, and the natural next step was to experience Paul.

"Amy, stop!" No-nonsense Claire showed up in the nick of time, swatting the devil away and settling Amy's libido.

Claire was right. She was into Paul and didn't want to mess this up. As she pulled up to her townhouse and got out of her car, she put her trust in Mother Universe to guide Amy with her wisdom.

Long and lean, Paul unfolded himself out of his car and grinned from ear to ear at the sight of her.

"You look beautiful in the moonlight."

Did he seriously say that? Her devil retched, rolled her eyes, and accused Amy of being a basic bitch.

But Claire held steadfast and told Amy to chill and enjoy this campy rom-com moment. Amy deserved to be adored. And perhaps if Amy told herself enough times, she might believe it.

They walked up to her door with pinky fingers entwined, and Amy felt — what? Safe. She was safe with Paul. They slipped off their boots and jackets in her little foyer, laughing and bumping into each other. Then Paul asked to use the bathroom.

Amy seized the opportunity to run to the kitchen and grab a bottle of Valpolicella and two cobalt-blue wine glasses. Then, nimbly, she put her cat Orgasm into her bedroom, lit several candles, and jumped onto her ratty couch.

I can do this. No sex. Just talking.

"You have a great place. It's you." Paul sat beside her as Amy watched her no-sex resolve ebb away. She poured them a hefty measure, and their fingers touched as she handed Paul his glass. The frisson went up her arm and straight to her vag. And just like that, her devil won.

"You said you renovated?" Paul asked as he took in her living room.

"I like you, Paul," Amy was a black widow, sizing up her prey.

"Um, I like you too, Amy." He blushed, his crooked smile scrumptious.

"Can I kiss you?" With sex, Amy was direct, no-nonsense, and take-no-prisoners.

When he nodded, she didn't hold back. In a flash, they returned to the same intensity they'd had by the snowy parked cars. The hit of hormones, like a potent drug surging through Amy's veins, gave a heady rush, a body tingle, and a wet vag. His free hand tentatively caressed her waist and hips.

Is he shy or worried about touching me without my permission?

Consent being what it was, she breathed, "I want to have sex with you. Do you want to have sex with me?"

"Uh, yeah, of course, but I'm not used to this ..." he sheepishly confessed.

"To what?" She giggled as she nibbled at his earlobe.

"I can't decide if I should be scared or turned on. Truthfully, I'm both." His uneasiness was lost on Amy as her hands glided over his gloriously muscular chest.

"Good. You need to be on your best behavior. Now do this to me," Amy directed, caressing her ample breasts and massaging circles around where her nipples protruded through her top.

He sat frozen, hesitating a beat too long, as if he were having a conversation inside his head about what to do. This wasn't the first time she'd needed to take charge and put his wineglass with hers. Then, she placed his hand under hers so she could show him.

His touch was amazing, and she leaned into the body buzz, whispering, "Can I do the same to you?"

He nodded, his pupils dilated, as he said, "If this is a dream, don't wake me." His long fingers fumbled, unbuttoning his shirt, exposing that delicious, muscular chest.

"I want you to kiss me here." She pointed to her neck, just below her earlobe. Obediently, he leaned over, nuzzled his nose on her neck, and gently kissed that sweet, sensitive spot. She breathed, "Where would you like me to kiss you?"

He stopped mid-kiss and pulled back, looking lost for words. Maybe a little lost in general.

He's never been with a real woman. Amy's devil chuckled.

"How do you like this?" She kissed him slowly on his exposed chest and up to his neck. Squeezing the sizable bulge in his pants, she knew it was time to get the adulting over with.

"I recently had an STI check. I'm clear. Are you clear?" She asked, taking her time tasting him.

"Oh, I haven't been tested," he answered, confused.

"That's okay. I have plenty of these." Amy reached into an ornate mahogany box on her side table and pulled out a condom. "I'm going to undress you first. I want to see your naked body."

He stood up, taking off his black shirt while she undid his belt and pushed his loose jeans over his hips so they fell to his ankles. She took a moment to admire his naked, athletic body.

He blushed from the chest up at her intense inspection but managed, "I want to see you naked."

"Well then, undo my buttons."

As he undid each button, he kissed her body. A low, satisfied growl rumbled deep in her throat. When he was done, she pushed the skirt over her ample hips and did an unhurried twirl, wanting him to take in her lovely curves. His deep, appreciating groan was like a snort of cocaine straight into her veins, and Momma needed more.

"Mmm, you're gorgeous," he murmured as he caressed and kissed her soft torso while pulling down her panties.

"I want to lick you," she said, gently pushing him onto the couch as she pulled his pants legs free. Taking the wrapper off the condom, she asked, "Do you like it fast or slow? Up or down?"

The blush deepened as his throat made gulping motions. Somehow, he said, "Um, lick the tip and stroke it slow," as he leaned back on the couch. "Uh, please. And thank you."

Placing the condom on the edge of her lips, she expertly rolled it down the head and shaft of his penis with her mouth. Immediately, his body tensed, and she heard a strangled groan that could mean only one thing. Amy pulled back to look at him.

"It's been a while." A mortified Paul covered his beet-red face with his hands.

"That's okay. It's not a big deal. We have all night. You can finish me." Amy shifted into position on the couch just as Paul got up.

He grabbed his clothes and stomped out of the living room, leaving Amy breathless and open-mouthed as she heard the bathroom door shut.

Jeanette

Class Two

Why does God want me here? Jeanette asked for the millionth time since He gave her the marching orders.

Dr. Gwen tapped her long fingers on the table to make a point.

"Negative emotions take up valuable real estate in your thoughts." Dr. Gwen pointed to her head, unaware of how her scholarly words affected Jeanette. "The fastest way to remove their stigma and emotional charge is to forgive and share."

The shame never goes away. Jeanette wanted to shout at the top of her angry lungs, struggling to keep a relaxed posture.

Her resolve was thinning after a long day of psyching herself up to be there. She shifted in the uncomfortable chair, willing the class to be done.

"If you are questioning whether working through your shame is worth it, ask yourself: Are you worth it?" Dr. Gwen unfolded her large frame from the desk. "The answer is a big, resounding yes. Think of it as an internal spring cleaning and having your sexual self reborn."

Jeanette glowered at the reborn comment. This class was the furthest thing from spiritual rebirth. She crossed her arms, then promptly uncrossed them, remembering that her Ralph Lauren linen blouse wrinkled at the thought of movement.

"One last thing." Dr. Gwen was handsome; Jeanette's appraising eye did a once-over, distracting her from the lecture. Not good-looking in the traditional sense, but attractive. "Negative emotions differ from sexual dysfunction. This course does not address and cannot fix if your body has a dysfunction. Or if you are processing past abuse or trauma. Or dealing with serious personal or relationship problems. I encourage you to speak to your spiritual leader, to seek counseling or therapy."

Jeanette's stomach cramped, and she had to lean forward to stop the pain, creasing the linen blouse.

"That is it for tonight." Dr. Gwen looked at her watch. "This week's homework is to write out your sexual shames, negative thoughts, and feelings. To thoroughly forgive and move on to the next one. You will find more details in your handout. I am here for the next fifteen minutes."

I can't do the homework. I don't have the strength to unleash the geyser. Jeanette let out a ragged breath.

Days earlier, she had watched a science YouTube video in which 13 Mentos candies were dropped into a giant Coke bottle. The dark liquid instantly erupted into the air, six or seven feet high. If Jeanette were to do this homework, she would be that Coke bottle, spewing out her twenty-eight years of angry emotions.

She watched the class rise as one. Her group gathered their stuff, not noticing Jeanette's pain. She should be happy; she didn't want these women in her life, but she needed someone to see her.

"Jeanette, will you email to organize our next meeting?" Efficient Claire asked as she checked her cell, and Jeanette managed a slight nod.

"Thanks." Isabella gave her a grateful, distracted smile before she and the other two women took off.

Jeanette had been sitting still for so long that her butt cheek fell asleep and started tingling. She tried to stand, but her legs wouldn't cooperate. Slowly gathering her things, she was so wrapped up in her pain that it was easy to overlook the pale young lady. She was the same age as her younger son, waiting at the front, anxiously shifting from one foot to the other. Jeanette couldn't help but hear her question echo in the empty, windowless room.

"Can I talk to you about something?" At the professor's slight nod, the young lady lowered her voice. "When I wrote my sex history, a memory came back, and at first, I thought it was a shame, but now I'm not sure."

"Are you willing to share that memory?" Dr. Gwen asked as she sat in her chair. "Take your time."

"Sorry, I don't know why I'm getting so emotional." She looked up at the ceiling to keep the big tears filling her eyes from flowing over. "So, uh, when I was like fifteen, I had a friend of the family touch me in a way that I wasn't comfortable with. It's nothing." Her timid words made the tears spill out, and she wiped her tears with the back of her hand. "I'm so sorry."

"Never apologize for acknowledging your feelings. I can handle big emotions." Dr. Gwen gave her a wry smile. "Did you tell your parents?"

"No! They would have freaked out." Her words gushed out like a broken dam. "He was, like, my dad's good friend from university. I thought I would get blamed because he had flown in for a business meeting, and my father made a big deal of having a barbecue for him. Everything happened so fast." Her breath caught in her throat as she relived the memory.

Jeanette huddled at her desk, making herself invisible.

"You know this wasn't your fault, right?" It wasn't a question.

"I guess, but ..." Her face contorted into an ugly cry.

"Take your time. Breathe." Dr. Gwen took a deep inhale through her nose, and the young woman followed suit.

"I wanted to look nice, so I wore a cute dress. My father kept telling me that if I dressed like that, it would get me into trouble." Her straight blonde hair fell into her face as she looked at the floor. "He was right."

"Please look at me," Dr. Gwen urged, remaining silent until the young lady raised her gaze. "How you dress has nothing to do with how you deserve to be treated."

"Yeah, well, I keep thinking that if I had been, like, more covered up, he wouldn't have been interested. It would never have happened." Another tear escaped. "He said I was too tempting, my smile too seductive, and it brought out the bad boy in him."

"It is time to stop blaming women's looks and recognize misogyny as the problem." The young lady shrugged as Dr. Gwen grabbed a pen and a piece of paper from her attaché case. "I think you've already guessed that this course is not a good fit for you. Here are the names and numbers of agencies that provide free counseling. Your parents do not need to know if you are uncomfortable telling them." Dr. Gwen handed over the slip of paper and asked, "Can I come with you on your first visit?"

"You would come with me?" The young lady sounded relieved that someone believed her and would help her.

"I would like nothing more than to go with you," Dr. Gwen said sincerely. "Now make that appointment, and let me know when I need to show up. My email address is on that piece of paper."

"Okay, thanks." She wiped the tears away and slowly walked out of the room.

Jeanette watched the young woman leave and prayed hard for an angel to follow and look after her. Then, she prayed for her angel.

They would both need extra protection tonight.

Jeanette's Divine Intervention

January 24

Three weeks earlier.

Max's excited bark in the middle of the night meant Andre had found his way back to his separate bedroom. It was Sunday morning, and as she went downstairs, Jeanette smoothed her pajama pants, the silk soothing on her skin.

She found Andre drinking his morning protein shake, perched on the custom-built bar stool at their modern marble kitchen island. He didn't bother to look up or acknowledge her, as if everything was normal and he hadn't spent the last few days AWOL. She narrowed her eyes in loathing. He could do whatever he wanted, whenever he wanted. But she kept her mouth shut.

I'm tripping over the big lumps I've swept under the rug. Telling herself once again that this episode would blow over like it always did. Jeanette's slow-burning rage, a rage she had kept locked up for years, was surfacing, ready to drag her down and consume her.

Max broke the tension, running up and giving her a cheerful morning greeting. Bending to scratch behind his white-with-brown spotted ears, she told Max, "I want to go early. The prayer group is at nine."

"Sure," Andre replied.

They went to church together, no matter what else was happening in their relationship. Looking up from his tablet, then at his limited-edition Rolex, his handsome, full mouth formed a thin line at the sight of her. They gave each other a long, contemptuous stare. Jeanette blinked and looked away as a headache crept up the back of her neck.

"Please feed Max." She exited the kitchen, using every ounce of strength to hold her head high.

Her body gave out as soon as Andre couldn't see her. Heavy and bone-tired, she counted the minutes until her church would prop her up and give an injection of emotional strength. She needed a one-on-one with Pastor Matt, but since it was his busy day, she had to go to her prayer group.

Hopping into the cavernous gray marble shower, her mind churned. How could she ask her prayer group for help without divulging too much? It was okay to admit a fight, but this was far beyond a typical marital spat. If her church knew the truth, they'd never look at her the same way. Stepping out of the shower, she refused to glance at her reflection in the misty mirror. She woke up this morning with a bloated stomach because she couldn't resist having a glass of wine and eating carbs last night.

Meticulously dressed in a chic black Prada pantsuit, she wore a dramatic, chunky gold necklace that glowed warmly against her skin. She pulled her dark hair back into a simple low ponytail to best show off the necklace. The finishing touches were three-inch black patent Louboutins and red lipstick for a pop of color. Inspecting her reflection in the full-length mirror, she saw that her roots showed ever so slightly, and there were a few faint lines around her eyes. She needed to make appointments on Monday.

Dressed in her armor, she headed for the kitchen and sat immobile, refusing to let Andre see her agitated. She heard Andre's shower stop. Minutes later, he came down the stairs with fragrant, damp, combed hair and wearing a sports jacket. Without so much as a glance in her direction, he headed for the garage. Jeanette grabbed her coat and followed like an obedient dog.

They drove in his Jag in awkward silence, listening to the Sunday morning show on French Sirius radio. Once parked in the church parking lot, Jeanette hopped out, negotiating the icy gravel in her slim heels. Andre took his time getting out of the car and had to jog to catch up. They always showed up as a unit. Pam was at the enormous oak door, her plump body even larger with her puffy winter coat. She greeted Jeanette with a motherly hug.

"Oh, good, you're coming to the prayer meeting." Pam drew back, sharing a warm smile that crinkled her bright brown eyes. Then she hugged Andre's large, lean, muscular frame.

How could she touch that man without retching? Jeanette's face must have shown her disgust as a flicker of confusion passed over Pam's pleasant, round face. Still, like most people, she politely ignored it and moved on.

The moment Jeanette walked into the prayer room, her walls fell. With its warm brown tones accented by the soft filtered sunlight, the smell of books on the bookshelves reminded her of her parents' home in Montreal. She was with her people in a safe space. Faith and community were a robust, healing balm, slathered generously over many relationship wounds. These ladies had her back and would support her through this situation.

"Jeanette, you look amazing," Hitomi gushed.

Jeanette sat in the circle of chairs beside her friend, Jolie.

"She always looks amazing," countered Andrina, the newest mom in their group.

"How are your boys? How did the special dinner go for Pierre?" Jenny joined in.

Jeanette was about to answer when Katherine, who headed up the prayer group, spoke up. "Okay, ladies, are we ready?"

The extensive library, which doubled as the prayer room, quieted. The women's eyes turned toward Katherine, whose compact frame exuded an ethereal quality. Everyone followed as she bent her dark, pony-tailed head and prayed with strength and compassion.

"Holy Spirit, we invite You here. We worship You and glorify You. Thank You for every answer to our prayer. Please lead us this morning. Amen." Opening her light-brown eyes, she asked, "Are there any prayer requests?"

Jeanette raised her hand.

"Yes, Jeanette. What would you like us to pray for?" Katherine gave an encouraging smile.

"Andre and I are having a few, uh, marital issues, as every marriage does. I think a big part is empty-nest syndrome, the kids being gone, and we are figuring out who we are as a couple." A few women nodded their heads empathetically. "I want to ask God how to handle this."

"Is he threatening or hurting you, Jeanette?" Katherine asked carefully, as her thick, dark brows creased in concern.

"No, it's nothing like that," Jeanette appreciated the check-in.

Katherine's kind eyes gave a lingering look, knowing there was something Jeanette wasn't admitting, but she didn't press.

"Heavenly Father," Katherine began, "Our sister Jeanette needs Your guidance. Her heart is heavy, and we want her marriage to come through this time with renewed passion."

As Katherine spoke, the prayer washed a calm over Jeanette, giving her toxic thoughts a peaceful reprieve. Her entire body became weightless as her mind blissfully and freely moved to another plane. Jeanette cherished this sacred space, wishing she could set up a house and stay, grateful this was the heaven she would one day be in forever.

The message was sudden and unmistakable. It was as if someone were speaking to Jeanette.

"You must do it."

Jeanette shook her head. "No." It wasn't the answer she wanted or expected, and she gulped in sharp breaths as the loving and healing evaporated.

"I must do it?" Jeanette mouthed, confused but not questioning the edict. A word from God wasn't debatable. She must take the sex course.

But why?

"Did you get your answer?" Katherine asked quietly. Jeanette nodded, unable to speak.

Katherine's empathy kicked into high gear, and she got up from her chair, walked the short distance, and embraced Jeanette with all the love and protection she could give. Jeanette wished she could bottle it for when she was alone and needed it the most.

In her dilemma, Jeanette missed the prayer group's conclusion and didn't hear a word of the sermon. Somehow, she made her way back to the Jag after church.

"I asked God, and He told me I need to take the course," Jeanette said to the window as they drove home.

"That's good news." From their countless arguments, Andre knew better than to gloat over the victory.

The silence for the rest of the drive was unbearable.

Isabella

Group Meeting, February 22

THE WHOOSH OF FRESHLY ground coffee hit Isabella's nose as she walked in, and the shop's cozy warmth wrapped around her. Jeanette had picked this charming French-inspired cafe for their second group meeting. Isabella smoothed her dressiest light-blue mommy tunic over black leggings as she scanned the costly overhead menu.

I'm so glad the magazine is paying for this.

To celebrate the success of her first article, Isabella treated herself to a twelve-dollar coffee and a six-dollar scone. Her weary body sank into the comfy earth-tone-colored sofa as she looked around at the elegant decor. She was grateful not to have a child hanging off her like an appendage. When was the last time she was by herself in such a fancy place? Just as her shoulders relaxed, her anxiety pushed its way to the surface.

"You have time, and you have a choice." Dr. Gwen's vexing words gnawed at her.

She was a busy working mom. Her day was constantly putting out fires. Going through and sorting her feelings of shame took time and energy she didn't have. But this was her job, and she had to do it.

I'm way over my head.

Isabella took a bite of the best, buttery, flaky, raisin scone she'd ever eaten. Savoring another bite, she looked around at the moneyed clientele dressed in an urban, ultra-chic, casual way.

What kind of sex lives do they have? The journalist in her wondered as the subsequent anxiety, impatiently waiting its turn, moved to the front of the line.

Do I tell the group that I'm *writing these articles?*

Would she want to know? Probably not. Telling them would make for a weird group dynamic. She did try to say something during the first group meeting, but her kids found her in the closet, and the opportunity slipped away. Or, if she was being truthful, she was relieved to have the excuse.

The articles were about her experience and had nothing to do with the others. She would be done with the course in five weeks, and the group will be none the wiser.

Unless they catch me, Isabella was confident that none of the women read *Femme.*

A gust of wind announced Jeanette's arrival. Waltzing in as if she owned the place, she took off her cashmere wool jacket and told Isabella she would put in her tea order and be right back. Isabella watched her seriously great ass in wine-colored slacks walk toward the counter. She laughed at something the barista said, her face transforming from severe to luminous.

Jeanette was intelligent, confident, and beautiful, but clearly, she didn't want to be in the course. Yet she organized their group meetings. What was her deal?

"How are you?" Jeanette sat down beside Isabella and blew on her mint tea. A subtle, stylish gold cross twinkled on a delicate bracelet around her slim wrist.

"Good. I'm so happy to leave the house and have a break from my kids." A bolt of inspiration unfurled a pitch on religion and sex, but she needed to tread lightly. Jeanette was cagey and perceptive. "I always feel like such a bad mom for saying that." Isabella chuckled at her Jeanette-approved topic to keep Dr. Jekyll from turning into Mrs. Hyde.

"Hang in there. This season of your life will soon be over." Jeanette assured kindly.

A cold gust of air announced Claire and Amy's arrival, and they waved as they passed to order their coffees.

Isabella turned to Jeanette before it was too late. "The homework helped me understand why I'm having marital issues. There was one thing I thought you could help me with. Can I ask you something?" Jeanette nodded as Claire and Amy approached the table.

"When I wrote out my sex history, I kept returning to my religious upbringing. My parents emigrated from Mexico and are devout Catholics. They expected me to be a good girl, not to date, and not to have sex. So now, after many years of marriage, I still carry Catholic guilt."

"My parents weren't super religious." Claire joined in as she put her coffee on the table and draped her Burberry wool coat over the chair.

Amy jumped into the conversation without bothering to take her coat off before sitting down.

"Religions encourage people to wait for marriage to have sex. But then, because they suppressed their sexual desires, they can't open up to the sexual experience. Which is what your Catholic shame centers on. It's such bullshit." Amy took a hesitant sip of her hot coffee and finished her sentence. "Religion has messed up millions, probably billions, of people's sex lives."

"I guess it depends on how you look at it," Jeanette put her tea down, then turned to Amy, ready for battle. "My faith believes once you get married, you can have all the sex you want. A big part of a healthy marriage is having a good sex life. There's support, teaching, and acceptance for Christian sex education in our community."

"Really? I did not know." Isabella made a mental note as her column came together.

"We are open to having a healthy sexuality," Jeanette said loftily.

"If there's support within your community, why are you in this course?" Amy matched Jeanette's tone, and Isabella saw a shadow cross Jeanette's face as her ice-queen veneer faltered.

"Why are any of us taking this course?" Isabella came to Jeanette's rescue.

"It's well documented that religions have used sex for hundreds of years to control people's — women's — lives," Amy countered. "That's why there is an overriding belief, almost a default, that religion messes up people's sex lives."

"Sorry, Amy, but you've hit a nerve," Claire countered. "You believe in New Agey stuff. That goddess shrine in your bedroom means you pray to a higher power. You may think the Universe differs from Jeanette's God, but it's the same thing. So, why am I expected to respect that you're 'spiritual' but then admonish someone in organized religion? That's hypocritical."

"The difference is I can be a bisexual sex worker, and my God would love me." Amy enjoyed the debate. "Would Jeanette's God love me?"

Interesting, Isabella thought.

"That's not what I'm talking about. You're being the same judgmental person that you claim bothers you. You want everyone to have a right to choose unless it goes against your beliefs," Claire threw back, also enjoying the debate.

"But is sex their choice? More like they're brainwashed to believe sex is dirty and shameful." Amy countered.

"Excuse me." A blond version of Jeanette, dressed in an expensive tracksuit and designer high tops, turned in her chair to glare at Amy's outburst. "Can you please keep it down? Your conversation is bothering us."

"Sure," Amy gave the entitled, white, wealthy woman-of-a-certain-age a slow once-over. Then she turned away, shouting to everyone in the coffee shop. "Hey ladies, we're not supposed to talk about religion and sex because it bothers her."

"I don't think women inside or outside of religion are much different when it comes to sex." She said as softly as possible. "Every woman has her shame, which can come from several places. Religion is one of those places, but I also think religion has become an easy scapegoat."

"I agree. If we put a magnifying glass on one person's sex life and compared it to another's, they'd have similar issues." Claire glanced around to ensure she wasn't bothering anyone. "We should tone it down, keep it to polite conversation."

"Fuck polite conversation. We need to talk about this loudly. If we don't, no one will. Everything will stay the same, and nothing gets solved. We need to fight for women's sexual happiness." Amy shouted, and everyone in the small coffee shop turned to look. "And everyone is welcome to join in."

"I agree with Amy," Claire said in a louder-than-normal voice.

Isabella looked at the defiant Amy and Claire. She wanted to raise her voice but couldn't. Why couldn't she?

Because it's easier to put up with the BS and do nothing about it, Allison's voice came into her head.

Women choose to stay silent and stuck, only to rot in her resentments. Dr. Gwen's powerful voice came to her.

It was a bitter thought, and she, for one, would never make that choice.

Oh, but you are. Allison countered, and Isabella reluctantly agreed.

She'd been living under everyone's expectations of what her sex life should look like. Silenced by other people's need for polite conversation. She had to do something different if she wanted things to change.

But what could she do?

"I agree, too," Isabella said as loudly as possible. Which wasn't loud, but it was the best she could do.

Amy

Group Meeting

"Society is forever searching for its next moral panic." Amy clutched at an imaginary pearl necklace, speaking to the blond woman who got up in a big show of you're-inconveniencing-my-coffee-time and went to the counter, presumably, to talk to the manager.

Bring it on. Amy fumed as a vision of her starting a protest in the coffee shop took shape.

Standing on her chair, she would give an empowered speech about not letting the patriarchy rule their sex lives. Someone in the shop would record her on their phone and post it to their social media. It would go viral, inspiring women all over the world to lock themselves in their local coffee shops and stand up for their sexual rights! To use the hashtag #NoMoreSexualShame in her honor.

"Earth to Amy. The woman went back to her seat. You had your moment." Claire's face tried to be stern, but couldn't hide the smirk. "We're here to talk about shame, not to get kicked out."

"I read our shame comes from thinking everyone has a better sex life than you." Isabella offered, steering the conversation in a calmer direction.

"People don't think others have better sex lives than they do." Amy guffawed, not believing that for a second.

"Not everyone has your sex life." Claire sipped her complicated, low-cal coffee.

"But every woman could have a sex life like mine," Amy said sincerely, eager for another debate, but the group avoided eye contact.

"How did you find the homework?" Isabella tried again, and Amy sighed and sagged back in her seat.

"I found it challenging," Jeanette answered, noticeably subdued. "I don't know if I can share. It's just too raw."

"Me too!" Isabella chimed in. "Why would Dr. Gwen give us such difficult homework?"

"I almost ditched this meeting because —" Claire faltered, unable to finish her sentence. "You're right, Amy. We need to be comfortable standing up for ourselves. But talking about my shame is so uncomfortable."

"That's the point." Amy threw her hands up in the air. "We never dig up these emotions because we're afraid —"

"Exactly," Isabella cut Amy off. "It's completely unrealistic to go from zero to one hundred. This homework was way over my head. Too much, too soon."

"That's not what I said. Please let me finish." Amy settled into professor mode. "By sitting together as a group and discussing the shame monsters we've built up in our heads, suddenly they're not monsters anymore. They're tiny little trolls. Sharing is about you controlling your thoughts instead of allowing your thoughts to control you."

"It doesn't make going through this any less difficult." Claire leaned over the arm of her chair and pulled her laptop out of her oversized cream-colored Michael Kors bag. "I read the supplementary notes and found something similar to what you're saying." She opened her laptop and scrolled. "Okay, I can't find the exact quote, but to paraphrase: Most people struggle with their sex lives but are too ashamed to talk about it. If they do, they lie about what is going on because shame silences them."

Claire looked expectantly at each woman as she took another sip of her complicated coffee, but got nothing. Amy nodded, as if this were old news, while Jeanette and Isabella looked on edge, squirming in their plush chairs. Claire gave it another try. "It's pretty twisted that even knowing this, if a stranger asked me about my sex life, I'd lie."

"I would, too. Shame comes from so many places," Isabella picked up her phone and started scrolling. "I'm on Instagram, and the second headline to pop up is: 'Popstar slams back at troll for body-shaming her.' That's one in a thousand messages we take in daily."

"It's also our lived experience that creates our perception," Jeanette said, sitting up straight. "We have different lives, so our sexual shames will be different."

"I have to leave in forty-five minutes for the babysitter," Isabella interrupted as she looked anxiously at her phone. "This is so interesting, and I don't want to miss anything, so can we move on to the homework? But I don't want to go first."

"I have my laptop open already. I'll find the assignment." Claire tapped the keyboard and then read from her notes. "The first step is to identify what makes us feel shame. Once we face shame, we move to the next step: forgiving. The deeper the shame, the more time it will take, yadda, yadda, yadda. Amy, you go first?"

"Sure. Hey, here's an idea. Let's do a before-and-after check-in to get clear." Amy looked at the women, who gave dubious nods. "Okay, so I've told no one this, not even Claire. Right now, I'm surprised at the amount of shame. My throat wants to close up, and my stomach is upset, like a fight-or-flight response. My brain and my body are begging me not to do this." Admitting this was harder than she imagined, but the professor in her wanted to normalize these emotions for the group when it was their turn.

Amy closed her eyes and let herself experience the shame as it washed over her. "As you know, I was married. After about nine months together, my husband's sex drive dwindled. At first, he had excuses like he was swamped with research. After a couple more months, our sex life got worse. I blamed myself and did everything, but the more I tried, the more he withdrew."

A vise-like grip tightened around Amy's chest. "So then I gave him space, but that backfired, too. After six months, it came to a head, and we got into a big fight. He accused me of not being normal and that I had way too much sex drive, and should have my testosterone checked. Because I was knee deep in the drama, I believed him."

"But you know better," Claire said protectively. "You know this wasn't your fault."

"I do now, but I didn't back then. To no one's surprise, our marriage unraveled fast. One day, he secretly boarded a plane and returned to his home country, China. The only thing he left me was his debt. I received the divorce papers a month later, citing his parents' disapproval of him marrying a white woman, a Gweilo. Which is rich because I'm second-generation Asian-Canadian." A bitter taste filled her mouth.

"I've never met a woman with a higher sex drive than a man." Jeanette looked comically perplexed.

"That's your takeaway?" Amy laughed cynically. "I learned men are assholes. Sorry, I know that's immature, but being abandoned still hurts." It was Amy's turn to squirm, her equilibrium off balance. "Admitting this makes me want to jump out of my skin."

"Of course it would. It must affect your ability to be in a relationship." Isabella leaned in while Claire gave Amy a pointed look.

"It has. I haven't had a long-term relationship since." A tingling along her spine made Amy move her head, and she glimpsed the blonde woman's snigger. Was she listening to their conversation and judging Amy for her most shameful and vulnerable secret? She then saw the blonde lady turn to her tablemates, pointing in her direction, and tilt her head back with laughter.

Amy sat stunned for only a moment when a righteously indignant roar erupted. Women like her kept other women down, and it was up to women like Amy to put her in her place. Amy said loudly enough for the entire cafe to hear. "Fuck you, shame. You're my bitch today."

"We should have that made into a T-shirt," Claire said dryly, raising her oval chin and giving Amy a wink.

"So yes, Isabella. I've been on a few dates, but none of them worked out. Luckily, I've been happy with amazing and satisfying casual sex."

Amy grinned at the blonde woman, who stopped laughing and looked angry.

"Amy, you know I love you." Claire began. In Amy's experience, Claire only said this before landing a big punch. "Since shame is your bitch today, I wonder if you only ever 'hit it and quit it' because you're too afraid of being rejected."

What the hell is going on?

Amy gaped at her group, who stared back with concerned eyes. Even Jeanette leaned forward in the way women do when they want to protect and nurture.

I'm over my marriage and perfectly fine.

Amy and Paul Try Again

January 14

BACK AT AMY'S PLACE.

"We shouldn't have rushed things." Amy gingerly knocked on the bathroom door, scrambling to button her shirt. It wasn't a big deal to *her* that Paul came fast, but it must have been a big deal to him. "Can we start over?"

The door opened a crack, and Paul was an adorable mess; his shirt tucked partway into his pants, the buttons askew, one sock over his pant leg.

"That was humiliating," Paul admitted, raking his fingers through his thick hair.

"It's no big deal." Amy took one look at Paul's face and changed course. "The amount of chemistry between us, I mean." Amy's hands made an explosive motion over her head.

He gave her a "Really?" look, but a tiny smile appeared. Seeing him cave, Amy took his hand and led him back into the living room. Sitting on opposite ends of the small couch, she tucked a blanket around them and handed Paul his glass of wine. Relaxed, they talked like two people eager to learn everything there was to know. An hour later, Amy held up an empty wine bottle.

"Should I grab another?"

"Another time." Paul took the bottle out of her hand. "I have other ideas." He angled closer. "Since you're such a talker, Amy Tam, tell me this," he said so seductively that Amy almost passed out. "What do you want me to do to you?"

Amy could list about a thousand things she wanted Paul to do to her, but kept her response light. "I want you to ravish me, like in the movies." Amy touched her forehead like Scarlett O'Hara in *Gone with the Wind*.

"Is that a thing?" He unbuttoned her shirt, letting it fall open at her shoulders. He kissed her naked shoulder and along her collarbone, leaving her skin tingling where his lips touched. "Ravishing to commence."

He kissed her neck right beneath her earlobe, where she had asked him to before, and her whole body shivered. Moving his hands down her body, he placed them under the waistband of her panties and slowly moved them downward. He pulled back, his eyes devouring every inch of her naked body.

"Oh, Rhett. I'm a lady." Amy giggled, then gasped as he caressed her, his fingers as light as a feather. "Where did you learn that?"

"I have my moves. Thank you very much, Amy, who likes to talk during sex." He gently swatted her hand away as she reached down towards his penis. "Oh no, it's about you this time." He eased onto the floor.

She was more than happy to comply as he softly pulled her bum to the edge of the couch. He kissed her mouth, then made his way down to her neck, kissing and sucking her right breast and then her left. Amy had been with more experienced lovers, but the intense emotions combined with her body's sweet reaction put her into a full-on sex haze. She enjoyed every single sultry second, luxuriating in her sensuality. His downward trek slowed when he opened her legs. Clumsily, he licked her labia.

With past lovers, it was up to her to teach them what she liked.

"Lick me with longer strokes. More pressure on the left."

She could feel him tentatively move his tongue over her inner labia, searching for the spot. When he found it, she held his head steady.

"Right there."

He moved into a rhythm of licking her labia, then sucking her clit. It wasn't long before an orgasm rose, but she needed more stimulation to tip her over the edge.

"Use your fingers to stimulate my clit." In earnest, his fingers massaged her labia and clit. "Yes, like that. That's good." Amy groaned her approval.

Paul confidently switched between using his fingers and mouth on her clit. A moan escaped Amy, and her body tensed ... but it was only a small orgasm? Even so, she basked in her body's wondrous sensations. As her orgasm finished, Paul pulled away, but she stopped him. "Keep going."

Paul looked at Amy, his face like a glazed doughnut.

"Can I kiss you first?" he joked.

"Try me," she called his bluff.

He got back to work. As Amy rode the multiple orgasm wave, her body told her she could push herself over the edge and have a G-spot orgasm. Indecisive, not wanting to freak Paul out, she hesitated, and the G-spot orgasm was gone. When the last blissful multiple orgasms reached its conclusion, she put her hand over her vulva and said, "I'm too sensitive. No more."

"Did I vindicate myself?" Paul looked like a kid in a candy shop, super proud of himself.

"You did." Amy moved off the couch to undress him.

"I want you inside me." She said with fresh intensity.

"I want that too."

She grabbed a condom from her ornate box and gave it to Paul, watching him slide it on. "I want to ride you, cowboy. Or are you a captain?" She mounted him and slipped his penis into her sensitive and engorged pussy as he suckled on her breasts, groaning with pleasure.

"I thought I was Rhett." He breathed, his hands on her ample waist, helping her to move slowly up and down.

"Frankly, my dear, I don't give a damn." She joked, but they both were panting.

"I don't want this to end," Paul said, pulling out his penis.

He gently moved her off his lap, turned her around, and leaned her over the edge of the couch. Entering her from behind, they moved in a natural rhythm. Paul's penis was at the perfect angle, putting pressure on her G-spot. And this time, she let her body go there.

"I'm close. G-spot. Keep going," Amy could barely whisper. "Here it comes. Watch me," she gasped as she ejaculated.

Paul pulled out and watched her squirt, murmuring that she was amazing.

A shaky and wonder-filled Paul reentered Amy. She was more than placated, content to go along as Paul rode to his orgasm. When it was done, he nuzzled and kissed her neck, whispering that it was the best sex of his life. He took off his condom, tied the end, and dropped it on top of his sock. Crawling onto the couch, they snuggled under the blanket.

"Can you always do that?" Paul's face was pure awe.

"The G-spot? Only when my body is properly ravished." Amy loved the feel of his lean body against hers. "Are you thirsty?"

"Thanks, but it's much too nice cuddling with you to get up."

Soon, they were both asleep. Amy woke, still in a sex haze, wanting to go a third time. Stirring, she woke Paul, who kissed her forehead as he untangled his lanky frame from her body and the covers.

"This was a night to remember." He bent and kissed her with passionate fierceness.

She wanted to watch his toned arms pull his underwear over those toned legs, but her bladder had other ideas. "I have to pee."

He gave her another long, lingering kiss before she eased away. She could only shuffle to the bathroom with the warm blanket wrapped around her cold body. He laughed as she shuffled out of the room. A few minutes later, she shuffled back into the living room, but he wasn't there.

"Paul?" she called out to the empty townhouse. Throwing off the blanket, she hurried to the front landing.

His coat and shoes were gone.

Claire

Back At The Group Meeting

"I GET YOU'RE UPSET about Paul." Claire's eyes widened as her hand flew up to her mouth, and she braced for Amy's blowback.

"I'm not upset." Amy feigned a smile as she brushed an imaginary crumb off her arm. "I've already forgotten him."

Claire's eyebrows shot up at hearing her friend's lie.

This right here. This was why she had given Amy the three-date rule. Claire had been direct and specific about Amy's "hit it and quit it" habits, yet Amy was still in complete denial.

"That's me. Let's talk about you, Claire." Amy, the master of taking the focus off herself when emotions got too close, glared at Claire.

Standing at this oh-so-familiar Amy's not ready-to-hear-the-truth impasse, Claire turned to Jeanette and Isabella, one perfectly polished and one disheveled, wishing they would back her up, but got nothing. So, instead of convincing her friend, she huffed, scanned her laptop, tapped the keys, and opened her homework. After reviewing her notes, the heaviness and dread returned to her chest, and she had to close her eyes.

"Everything okay?" Amy switched from belligerent back to her best friend.

Claire put her hand up to show she had this, keen to work through whatever this was. "I was fine writing out my sex history, but it must have set off something. I don't know how to explain this. A subconscious chain reaction? When I wrote about my shameful memories, it was like I had this visceral reaction. My body was on pins and needles."

"Did you get all your thoughts down?" Jeanette asked, sipping her tea.

"Yes. At least, I think so. It was like dominoes; once I admitted one shame, the others fell. I would write something and then walk away, so it took several days. I'm not done, but I wrote as much as possible."

"Is there something you want to work through with us?" Isabella's curvy bum sat on the very edge of her seat.

The last thing Claire wanted was to share her shame with the group and work through it. The thought triggered the same intense fight-or-flight response she had while writing out her shame.

"Oh my God, they're talking about shame?!" The blonde at the next table fake whispered to her friends, who smirked. Claire's guts clenched as she heard a stranger mock her. Why did she care what that horrible woman thought?

Shame is controlling me.

The realization clunked itself ungracefully into Claire's analytical brain. If there was one thing she would not tolerate, it was something controlling her. She sat up straighter, forced herself into the tackling-difficult-things zone, and nodded to Amy.

"First, tell us what's going on," Amy gently probed.

"I don't understand why this is so difficult to admit." She looked at the group of women who were rooting for her success. "I dread being judged." She looked at the blonde woman. "But, like Amy, I want to make shame my bitch."

Jeanette raised her tea and toasted. "Here's to Claire, making shame her bitch."

"Bend shame over the table and fuck it hard up its ass!" Amy added loudly. The blond lady whipped her head around and gave Amy a filthy look. Amy winked back and toasted to her as well. Her unapologetic moxie made the group grin and helped Claire relax.

Squaring her shoulders, she launched.

"My boyfriend, Carlos, might be the one, but I can't relax when we're having, you know, sex. I know I said this at our last meeting, but I need to work through —" Her stomach gave a loud gurgle in protest, and Claire blanched but kept going. "Why, I can never relax. The real problem is that the more he pleasures me, the more irritated I become. If I'm not going to enjoy sex, I want it to be over with."

"Oh, that's not good," Isabella exclaimed.

"Right? I feel so ungrateful. Guilty. Ashamed. He's working hard to make it a good experience for me. For us. But my body doesn't cooperate. Sometimes it's good, but most of the time, I want it to be over with."

"That's normal," Jeanette said, but Claire kept talking.

"I've gotten into the habit of faking my pleasure, and it's exhausting. So now, when sex is initiated, and I think about how much effort I will have to put into faking, it's not worth my time." With each word, a weight lifted off her shoulders. "I'd rather be working."

"Ding, ding, ding, we have a winner!" Amy lurched forward. "That's your problem."

"Yes, faking orgasm, I know —"

"Not that. It's about you putting your focus on your career." Claire must have looked as bewildered as she felt because Amy said earnestly, "It doesn't leave any space to enjoy sex. Instead of focusing on faking or how to have an orgasm, you need to focus on making your sexual enjoyment a priority."

What was Amy going on about?

Of course, she focused on her career. Amy focused on her career. Every person her age focused on their career.

"What am I supposed to do? Quit everything so I can devote my attention to Carlos like a 1950s wife?" Claire thought this must be a practical joke, but Amy wasn't laughing. "Amy, you know how hard I've worked for fifteen years. Besides, you're one to talk. You worked just as hard as I did to become a professor, and your sex life is great. So it can't be about the career."

"Claire, we're both excellent at our jobs but failing at our relationships." Amy's voice faltered, and Claire caught the sad shadow pass over her face.

Claire had a serious boyfriend; Amy's dating life was a mess. There were a thousand miles between what they were experiencing in the relationship department.

"Amy, you know my ten-year plan. There won't be as much pressure once I make partner in my law firm, and I can focus on other things." Claire was so proud of how her ten-year plan unfolded precisely as expected. "Like making my relationship a priority."

"Do you seriously believe that?"

"Yes, I seriously believe that." Claire mimicked Amy's condescending tone.

"You're not the only one going through this, trust me," Isabella said shyly. "Balancing a relationship and a career. Speaking from experience, it isn't easy. I can share my ups and downs if you're interested."

The sympathy in Isabella's voice made Claire's emotional side snap shut. She gave Isabella a cool once-over, confident she would never be like her. She had a plan. She had her life together. She would never be constantly frazzled with a perpetual big stain down the front of her shirt.

"Of course, a work/life balance is tough. Anything worth having will be work." Claire didn't notice Isabella's stricken face. Her only concern was to get through this exercise. "I want to tell Carlos that I'm, well, you know, faking. Orgasm." She heard a collective intake of breath from the group. "What? If he's the one, we shouldn't have any secrets."

"Telling Carlos you're faking is a terrible idea," Amy warned. "And for the record, you're focusing on the wrong thing."

"Noted." Claire was so done with Amy's nonsense. She looked at her laptop notes and exhaled slowly. "The homework says the next step is to forgive." She slumped back into her seat. "I don't think Dr. Gwen covered how to do this. I don't know where to start or what to do. Who am I supposed to forgive? Myself? Carlos? He's done nothing wrong. Forgive my vulva? I'm not being glib. This is confusing."

"I don't know either, but you must figure it out." Jeanette chimed in, giving Claire a stern, motherly look. "If you want your relationship to work, forgiveness is the most powerful tool in your toolbox."

Claire believed Jeanette, but forgiveness was a nice-to-do rather than a must-do, and she tucked it in the when-she-had-a-free-moment-to-think slot. Along with Amy's ridiculous thoughts on her career. Out of everyone, she would never expect Amy to tell her she needed to prioritize her relationship over her work.

Claire looked around the warm, cozy cafe to see if hell had frozen over.

Jeanette

Group Meeting

"I've taken courses at my church about forgiveness." Jeanette ignored Amy's mocking eye-roll. She may not know about sex, but in this group, she had a monopoly on forgiveness.

"The best definition I've heard is that forgiveness is to give up the hope that the past could have been any different. To let go of a past we thought we wanted."

"Letting go of the past we thought we wanted," Isabella repeated under her breath as she frantically wrote.

"Letting go is a choice. You can choose to limit yourself and your relationships by holding onto resentment and pain. Or choose forgiveness to no longer let that feeling have power over you." Jeanette dictated slowly so Isabella could keep up.

"Sure," Claire still looked perplexed. "But how?"

"The best way I've heard is a Hawaiian healing mantra. You need to say, 'I forgive you." Thank you. I'm sorry. I love you.'"

"I'm not being difficult, but how is that useful?" Claire threw her hands up in the air.

Jeanette contemplated Claire, who could never forgive herself while pursuing perfection. She wanted to tell Claire that perfection was an illusion with a trapdoor and a long fall into loneliness and anxiety.

"I'm figuring this out too, Claire." Isabella finished taking notes and looked up at her group. "To recap what Dr. Gwen said: When we forgive our shameful experiences, we eliminate our baggage to create a space. I'm not sure what Dr. Gwen meant when she said sex is neutral. After we stop looking at sex in a negative way, then what?"

"Dr. Gwen said it was a vacuum." Amy took up the torch. "Shame needs to be replaced with something else. I'm assuming it should be with a positive emotion."

"Like enjoying sex?" Claire sighed as she glanced sidelong at Amy. "Look, I don't want to be the cynical one, but positive thinking can not turn around thousands of years of shameful socialization."

"Hold on," Isabella jumped in. "I read an article yesterday about how couples would rather focus on relationship symptoms, like an inability to orgasm or a lack of sex, when the actual problem was emotional connection and safety. This vacuum can create a space for couples to be vulnerable, focus on their connection, and practice communicating. That's not positive thinking, that's practical."

Jeanette took a long sip of lukewarm tea to steady herself. There had never been an emotional connection with her husband, and she was sure there never would be.

"Dr. Gwen might be setting people up for a letdown. Turning a lifetime of thinking around in a month is unreasonable," Claire said.

"Okay, what's the alternative?" Amy sat up, excited to debate.

Isabella looked at her phone again and started packing up. "Can we move on to Jeanette? I have to go."

Jeanette nodded to Isabella, then leaned over to pull her notes out of her black Hermès handbag.

"Did you want to do a before and after?" Amy asked.

"Sure. I'm nervous to tell you about my discovery." Jeanette looked down and read from her typed, double-spaced notes. "I researched online and found out I have a hormone imbalance called HSDD. It's such a relief to have a name for what I'm going through." She sank back onto the couch, surprised at how relieved she was to say it out loud.

"What is HSDD?" Isabella asked, intrigued, thinking this could be a solution for her, too.

Jeanette wanted to help, but Isabella's situation was the problematic season of young kids, not hormones. Then again, Jeanette wasn't a doctor, and it might be hormones — or both.

"HSDD stands for Hypoactive Sexual Desire Disorder," Jeanette read. "After researching, I found this website with an online quiz about my symptoms. I answered the questions, and it confirmed I have HSDD. It's a biological predisposition. My brain is wired differently," Jeanette finished triumphantly. She glanced at the group, who looked nonplussed.

"So, where's the shame part?" Amy asked, sipping the dregs of her coffee.

Jeanette scrambled, unable to admit the truth, settling for a half-truth. "I've always carried shame about not being sexual."

"Let me guess. This website promotes a drug to cure HSDD," Claire zinged sarcastically.

"Yes, in fact, it's an FDA-approved drug that needs to be prescribed by a doctor to help postmenopausal women with HSDD. Which is me. Just because a website sells something doesn't mean it's snake oil." Jeanette shot Claire a stinging look that bounced right off her.

"Have you made an appointment with your doctor?" Amy asked, a fair question that Jeanette wanted to dodge.

"Not yet. I only found out about it." Again, Jeanette had to use another half-truth to avoid a more profound truth. If she started taking the drug, Andre would expect her to have sex. And she was never having sex with him again.

"Holy, I've got to run. I promised the babysitter I'd be back in fifteen minutes." Isabella tapped a quick text, pulled on her black puffer jacket, and waved goodbye. "Sorry, we didn't finish your turn, Jeanette."

"I have work due tomorrow, so I've got to run too. I'll call you." Claire and Amy exchanged looks as Claire threw on her Burberry winter coat, grabbed her bag, and left.

An uncomfortable silence followed after the two women's quick departure. Jeanette couldn't handle chitchatting with Amy, so she grabbed her things.

"I'm still working out why you're in this class." Amy examined Jeanette thoughtfully as she buttoned her high-collared cashmere jacket.

"I have my reasons." Jeanette leaned over to pick up her purse, keeping a tight hold on her emotions. "Why else would I put myself through this?"

"Do you believe that?" Amy threw her hands up in disbelief. "The three of us spilled our guts. While your 'big shame' is filling out a website questionnaire that says you have a medical condition, you won't go to a doctor for."

"You have no idea about my life." Jeanette's walls were crashing in, and she had to escape.

"It's your choice to live in denial," Amy said to Jeanette's back as she fled the coffee shop.

Jeanette's "Gift"

February 22

"The nerve of that woman."

Max's white head tilted back and forth, watching Jeanette as she paced the living room floor, then perched on the edge of the couch cushion to bounce back up and start pacing again.

The confrontation with Amy at the coffee shop had unleashed something weighty and shameful she could no longer run from. Jeanette was well aware of what her life was like — a big lie wrapped in a pretty bow.

She stopped mid-stride, almost tripping over the glass coffee table as the memory came rushing back. The awful night when she and Andre fought. Scratch that. It wasn't a fight. It was an ultimatum that would change the trajectory of her life forever.

Reliving the memory from a month earlier, Jeanette's knees buckled as she sank onto the couch and let her heavy head rest in both hands, big, messy tears falling onto her lap.

"Quelqu'un à la maison?" Jeanette called out, opening the side door from the garage into the house, tired but satisfied after getting Pierre's big date night ready.

"Salut, mon petit chou!" She greeted Max, whose tail wagged so hard it might snap off.

"I'm upstairs."

She heard Andre's muted yell, and then the shower turned on. Jeanette's dark eyebrows met in a scowl; she hadn't expected him home and would have to pull supper together on the fly. Worse yet, spend time with him. She kicked off her kitten heels and put the multiple shopping bags on a piece of paper on the white marble counter.

She took a long breath through her nose and out of her mouth. She needed to refocus and reframe her attention to avoid a fight. Her eyes roamed the immaculate kitchen, taking in the white-tile backsplash, pristine cabinets, and stainless-steel appliances. Designing the house had brought her immense pride. Now, there was little joy in the house that lit up the pages of home-design blogs; too many bad memories lingered within these walls.

She blew a ragged breath and tried again — refocus and reframe — busily clearing away the shopping bags. The slip of paper under the bags fell to the floor, and when she picked it up, she couldn't read what it said. Another unwelcome reminder of how she was aging. She took another breath as she grabbed her newly purchased reading glasses.

She first noticed the university logo and assumed it was a registration for her younger son, which was strange because he didn't live with them. She looked more closely and saw that the registration was in her name? Confused, she read further down. Her arm braced the side of the counter as her body went off balance, the air sucked out of her lungs, and the blood drained from her expertly made-up face.

This can't be right.

Jeanette thought as she reread the registration.

"Have you seen my dark blue shirt? The one from Harry Rosen?" she heard from upstairs. "Never mind, I found it."

Like a jack-in-the-box, the hinge on the tightly contained box of her emotions loosened, popped open, and the years of fights exploded out. The times Andre would hassle her for sex. The hundreds and hundreds of times she refused. Saying yes out of guilt and resentment. The thousands of times he held her lack of sexual desire against her, insinuating there was something wrong with her. How he mercilessly shamed her for not wanting sex as much as he did.

Now this?!

She crumpled the paper into a compact ball and threw it on the ground.

This is going to fix it?

She had made enough concessions in their marriage, thank you very much.

"He can go to hell." She meant that literally.

Grabbing a bottle of Bordeaux from her shopping, opening it, taking two glasses from the overhead cupboard, and pouring herself a hefty glass. Screw her perimenopausal body rebelling tomorrow. She needed a drink tonight.

"Andre!" she yelled, suppressing the enraged tremors in her voice. "I bought a new wine today. It's a Château Figeac 2010 Bordeaux." She knew her husband, the wine snob, could not resist.

"Okay, I'll be down in a minute."

He sounded, what, cautious? He's going to play this as if *it's no big deal.*

Her foot tapped impatiently as she contemplated the ways she would tell Andre to shove this up his ass.

The exquisite scent of Andre's imported Italian shower gel announced his entrance. With his salt-and-pepper, tousled, damp hair, he still had major sex appeal. Jeanette gulped her fine wine, now vinegary, to her taste buds and almost spat it out. In photographs, they were a beautiful couple. To the outside world, they had it all. But she'd never found him attractive, and after twenty-eight years, she found him repulsive.

"How did it go helping Pierre with his date night?" Andre's eyes darted to the balled-up paper on the marble-tiled floor.

His sly question stopped Jeanette's anger in its tracks. Talking about the kids was their Switzerland. Despite being incompatible, they were an excellent parenting team. Always in sync when doing the best thing for their boys.

"He wasn't there, so I let myself in with the spare key. I spent a little extra buying everything ready-made, but that way, he can put things in the oven."

"Good thinking. You're such a great help to him."

Even though Jeanette knew Andre meant every word, she refused to be sidetracked and resumed tapping her foot. Andre poured a generous glass of wine and left the kitchen without a word.

He doesn't want a confrontation. He never wants a confrontation.

She snatched the paper ball off the floor and ran after him into the living room.

"What's this?" She stuck the crumpled paper in his face. "Or were you going to forget to tell me you signed me up for a — for this?!"

"I thought it would be a fun gift," Andre replied, dismissing her concern but unable to meet her gaze. She had learned a new term at her church women's group: gaslighting. She was pretty sure he was gaslighting her.

"This is your idea of a gift?"

"You didn't like the lingerie I bought you one year ago." He listed on his fingers. "Or the jewelry. Or the flowers. Or the candy. Or the vacations. You like nothing I buy for you. So why should this be any different?"

"Don't you dare deflect." Her eyes narrowed to slits.

After twenty-eight years of marriage, she had learned to pick her battles. She didn't want to fight, but that ship had sailed. She was ready to go down with this ship, grateful the triple-glazed windows meant the world outside wouldn't hear.

"This gift is about you, not me."

He sat on the plush couch and pinched the bridge of his nose. A classic Andre move to imply Jeanette was so stupid she couldn't understand basic logic.

"I don't know what else to do," he said reasonably, as if calming a deranged person. "That we haven't had sex for at least a year should give you enough reason to thank me for taking the initiative. You refuse to go to a therapist."

You are having sex, but not with me. She wanted to scream, but they both knew she wouldn't bring up his mistress.

Instead, she said, "So, it's up to me? I'm supposed to fix this while you sit back and wait for me to make it happen!"

If she could breathe fire, her stylish sitting room would be in ashes.

"Well, you're the one who doesn't want to have sex. I'm a willing partner."

"That's such a cop-out." This wasn't about sex. This was about wielding the power dynamic in his favor.

"Is it?" He sighed, signaling that he was growing tired of the conversation. "I am a fifty-four-year-old man in his prime in a sexless marriage. You're the one who doesn't like sex. What am I supposed to do for the next twenty-five years? Not have sex because it's too inconvenient for you to take a course?"

"Do you think a sex course is going to fix this?" She waved her arms between them, no longer caring if she looked hysterical. She was distraught and rapidly becoming unhinged.

"I don't know. But you need to do something," he replied in his calm, condescending voice. "I'm willing to see a therapist. You're not."

"Don't drag out that old excuse." But he was right. She loathed the idea. Over the years, Andre had convinced her she was frigid. There was no way a therapist could fix that, so there was no point in going.

"Look, it's your choice." Finishing his wine, he put the glass down and stood up. "Good wine, by the way. Please get more." He put his hands in the pockets of his tailored khakis. "Take the class or go to a therapist. If you don't fix this, I'm done."

"What do you mean done?" She crossed her arms in disbelief, the taste of bile rising in her throat at the finality of his tone.

"I've initiated talks with my lawyers, and I'm sure we can work out a fair deal if it comes down to divorce." He straightened the cuffs on his shirt.

Shocked, she stood rooted, as hard and unyielding as petrified wood as he strode from the room, his oh-so-recognizable scent following. Good riddance. It made her nauseous.

A few seconds later, maybe a few hours later, she heard Max bark as the garage door opened and Andre drove away. To his mistress, no doubt.

"He can't be serious." Jeanette said weakly to Max.

They'd been married for twenty-eight years. They'd raised a family. They were pillars in their church and community.

She forced the jack-in-the-box lid closed, as she had countless times. Shoving the shameful truth, which was far worse than any fight, about what was wrong with her as far down as it could go. Jeanette picked Max up, his warm little body calming her frazzled nerves. She'd sacrificed so much to keep her marriage together, acquiescing, surrendering her happiness to live this lie. A course could never fix her.

He's bluffing to get his way. He never follows through.

She needed to let things cool off. They slept in separate bedrooms and could avoid each other for the next few days.

Claire Tells Carlos She's Faking

February 25

CLAIRE SHIFTED HER TIRED body into a comfortable position under her bed's warm-down duvet. She was so absorbed in reading the deposition on her laptop that she barely registered the lips skimming her neck. She brushed Carlos's face away, not noticing when he changed tactics and leaned over to caress her shoulder. As his hand made its way down to her breast, it was irritation that tugged Claire out of her focus.

Carlos left a trail of kisses just under her ear, and she was about to say, "Sorry, not tonight," but stopped herself.

She and Carlos were young, and their relationship was still new. They should be having the best sex of their lives. Somehow, with eyes wide open, she got snared into faking her pleasure. She let faking become her get-out-of-jail-free card, with shame holding her hostage.

TF? Like, what the actual F! Claire thought. *Not today, shame. You're my bitch,*

There will never be a good time to bring faking up, so it might as well be now. Carlos deserved the truth, and if telling him caused them to break up, perhaps it was for the best. She forced herself into the 'tackle difficult things' zone and turned to him.

"I'm bushed. I have a big day tomorrow."

What the?! Were her brain and mouth on different frequencies?

She was about to correct herself when Carlos mumbled something snarky, gave a pissed-off sigh, and rolled over. His reaction teased out a mix of guilt and resentment, stoking the flames of a repressed resentment she did not know existed. In one fluid motion, she snapped her laptop shut, gave a chilly goodnight, and rolled over to her side of the bed.

Less than a minute later, the chasm between them felt like it would swallow her, so she moved to his side of the bed. When she spooned into Carlos's disgruntled body, he grabbed her hand as an olive branch.

They had so much to say, but neither could say any of it.

Sex takes, like, ten minutes, so why the drama? She asked herself.

If she had sex right now, this weirdness would vanish.

But I don't know how to have sex without faking it.

She didn't know what to do or how to act, and she needed more time to devise a plan. And so went the argument in her head until Carlos's breath deepened in sleep.

Claire rolled out of bed, agitated and guilty at not seizing the opportunity to have sex. She shoved her arms into the comfy robe that wrapped her in a much-needed hug. Quietly, she padded to the living room to flop into her beloved comfy chair.

She didn't know what was worse: Going through this guilt trip or being obligated to have sex when she kind of didn't want it. She should only have sex when she was in the mood. But then she remembered Dr. Gwen's lecture about responsive desire: she needed to put her body in motion, and then her desire would catch up. If her desire caught up, she wouldn't need to fake it? Or was it the other way around?

She stretched her shoulders to loosen the tension.

No longer faking and performing like a porn star was the way through this.. Of course, it would be bumpy, but it couldn't be as complicated as her imagination made it out to be. She just needed to have sex and get it over with.

"I thought you said you were bushed?" A deep, resentful voice came out of the shadows, making Claire jump.

Carlos scratched his semi-erect penis with one hand while he held out the other to her. Putting her hand into his firm grip, their touch spoke a thousand words. They needed to work as a team to go the distance. As he let go of her hand, saying he needed a drink of water, she made a vow never to fake an orgasm again.

They walked back to bed hand in hand. Claire climbed in and admired Carlos's mostly naked body as he sat on the edge. She was so attracted to him. He kissed her right shoulder as he handed her his water. As she drank, water dribbled down her chin and onto her chest. Carlos waggled his eyebrows and playfully went to lick it away. Claire giggled, put the water down, then threw her arms around his neck and kissed its hollow as desire tugged at her nether region.

When Carlos touched her breasts, Claire was fully aware — for the first time — of what her breasts felt like being touched, but she remained silent. Not getting the usual response, Carlos put more energy into massaging her breasts, and Claire willed her body to enjoy the touch, but there was too much going on in her head, and it barely registered. She refused to fake a groan.

My pleasure is a big part of his pleasure, she realized.

His hand slid down to her clit, and from the first rub, she knew she wouldn't orgasm. She started to tell him, but he kissed her, and she lost her nerve.

As if having an out-of-body experience, she watched the dance as he went through the motions to get her off, but this time she didn't moan. She did nothing. She just lay there, trying to feel her body. The harder

Carlos got her off, the more her body retreated, her body and brain at a stalemate.

"Is everything okay?" Carlos whispered.

Claire tried to speak but could only nod. She didn't like this knowing. It was awful and awkward; the burden flatlining her libido. She wanted to show him where she was authentically. She did. But inadequacy and shame were poor bedfellows, and it took everything she had not to fake again.

Carlos gave up the foreplay and lay on his side, angling her hips at forty-five degrees and resting her legs over his hips. It was a nice, lazy way to have sex, but not orgasm-nice. Mercifully, it didn't take long for him to cum. Which meant he could cum without her faking.

"So glad you stayed up. That was great." He gathered her into a cuddle and kissed her cheek.

You thought that was great? Great for whom? She wondered, but at least their fight ended, and they were happy again.

Listening to Carlos drift back to sleep, Claire reflected on the tedious, cringe-worthy, and far too awkward sex.

As terrible as it was, she was glad she had done it and fell asleep with a glimmer of hope that sex could get better.

Isabella

Class Three, February 24

Isabella trudged into the hot classroom, wound tight in her thoughts and too many winter layers. She'd mistakenly taken Jeanette's advice and set boundaries with Alex, putting her foot down and making him care for *his* kids. She lost it when he whined about having important deadlines and refused to babysit the children.

His deadlines meant something; her deadlines meant nothing. She made money, but he made more, so his deadlines took precedence. He didn't say her actual job was supporting him and their kids, but he implied it.

What century do I live in? How did my life turn into this? Isabella fumed.

As Alex listed the reasons she should have called his mom, Isabella grabbed everything from the front closet and fled. She spent the entire drive calming her frayed nerves, but at the classroom door, her tired shoulders sagged in defeat. Why did sticking up for herself mean a battle?

Setting boundaries shouldn't be this painful.

Jeanette was already there, looking flawless, with her salon-styled hair, cashmere sweater, and stylish camel slacks. When Isabella sat down, Jeanette pounced, "Can I ask you something?"

"Sure?" Isabella didn't want to listen to Jeanette's situation. She wanted to vent about her failure to set boundaries.

"When we were in the coffee shop, Amy told me I was in denial." Jeanette chewed the inside of her cheek. Isabella didn't have the emotional bandwidth to clean up Amy's mess, but she didn't want any group infighting.

"Things got intense, and emotions ran high." Isabella noticed Jeanette's head snap to attention and followed her gaze to see Dr. Gwen walking down the stairs.

What was that about? Jeanette turned back to reply when Amy and Claire arrived.

"Hey," Claire smiled, her black, tailored Theory suit out of place in this crowd, while Amy's *Meditate, Medicate, Masturbate* T-shirt fit right in. Amy and Jeanette ignored each other.

Luckily, there wasn't time for an awkward confrontation because Dr. Gwen dimmed the lights and started a video. The credits showed it was a documentary about *Bodysex,* as a female voice spoke over the photo montage.

"Betty Dodson was 90 years young, a renowned sex educator, famous author of *Sex For One*, and a revolutionary for women's sexual equality."

Isabella had read Betty Dodson's book, *Sex For One*, back in university. For the first (and perhaps last) time in her life, she felt sexually empowered. What happened between then and now? Instead of embracing more confidence and equality, she moved backward into a traditional role.

"Since the 1970s, Betty's private practice from her New York apartment included workshops teaching women about their bodies and how to masturbate and orgasm. She coached over seven thousand women before her passing in 2021."

"I have a Betty Dodson art print in my townhouse," Amy whispered, almost levitating off her chair.

"Of course you do," the group chorused back, lightening the tension.

The video moved to a shot of Betty talking.

"You need to have a healthy relationship with yourself before you can be an active participant in your sexual experience." Dressed in hip, urban clothes, with a shock of gray, spiky hair, not looking or acting remotely close to her ninety years. "My workshops are a process. First, we get vulnerable. Then, comfortable in our bodies and our vulvas. Only then can participants move on to achieving orgasm."

Betty leaned into the camera.

"Men and women were told this lie: that women can effortlessly orgasm. A healthy man will become turned on and achieve orgasm with ease. Therefore, it's assumed a woman should effortlessly compartmentalize whatever happened in her day and be fully engaged in her sexual pleasure, become aroused, and easily orgasm. When, in fact, orgasm doesn't come naturally to most women. It takes work. Add to this, most women cannot orgasm simply with penetration, which leads many women to perform and fake her pleasure. She needs to stimulate the clitoris during penetration to make sure she also reaches orgasm."

Isabella heard Claire's sharp intake of breath and took her hand. Claire's hand grasped tight, and Isabella hung on, too, as a myriad of emotions swirled. How did an intelligent, strong woman like Claire get caught in this faking web of lies? Women needed to be more like Betty, open up, and be honest about orgasms and faking. It started with Isabella and her column.

Betty spoke over footage that now showed her naked, answering her New York apartment door to welcome in a new group.

"We sit in a circle naked, and there's no judgment, only acceptance. All of that awkwardness goes away right away. It really does."

Isabella watched in disbelief as the women removed their clothes in Betty's small apartment foyer.

"There is something so powerful and healing about this connection and to have these conversations with other women."

The next shot showed the women sitting in a circle on blue mats in Betty's living room.

A shiver ran down Isabella's spine. She wanted to be one of the women sitting on a blue mat?

Where did that come from? Isabella felt Claire squeeze her hand.

Betty continued, "The most important ritual on day one of our workshop is genital show-and-tell because so many women think, 'Oh my God, what could be scarier than that?'"

Beside Betty was an empty mat with an oval mirror and a small desk lamp. The video jumped to a captivated young woman with cocoa skin, sitting with Betty as they mapped out her vulva. Later in the video, the same young woman masturbated with a Hitachi wand vibrator. As Isabella watched her orgasm, it was the opposite of watching porn, and it left her both moved and queasy.

Off-camera, the interviewer asked Betty, "Any last piece of advice?"

"Learn to run the fuck, and if you can't say it, then you certainly can't do it," Betty concluded in her no-nonsense way.

The video ended, and Isabella blinked as the lights came on, her tired brain keeping pace.

"Today, class, you are going to learn how to run the fuck." Dr. Gwen announced, and Isabella's gut somersaulted.

What did that even mean?

Isabella had never run the fuck. Okay, a few times in university after she read *Sex For One,* and at the start of her marriage, but she did not know what to do or how to do it. Feeling pathetic, her underarms sweaty, she looked around the room. The young woman looked as terrified as her, like they never ran their fuck, either.

"Please join your group and discuss whether you would attend a Betty Dodson workshop." Dr. Gwen instructed the class. "If yes, what would you want from the experience? If not, why not? You have ten minutes."

Her editor, Jessica, would love Isabella to do the Betty Dodson workshop. But even if she could somehow fly to New York and take the workshop, she wouldn't do it.

So, you said you wanted to be one of those women on a blue mat. What are you afraid of?

Nothing, she replied too quickly to herself. She wasn't scared, per se. Okay, a little frightened. But there was a big difference between wishing to do something and doing it.

"I would LOVE to attend a Betty Dodson workshop." Amy was as eager as a Labrador puppy. "I am such a big fan, and it sounds like a healing experience."

"Naked in a room with a bunch of other naked women? Yeah, I'd pass." Claire's rigid posture squirmed. "Even to undress in a foyer with strangers is weird."

"It looks like you go to the gym." Jeanette gave Claire a quick once-over. "Do you undress in front of other women in the locker room?"

"Do you?" Claire threw back, not taking the bait.

Isabella eyed the long and willowy Claire, then the lean and buff Jeanette.

Of course, it's easy for them to get naked.

"I don't change in front of women at my gym. I wear a sports bra and yoga shorts to show that I've not gained weight. If I see a love handle,

I immediately control everything that goes into my mouth." Jeanette admitted, looking at her feet. "I've never told anyone that."

"If we're doing confessions," Claire gave Jeanette a look of solidarity, "I also work hard to keep in great shape because I have to earn feeling good about myself. If I can't exercise, I hide in loose clothing because it doesn't match my ideal body image. How much I work out dictates how much I eat."

Isabella did a mental stumble. The two women with Instagram-approved bodies were uptight, while curvy Amy was body-confident?

She heard Amy ask Isabella for her thoughts on the Betty Dodson workshop, and something unexpected popped out of her mouth.

"It was so empowering to see the women in the video so comfortable in their naked bodies with the other naked women. Not to mention the camera crew," Isabella confessed. "I wish I had that level of body confidence. Betty was a true pioneer and risk-taker, so I would take the class even if it scared me."

Amy put her hand up, and when Isabella went to high-five, Amy gave her a hand-hug.

"A plan is being formulated."

"Oh no. You've got that look in your eyes. Amy, reel it back in." Claire warned, but then Dr. Gwen spoke over the class.

"Is anyone open to taking Betty Dodson's workshop?"

"It sounds dated." A brave woman in the back admitted. "Sitting in a circle and looking at your vulva is 1970s retro, something flower children would do. Like, for my mom's generation."

Dr. Gwen turned to the young woman.

"If I asked you to come to the front and show the class your naked arm, it would not be a big deal. If your vulva is in the same category as your arm, then it should not be a big deal to show everyone your naked vulva.

Would you be willing to come to the front of the class and show us your vulva?"

Dr. Gwen motioned for the young lady to come forward, but she sank into her chair, turned a shade of purple, and shook her head no.

"Looking at your vulva may sound like a trite exercise, but it is a gateway to acknowledging, exploring, and accepting your body."

Dr. Gwen's last statement hit Isabella like a hammer. How could looking at her vulva be the gateway to body love? It didn't make sense.

The professor continued. "Although Betty Dodson advocated tirelessly since the 1970s for women's sexual equality, little has changed. Today, most modern women do not run their fuck. She still puts her sexual needs second. Have you ever considered why most women automatically put their partner's needs first? Tonight is about you learning what it is to be sexually equal and, therefore, to understand what you want out of sex."

I'm not ready to run my fuck.

The thought was just so ludicrous. Isabella pictured herself as a chain-clad dominatrix cracking a seven-foot leather whip. Running the fuck, she reasoned, was for single people, not for long-term couples with young kids.

But then frustration, anger, and resentment showed up, dropping the memory of Alex complaining about "babysitting" his kids. The trio told her equality was so much more than sex. That she and Alex had fallen into traditional gender roles was nobody's fault, but it needlessly complicated her life. Setting boundaries would be simpler if she were an equal in her relationship.

She might not know how to run her fuck, but she could learn.

Isabella heard that loud and clear.

Even though she was terrified of unlocking her sexual power, she turned to Dr. Gwen, ready to learn how to run her fuck. Unwilling to put herself second ever again.

Claire

Class Three

When Claire heard Dr. Gwen say, "Tonight, you will learn how to run your fuck," she almost threw her hands up and called it a day.

She learned a lot from this course and wanted to have a positive attitude. But come on! Run her fuck? That was an Amy thing.

Claire could totally see Amy sitting with other naked women on blue mats, engrossed in discussions and examinations of their vulvas. But it wasn't Claire's thing, and she couldn't relate. At all. As Dr. Gwen pressed the point, Claire's finger tapped the desk, deciding whether to cut her losses and leave the class early.

"The next time you walk into a sexual experience, pay attention to whose pleasure you focus on. Is it you or your partner?"

Claire's finger stopped its impatient tapping.

Had she ever focused on her pleasure? Sure, she had moments where she was into the sex, and it was hot. But there was invariably a part of her that was detached, thinking about something from work, or what she looked like naked, or whether the room was too hot or cold, or how bored she was of having the same sex on repeat.

"Chances are," the professor continued, "especially if you are a people pleaser, you focus on your partner's pleasure. On their orgasm. Since your birth, society has programmed you to put your sexual needs second." Dr. Gwen tugged on her jacket. "For example, the next time you watch a movie or read a romance book, pay attention to the sex scene. It will most likely show that the woman's ultimate sexual satisfaction and orgasm comes from a large penis. That as soon as the large penis thrusts in and out of her vagina, she is instantly turned on. She can effortlessly compartmentalize whatever happened in her day to focus on the build-up and experience a satisfying orgasm."

"There is a reason it is called fiction." Dr. Gwen paused as a look of intense frustration passed over her face. "The myth that women need a large penis to experience pleasure persists, despite efforts by sex educators to dispel it."

Claire closed her eyes, unwilling to tear up, as the information settled in. She wasn't broken!

"It is time to put your sexual needs first and run your fuck. Focusing on your pleasure means you create a sexual experience to meet your needs. It starts with asking yourself, what does good sex mean to you?" The class stared blankly back, expecting Dr. Gwen to give them the answer.

"If we went around this classroom, and I asked each of you what you wanted out of your sexual experience, my bet is you would want a powerful orgasm." Claire saw Amy and the other women nod.

"Although consistently orgasming is important, having an orgasm is only one small piece of your pleasure pie." Dr. Gwen put up a slide showing a large apple pie with a thin slice taken out. "You need to ask yourself what you want out of the sexual experience that does not include orgasm."

A confused murmur erupted from the class.

"For you to stretch your sexual boundaries and tap into your unique pleasure spectrum."

Pleasure spectrum? What kind of nonsense was this? Claire's goal for this course was to have an orgasm during sex. Period. She wasn't like Amy, who could tap into her pleasure spectrum.

"What's a pleasure spectrum?" Isabella leaned forward, listening to Dr. Gwen with her whole body.

"Your pleasure spectrum is a vast range of the sexual satisfaction your body contains. And you have a ton of sexual satisfaction waiting and wanting for you to access it. Your pleasure spectrum is fluid and ever-changing, with nuances depending on your mood, menstrual cycle, outside distractions, etc." Dr. Gwen smiled at Isabella, who looked unconvinced. "No two women's pleasure spectrums are the same, which makes yours unique and interesting. Worth exploring. You are full to the brim with a lifetime of toe-curling sex. You need to learn how to tap into it."

Claire rolled her eyes, saw Dr. Gwen look at her, and immediately regretted it. Pleasure spectrums were way above her pay grade, and toe-curling sex was not already inside of her. She just wanted a good old-fashioned orgasm.

"Putting your sexual needs first starts with putting your focus back on you. Which means you need to unlearn and stop faking orgasms." Dr. Gwen put a black-and-white photo on the whiteboard. "In the 1970s, Masters and Johnson coined the term 'spectatoring.' This is where you are a spectator, watching yourself have sex, evaluating and worrying about your sexual performance."

Every nerve in Claire's body was standing at attention. There was a name for what had haunted her sex life, and this was the first time she had heard of it.

"Research shows that at least 80 percent of women fake orgasms sometime in her life." Dr. Gwen put up the next slide showing a close-up of Meg Ryan's face during the infamous orgasm scene in *When Harry Met Sally*. "Women faking orgasms is so common, its unspoken truth is the punch line."

Claire remembered laughing when she watched that scene in *When Harry Met Sally*, but now winced at the thought of *her* sex life being a punch line.

"When you regularly fake, you are so busy performing that you ignore your body's sexual cues. The longer you spectate, the more detached you become from your pleasure and body. If spectatoring goes on long enough, your body can stop orgasming."

Claire breathed a sigh of relief. Not faking was the worst kind of uncomfortable, but at least she stopped and dodged this bullet.

"A lot of women fake orgasms because, in the short term, it solves a tricky problem. However, this once-straightforward way to manage an awkward situation becomes a chore. It becomes work to fake your pleasure." Dr. Gwen sat on the table's edge as if stabilizing herself to throw the next doozy. "Why do most women still feel obligated to be passive and pretend to climax?"

Isabella put up her hand.

"Faking was never a conscious decision. One night, I was tired, so I faked it. It was simple, so I did it again. And, as you said, it was easier to fake than to get into a fight. I want to tell my husband that sometimes I can orgasm, and sometimes I can't. But that's an unpleasant conversation, and there's never a good time to have it."

Isabella was making shame her bitch, and Claire was living for it.

"What would be the worst thing if you told your husband?" Dr. Gwen probed.

"That I fake? Is that really a question?" Isabella looked flabbergasted. "It will start a big fight, and he will resent me for lying. And then every time we had sex, it would be the elephant in the room."

"I get this is difficult to share, so thank you. What is the cost to you and your relationship if you continue to fake orgasms and be a spectator in your sexual experience?"

"It's just that ..." Isabella's face was a mixed bag of emotions. "My husband can't move on to his orgasm until I've orgasmed, so I fake it. I don't know what else I'm supposed to do."

Another exasperated look passed over Dr. Gwen's face as she attempted but failed to suppress a sigh.

"You are supposed to run your fuck. To tell your husband the truth. That you have a whole pleasure spectrum waiting to be explored. To show and tell him what you want out of the sexual experience."

Isabella shook her head in disbelief, looking at Dr. Gwen as if she had three heads.

"My apologies. This topic triggers me. If you are already in the habit of spectatoring and faking orgasm, the best thing to do is take a step back. Notice your patterns and stop yourself when you feel compelled to fake. Transitioning from spectatoring to being engaged in your sexual experience will be challenging. The irony is, once you put your sexual needs first and focus on your body's pleasure, your partner will enjoy the sex more."

Isabella looked so miserable and ashamed that Claire decided to share her experience at the next group meeting and help her out.

Help her out.

Claire looked at Isabella, who'd made shame her bitch, screwed up her courage, then put up her hand.

Amy

Class Three

Amy saw Claire throw up her hand and quickly snatch it back down. It wasn't like Claire to vacillate.

"It is far harder to rewire your biology than to alter your beliefs." Dr. Gwen pushed a stray micro-braid from her face. "You cannot force your body to experience what society says should satisfy you. Presently, society dictates that a couple's sexual satisfaction is from orgasm-as-the-goal and the she-cums-first sex. Yet both have created an unpleasant conundrum for most women."

What was this?

Amy questioned Dr. Gwen's logic for the first time since the course started. Amy was a woman's orgasm advocate. Her mission in life was to make sure every woman could have a satisfying orgasm experience. Amy knew better than to have a knee-jerk reaction, so she sat back, crossed her arms, and listened to Dr. Gwen's full explanation.

"Typically, with the she-cums-first orgasm model, there is a polite prelude of foreplay to set her desire into motion and get her in the mood. Hopefully, during foreplay, she can orgasm, but if not, oh well. It's time to move on to the main event: her partner's orgasm."

Amy wanted to put her hand up and counter this broad generalization. She would never put her needs second and couldn't understand why any woman would.

"Expecting women to cum first has the majority of women tying themselves into knots because most are dealing with a delayed sexual response. Meaning it takes extra time for most women to shift from her brain and into her body's arousal. Generally, that brain-to-body lag in time means she cannot orgasm within the she-cums-first foreplay time frame."

If women didn't cum first, then they wouldn't cum at all. Amy thought defiantly. Then again, she'd never heard of this delayed sexual response and needed to look into that.

"Orgasm-as-the-goal sex is, generally, how men want to experience sex. However, women's and men's orgasms are not the same, and their experience of reaching orgasm is different. Yet, orgasm-as-the-goal sex expects a woman's body to experience orgasm the same way as a man's."

Amy had had enough, and the words flew out of her mouth.

"But women want to orgasm."

"Yes, of course, women want to orgasm," Dr. Gwen bristled at being interrupted. "As I was about to say, although women have active and robust sexual desires and libidos, it is less linear, with more variable patterns of desire, arousal, and fulfillment. Her ability to get in the mood and orgasm is, typically, inconsistent."

Amy was just about to counter, ready for an orgasm debate, when Claire put a steadying hand on her arm.

"I want to hear what she has to say." For her friend's sake, Amy relented and sat back in her chair.

"With orgasm-as-the-goal and she-cums-first sex, most women do not want and eventually resent the pressure to perform and orgasm first, on command, with every sexual experience. Instead, her orgasm needs to happen on her terms rather than be dictated by someone else's expectations. Does that make sense?" Dr. Gwen asked Amy, who looked at Claire, listening attentively and processing the information.

"In cultures that expect women to enjoy sex as much as men, anthropologists observed that those women have regular orgasms. Masters and Johnson documented that women's range and depth of sexual pleasure infinitely surpasses that of men."

Finally, something that made sense. Amy knew women experienced sex more intensely than men. She nudged Claire, whose brow furrowed as she chewed her lip.

"We have already determined that orgasm is only one facet of your broader pleasure spectrum." Dr. Gwen turned her attention away from Amy. "When your body is no longer forced to do something it may not want, and the pressure to perform and to orgasm is gone, it leaves a space where you can bring in the things that you find arousing, sexual and sensual."

"Let's compare your options." Dr. Gwen put a two-column diagram on the whiteboard. "Orgasm-as-the-goal and she-cums-first sex, usually, will not produce an orgasm for you. Rather, they put your sexual needs second because no matter what happens, your focus is on your partner's orgasm. Any sexual pleasure you might experience is truncated. Versus, you tap into your pleasure spectrum, and instead of forcing an orgasm, you bring a fresh, new dimension that gives your sex texture and sensual depth. You put your sexual needs first and let your partner worry about their orgasm. As you get better at putting your needs first, you experience a deep sensual pleasure."

Claire blew out a frustrated breath, and Amy grabbed her clenched fist.

"You don't get it," Claire whispered through pursed lips.

But Amy did get it. She'd always gotten it. She could easily tell any partner what she wanted, and Claire could not. That's why they were taking this class. Together.

"Is there anyone who can give a concrete idea of what you want out of sex?" Dr. Gwen's hopeful face scanned the class.

Looking resolute, Claire raised her hand, and Amy propped up her elbow so she couldn't snatch it down.

"I want my boyfriend to play with my clit while we're having, uh, intercourse," Claire's voice wavered.

"Great example. What is going through your mind, saying it out loud in front of the class?"

"Honestly, I can barely breathe. My chest is tight, and my thoughts are a jumble." Claire's lawyer's face was unreadable.

"Your courage is helping someone in this class work through their situation. I want you to appreciate that."

Claire gave a slight nod before speaking. "Okay, so, uh, when we're in the middle of things, and I'm on top, depending on how I'm, you know —" Claire stopped. Amy wanted to rescue her, but respected that this was Claire's journey.

"Thrusting?" Dr. Gwen prompted.

"Yes, that. My clit rubs against his body, and I love the sensation and want more. But it never lasts long because I go back into my head and lose the sensations in my body. It's like a teaser. I keep thinking that if my boyfriend helped me out, I could orgasm."

"Perhaps it's simply a matter of shifting your perspective and helping yourself instead of waiting for your boyfriend." Dr. Gwen gave her a look of encouragement. "Do you think you and your boyfriend would enjoy the experience more if you did?"

"Well, he thinks I orgasm now because I, well, I used to —" Claire blew out an uneven breath and barked out the word, "Fake. I used to fake but recently stopped." She shrugged. "That's it."

"Claire, that was superb. Well done." Dr. Gwen beamed. Amy knew her praise was the perfect balm for Claire's fragile ego. "See me after class if you want to talk it through."

Dr. Gwen turned back to the class. "The possibilities of your sexual satisfaction expand or contract in direct proportion to what you can imagine for yourself. There is nothing wrong with men desiring orgasm-focused sex. Just as there is nothing wrong with women tapping into her pleasure spectrum. True sexual compatibility is about merging these two ideals."

Amy was nodding so hard she must have looked like a bobblehead. "Your pleasure spectrum is your birthright. Putting your sexual needs first and having the sex you want is the basic minimum of what you should expect from your sexual experience. You deserve every sexual encounter to satisfy you."

"Amen," Amy whispered as she envisioned millions of women making up their minds that sex was about her needs and how amazing that would be for them, for their partners, and the world.

She looked at Claire, Isabella, and Jeanette, every fiber of her being wanting them to know the power of never putting their sexual needs second again. But how?

And then the plan came together in her head.

This was going to be epic!

Jeanette

Class Three

"If your sexual situation is not what you want, you can change it," Dr. Gwen said. "You are in the driver's seat. You are in charge of how much and how often you experience sexual pleasure."

I don't have a choice, and I can't change it.

Jeanette sat stone-faced, unable to catch her breath, as if she were underwater, surfacing for air. Every time Dr. Gwen spoke, it pushed Jeanette back under the water, and she struggled to breathe. She believed in taking responsibility and being the change she wanted to see. However, her situation was different.

"There are hundreds, possibly thousands, of things that can bring you a deeper sense of sexual satisfaction that do not include having an orgasm."

Dr. Gwen turned and put up a slide with the word "orgasm" in the middle, surrounded by pleasure spectrum ideas.

"If you were to take only one of these ideas and implement it, your sex would become three-dimensional and more interesting."

Jeanette looked at the whiteboard, which was full of suggestions. That she could ever experience sexual satisfaction was an utterly alien concept, and the idea of it pushed her back under the water.

"My partner would never go for this," came a defiant voice in the stuffy, windowless lecture hall. "I've brought new ideas into the bedroom, and my partner stomped out."

"You bring up an important point." Dr. Gwen said, turning toward the voice. "Can I ask what you did after your partner stomped out?"

"I dropped it. But now I resent him even more." Her words hung in the air, and in a weaker voice, she admitted. "I don't like being rejected."

"No one enjoys being rejected. But was it rejection, or were they uncomfortable trying something new? There's a big difference. Excellent share, thank you," Dr. Gwen turned back to the class.

"It is normal and okay to have your partner push back. Bringing in change and setting boundaries might initially threaten your partner, and it will take you both time to ease into this new idea. Because you are creating a new couple dynamic, it is your job to give them a hand up and help them meet you at your new level. Most partners want you to be sexually fulfilled. However, if your partner is against your sexual fulfillment, you need to ask why and consider seeing a counselor, therapist, or minister."

Jeanette had wanted to speak to Pastor Matt over the years, but shame and humiliation stopped her. It was time to set up an appointment.

Dr. Gwen's brows furrowed as she looked at her watch.

"That is our time for this evening. For your homework, you need to discover what you want out of the sexual experience that does not include an orgasm." She walked around the desk to her chair. "What could your sex look like when you tap into your pleasure spectrum? Think big and way outside your comfort zone. Thirty years from now, what good memories do you want to have about your sex life? Because you are creating them now. If you notice any triggers or negative emotions, write them in your journal."

Jeanette didn't have a pleasure spectrum. She was numb down there, always had been, and always would be. She didn't think Dr. Gwen would accept that as her homework. Then again, maybe she would.

"Topics for your next group meeting might be: Why do women believe she only need an orgasm to be sexually fulfilled over a lifetime? Why have women set the bar so low? Or discuss how focusing on orgasm is a big reason sex becomes redundant and boring for women over the long term. Talk about why society encourages women to get trapped as a spectator. Or why do women still sacrifice her satisfaction to appease her partner's ego?"

Jeanette froze, provoked by Dr. Gwen's last words. Her entire sexual life had been to "sacrifice her satisfaction to appease her partner's ego." She was raised to believe her sexual needs didn't matter, and until tonight, she'd never questioned that.

A gentle understanding enveloped her body: her sexual pleasure did matter. Then, the understanding drifted away just as quietly as it came. Jeanette's arms wrapped around her body as she tried to make sense of the message and was, once again, plunged under the water.

"Thank you, and I will be here for ten minutes if you have questions." Dr. Gwen turned off the PowerPoint as chairs shuffled and the class prepared to leave.

Jeanette's body was stiff from sitting rigidly. She stood up, a fog of confusion, and gathered her things. She wanted this night to be over. To get to the safety of her home with a cup of tea and the comfort of her dog, Max. She was about to ask the group about their next meeting.

"I have an idea." Amy paused dramatically. "Promise to think about it before responding."

"No!" Claire put up her hand. "Whatever you are about to propose, my answer is no."

"We could do a Betty Dodson workshop at my place," Amy said, ignoring Claire. "Let's look at our vulvas!"

Much to Jeanette's relief, Isabella and Claire blanched and answered in unison, "No!"

"Hear me out," Amy went on, undaunted. "Doing something way outside our comfort zones will create faster results."

"Because *Project: Up My Sex Game* turned out so well." Claire looked knowingly at Amy. "I speak for the group when I say we're not ready to take that step. Why can't we go to a sex shop?"

"When will you be ready?" Amy had a zealous look in her eyes. "Next year? Two years from now? There will never be a good time in your life to do a Betty Dodson workshop. So why not now? Isabella, what do you think?"

"Yes," Isabella's mouth mumbled a hesitant yes while the rest of her terrified face screamed no.

Jeanette's jaw went slack.

"Okay, that's one. What about you, Claire?"

"You won't let this go, will you?" Claire pursed her lips and closed her eyes tightly. "I've got to run. Email me the details."

"Super. What do you say, Jeanette?" Amy turned to her.

Jeanette didn't want to go on any field trip, let alone something so bizarre as this.

"I don't see the point of showing everyone my —"

But that same compassionate understanding returned, gently telling her to do this and that it wasn't an option. Despite the roiling turmoil inside, Jeanette kept her impenetrable, calm shell in place.

Why would God want her to do this? It made absolutely no sense.

"Jeanette, I'm next-level scared, but this is exactly why we need to do it." Isabella leaned in and put her hand on Jeanette's arm. The light, intimate touch was like a shot of electricity through Jeanette's body. She had never known what it was like to be held and touched tenderly.

And then she got what Dr. Gwen meant. What Jeanette wanted out of sex was to be touched lovingly. It was all she ever wanted, deeply and desperately, from the depths of her soul. But other than holding her kids and her dog, Max, she had given up on that dream years ago.

"I'll do it on one condition." Jeanette regretted the shaky words as they left her mouth. "I don't have to get naked."

Saying the word naked was like a giant shovel scooping and hollowing out her insides.

"Done. I'll speak to Dr. Gwen to ensure we can do this," Amy went to the front and spoke briefly with Dr. Gwen, who nodded. Amy came back with a thumbs-up. "It's a go! I will host at my house. We can do the homework first and then look at our vulvas. Oh my God, I'm so excited! I'll email you with the details," Amy triumphantly slung her bag over her shoulder, waved goodbye, and left.

"Did we enter the Twilight Zone?" Isabella joked.

"What are you going to wear?" Jeanette was catching up to what she had agreed to.

"Nothing. I'll be naked." Isabella's face turned ashen white as they left the classroom.

Isabella's Femme Column

Lingerie

I'M ASTONISHED TO WRITE the following sentences.

Too many intelligent, strong, and ambitious women take charge everywhere in her life except in dating, initiating sex, and saying what she wants. We let our partners take the lead and do what *they* want during sex. We choose to fall in step and, in doing so, move backward into traditional gender roles.

Why are women scared to take charge of our sexual experience? It makes no sense. It's time to stop waiting for our partner to read our minds. We deserve to be in charge of our sexual happiness and pull ourselves out of the faking our pleasure trap.

I never once asked myself what I wanted from sex. My automatic response was to have an orgasm. However, this week, I need to raise my sexual bar and think outside of having an orgasm.

It brings up a lot of emotions to say that I want something different. For fun, why don't you look in the mirror and say, "I'm taking charge and doing what makes ME feel good." Saying those words out loud made me queasy. See what comes up for you.

The irony is that your partner will be so grateful that you've stepped up. They want to know.

This week, I cleaned my underwear drawer and bought new lingerie. A Feng Shui experiment to clear out the old and bring in the new. What I learned was unexpected.

What's On This Week's Sex Menu?

Class #3: What do I want from the sexual experience that doesn't include an orgasm?

Answer: I want to feel sexy again.

Problem: My body has changed since baby number two, and I haven't come to terms with those changes.

Let's see how this plays out in real life.

Comfort Versus Sexy

I thought buying a cute bra and panty set would help me feel sexy again.

Since university, while living on spaghetti and adrenaline, I had a drawer full of beautiful, expensive lingerie. It cusped on an obsession. In my naïve twenties, I swore that unless it had to do with period panties, I would NEVER, under any conditions, wear cotton undies.

I hand-washed the underwear, folded it carefully, and set it lovingly in the drawer. I scattered lavender sachets to give a lovely, fresh scent. Every time I opened the drawer, it was a delicious, sexy experience.

At the start of my marriage, modeling the bra and panty sets was an ego boost and a source of couple fun. Some mornings, I would ask my husband, "Which set do you want to see on me tonight?" Knowing he would go to work and daydream about me and the underwear.

Then I got pregnant, and everything changed. The little wisps of Italian and French lace stopped fitting my constantly expanding body. I'm too practical to buy expensive maternity lingerie for a temporary body. I caved and bought a ten-pack of cotton maternity underwear. They were oh-so-comfortable.

Thus began a new chapter of my life, choosing comfort over doing things to make me feel sexy.

Even after returning to my pre-baby weight, my body shape changed. My already small breasts became saggy. The beautiful bras in my immaculate drawer no longer fit. Slowly and with much angst, I tossed the Italian and French lace sets into the garbage. I bought more cotton underwear because washing and wearing it was the sensible thing to do.

Since baby two, my once-pristine underwear drawer has become a dumping ground. No gentle wash. No precise folding. No scented satchels. I dump the underwear straight from the laundry hamper into the drawer. My gut clenched each time I opened and saw the mess.

Is My Underwear Drawer a Sex Metaphor?

The underwear drawer is a perfect metaphor for how I feel about myself and my body. I used to take pride in my appearance. Now, I'm doing well by not going out in my ratty sweatpants.

This week's challenge was to take charge of my sexual happiness, so I went underwear shopping.

With my two toddlers.

Bad idea.

Walking in the cramped aisles with a double stroller, my children lunged at every bra rack. I wasn't shopping. Rather, I grabbed a set of black, lacy underwear I didn't hate and looked my size. Bringing a double stroller into the dressing room stall was impossible, and I bought the nonrefundable underwear.

When I arrived home, I put on my new purchase, filled with hope and anticipation. As I tried on the bra and panties—while picking crusty snot off my breast from when my daughter used my chest as a tissue—my other child pointed out, "There's mummy's vulva!"

The bra didn't fit well, and the panties were too tight and scratchy. Or the panties fit, but I'm now used to the comfort of how cotton panties stretch.

I wanted to look at myself in the mirror, but couldn't. At first, I thought it was because I'm still a few pounds over my normal weight and look marshmallow-soft. Then I realized there was something else going on. I've got a weird asexual mommy vibe happening. One more entry to the list of things affecting my sexual experience.

Although the underwear shopping was a bust, I did clean my underwear drawer. It has made a difference. Opening the drawer and seeing my cotton undies perfectly folded gives me a sense of calm. It's a small step in the slow process of me feeling sexual again.

The Bitter-Sweet Ending

Taking charge and going through that effort only to fail was discouraging. I tossed the expensive, never-to-be-worn bra and panty set into a nearby laundry basket and willed my fragile ego to forget the experience.

Even though my husband can't find milk in the fridge, he somehow found the newly purchased underwear in my laundry basket. Underwear in hand, he approached me like a kid at an ice cream truck. "Did you do that on purpose? So that I'd find the new underwear 'by accident'?"

I thought about the early days when lingerie was integral to our foreplay. Seeing his hopeful and delighted expression nudged open a door I had firmly closed.

I know what I want from sex that doesn't include an orgasm. I want to get that playfulness back.

Sadly, I didn't do a fashion show for my husband. I'm much too insecure.

Amy

Betty Dodson Night — March 1

AMY'S HOT-PINK KIMONO SWISHED along the floor as she puttered with the finishing touches on the Betty Dodson evening. She turned up the thermostat, laid out beach towels on her living room floor, and lit oodles of candles so the warm lighting would make the group's naked bodies look their best. Bright headlights from a passing car blazed into her living room, and Amy closed her curtains. She giggled, picturing her neighbors catching an eyeful of the nude women.

She swished to her kitchen, uncorked two bottles of red wine, and pulled a box of appetizers from the freezer. She dumped the frozen selection of generic pastries onto the cookie sheet and put them into the oven as if she'd won a spot on MasterChef.

As she congratulated herself on the kick-ass evening she'd created, her cat, Orgasm, strolled into the kitchen to oversee her progress. She gently picked him up, went to her bedroom, and lovingly placed him on her bed. Closing the door behind her, Amy heaved a sigh of relief. Potential disaster averted. She heard his angry yowls and crossed her fingers that he wouldn't poop on her bed in mad revenge for holding him hostage.

The doorbell rang, and a frisson of anticipation rippled through Amy as she untied the sash of her hot-pink kimono and tossed it onto the couch. When she opened the door naked, shock and horror zigzagged across Jeanette's bewildered face. Her mouth opened and closed like a guppy fish while her flabbergasted gaze did a once-over of Amy's ample body. A blast of snowy air blew inside her small foyer, nipping Amy's exposed flesh, and she had to pull the petrified Jeanette inside.

"Welcome!" Amy smiled as she helped Jeanette out of her jacket.

Jeanette's eyes frantically darted everywhere but to Amy before finally landing on the foyer wall. She blanched and threw her eyes up at the ceiling in disgust. "I don't know what's worse, you," she gestured at Amy's naked body, "or the glittery painted walls."

Expecting as much from Jeanette, Amy changed the subject.

"I see you brought your yoga mat." A mute and mortified Jeanette robotically handed over the mat while fiddling with the exquisite Louis Vuitton duffel bag draped casually over her arm. Being ever the good hostess, Amy tried again to put her guest at ease. "Do you want to change here?"

"No! Of course not," Jeanette barked as if Amy had lost her mind.

Amy swallowed a frustrated sigh. If Jeanette were to have the full Betty Dodson experience, undressing in the foyer was part of the process. But then, biting her lip, she remembered Jeanette's condition of not being naked and, resigned, pointed to the bathroom down the hall.

A few minutes later, probably after some serious self-talk and a few big breaths, given how long it had taken, Jeanette emerged in an exquisite Olivia von Halle robe. Clutching her Louis Vuitton bag close for protection, Jeanette stepped over the beach towels and warily sat on the ratty couch. Doing everything to avoid Amy's nakedness, Jeanette's gaze bounced from one nude painting to the next; she then ferociously tsked before looking up at the ceiling.

With her guest settled in, Amy did a last-minute check and smacked her forehead, exclaiming.

"Oops, I forgot the most important part."

She sat on her yoga mat, hiked up her legs, and let her knees fall open while positioning the round swivel mirror from her bathroom and the spotlight from her desk lamp. It took a moment to sort out the light and mirror angles before seeing her vulva at its most fabulous.

"I can't do this," Jeanette whispered as the doorbell rang at the same time as the stove buzzer.

Amy jumped up and asked, "Could you get the door while I flip the appetizers?"

Jeanette's zombie face nodded and went to open the door. The townhouse was small, and Amy could hear her guests' whispered conversations.

"Oh, hi," Isabella's surprised voice said at seeing Jeanette. "Claire's right behind me."

Amy heard a second person, presumably Claire, step inside the tiny foyer, and then Jeanette hissed something incoherently.

"What did you say?" Isabella asked, confused. "Naked? Who's naked?"

"Amy. She's naked. In that hideous kitchen," Jeanette no longer whispered. "Claire! Tell her. To get dressed!"

Claire laughed but added, "Jeanette, please stay. I'm not ready for full-frontal either."

When Claire walked into the kitchen, Amy purposely bent herself over the oven door while putting in the cookie sheet.

"Hey, Claire-Bear. How do you like me now?" Amy turned toward Claire, doing jazz hands with large pastel oven mitts.

"You're lovely, of course." Claire laughed despite the stern look. "But you're freaking the other two out. You need to reel this in before they do a runner."

Amy's face fell. "I'm doing an authentic Betty Dodson experience."

"Of course you were. But we're new to this and need time to warm up to the idea." Claire picked up Amy's kimono and put it around her shoulders. "Isabella, Jeanette, she's decent!"

Both women tentatively poked their heads around the corner.

"I don't suppose you two want to have the full Betty Dodson experience and undress here?" Amy asked hopefully.

"Amy! I'll go use your bathroom." Claire turned, but stopped and looked around. "Where's your cat?"

"Locked in the bedroom."

"Good. Keep him there."

Poor Orgasm, Amy thought, just because he attacked Claire, he got a bad rap.

"This is a lovely home, Amy," Isabella said, looking around at the bold choice of glittery blush wall color and the nude paintings. "It suits you."

"Thanks, I recently renovated." Amy nodded, pleased. "Would you like wine?"

"Yes!" both women chimed.

"I need wine to get through this evening." Isabella accepted her glass just as Claire came back in.

"The bathroom's yours," Claire announced to Isabella.

Amy noticed Isabella rooted to her spot as she handed Claire her glass. "Everything okay, Isabella?"

"Yes, yes, I'm good." But then Isabella stood up and sat back down hard. "I had a busy day and didn't have time to shower, so I grabbed my old robe." She looked down at the scuffed backpack in her lap. "I'm such a mess."

"Isabella, this isn't a fashion show," Jeanette tried, but Isabella gave her exquisite robe and Louis Vuitton bag the side-eye.

"I have an extra kimono that would look luscious on you. How about I get it?" Amy suggested.

"It's okay. Thanks." Isabella pushed herself out of the chair and, a few minutes later, returned in a worn flannel robe.

"I prefer a well-loved garment," Amy said as she unrolled Isabella's yoga mat and helped her onto it. "Besides, what's under the robe is important for tonight."

The oven timer went off again, and Amy jumped up and soon emerged with two plates of rather dodgy-looking gray appetizers.

"Are we ready?" Excitement thrummed through Amy's body, but as she looked at each woman's face, she saw full-on stress verging on terror staring back at her.

Feeling defeat's hot breath on her neck, Amy eyed the side table where she had placed the small, framed photo of Betty Dodson from her womyn's shrine. She silently asked Betty to make this a life-enhancing, memorable evening that would help each woman with her sexual self-esteem.

Maybe it was a trick of the light, but Amy could have sworn Betty winked at her. And Amy must have imagined Betty saying, in her no-nonsense way, to get on with it and show these women how to run their fuck.

That if Amy didn't know where to start, she should tell the group about how she ran the fuck with her post-Paul hookup.

Amy's Hook Up

February 27

A WEEK EARLIER.

> Please call me Paul!

Amy's fingers typed the desperate text. Her body and vag ached remembering that magical night, and she exhaled a long, sad breath at his radio silence.

Why did he ghost me?

The only cure for this kind of pain was to get back under someone. Amy ignored Claire's nagging voice, telling her not to return to her hook-up habits, and opened Tinder. Doing a quick scan through the app, tonight would be slim pickings, but she only needed to find one person.

Nope. Amy's experienced pointer finger smoothly swiped left.

Ew! Definitely not. Swipe left.

What did I do wrong? She hadn't opened up to anyone after her divorce. Paul's rejection hit like a bomb, creating a massive crater in her ego.

I already had that one. She'd been a good romp. But then she wanted to sleep over? Amy didn't think so. Swipe left.

With dogged determination, Amy kept swiping, but she'd banged half the men and women and knew the other half were assholes or catfish.

How could he believe that's a decent photo? Nope. Swipe left.

Amy never played games. Dating games drove great people over the edge, forcing them to harden and become cynical about relationships. She called Paul the next afternoon, asking his voicemail to talk about what happened. She waited a few days and then sent a cute, funny text. A week later, after too many drinks, she drunk-dialled him. He responded with a cryptic text.

> You're too much woman for me. I'm sorry.

What did that even mean?

Nice guy, Paul, turned out to be not so lovely.

Amy's finger hovered over a profile. She might be okay. Amy would check who else was available and circle back.

Claire had begged Amy to do things differently and look where it got her. Same shit, different pile. Feeling that level of pain was too much. If someone were to ask Amy what it meant to be in a relationship, it would be pain from people leaving. Her angry and frustrated finger took it out on the profiles as she swiped aggressively. No, no, and no.

But then her finger paused, hovering over Adesh. He was cute, but his profile said he was ten years younger. She wasn't sure she wanted to teach a boy how to have sex with a woman.

An image of waking up tangled in Paul's arms flashed before her eyes. The next thing she knew, she had swiped right and sent a quick message.

Less than three minutes later, Adesh accepted, and the serotonin hit helped soothe her battered ego. After exchanging a few texts, it was clear that Adesh was only interested in sex. Which was fine. They agreed this was transactional, and she appreciated his directness.

She had an hour to get ready, and the frenetic prepping of her body for sex helped block thoughts of how she had gotten Paul so wrong.

Amy

Back At The Betty Dodson Night

"Is everyone ready to take off our robes?" Amy clapped her hands, giving the three women her most encouraging smile. They didn't budge.

Jeanette focused intently on her wineglass in her snow-white silk robe. Claire shifted in a black cherry blossom-print robe to get comfortable with floor sitting. Isabella's fidgety hands did their best to cover her entire body with the well-loved gray flannel.

Amy looked over at the Betty Dodson photo and silently asked her how to bring this group out of their shells. Her eyes darted to the wine bottle. Yes, of course, give them more wine. She nodded a thank you to Betty as she topped each glass with the cheap Merlot.

"Okay then, how about the top half of our robes?" Amy tried, but the three still didn't budge. They squirmed nervously on their yoga mats, silently taking sip after sip of wine, eyes downcast so Amy wouldn't single them out.

Okay, Betty instructed, *It's time for Plan B.*

Jumping up, Amy grabbed something off the side table and, hoping she would get a laugh, wiggled her butt in an overly exaggerated way as she slid into them. She then faced the group and slowly undid her sash. In a burlesque striptease style, Amy rolled her shoulders and swiveled her hips suggestively, and ever so slowly dropped her hot pink kimono.

"Ta-da." Amy did a leisurely turn, showing off the baby-blue cotton underwear and every angle of her womanly body. "This can be our group's motto." With a hand-heart, she framed the panty's words "It's all about ME!". "Isn't that perfect?"

"Nice gitch!" Claire failed to keep a straight face.

"What's gitch?" Jeanette stared, transfixed.

"Underwear," Isabella replied distractedly, unable to pull her gaze away from Amy's curves.

"I've ordered each of us a pair," Amy announced. "We can wear them to class in solidarity."

Wine spurted out of Claire's nose from the unexpected laugh. She then raised her glass to salute Amy's underwear.

"Here's to our new mascot, the 'It's all about ME!' gitch."

As the women giggled and raised their glasses to christen their new mascot, Amy made a show of slipping the panties off and haphazardly flinging them across the room with her toe.

"So, ladies, we are ready." It wasn't a question.

Amy plopped her naked self down on her yoga mat, her legs folded beneath her, and looked expectantly at the three terrified women.

"I'm sorry, Amy, but I'm not ready to get naked." Isabella hugged her knees tighter.

"Sure," Amy swallowed the building frustration of letting the group set the pace. She gave Betty a look and suddenly came up with the perfect thing to say.

"As you know, I'm a try-sexual. I'll try anything at least once. And from my experience, sex is a bell curve; sometimes it's awesome, other times it's awful, mostly it's somewhere in the middle. But the thing is, I never know going in how sex will turn out. So, when Dr. Gwen has us focus on what we want, it changes our expectations. We go into sex knowing there will be something in the experience for us. We empower ourselves to make our sex feel good for us. And when sex is good for us, it's even better for our partners. That's the irony. Women keep their mouths shut and don't say what we want, even though our partners desperately want to know."

"That's easy for you to say," Isabella spoke softly, but her words had a biting edge. "I don't know what I want."

"It's a worthiness mindset. Sexual self-esteem is a belief in our right to sexual equality that we bring into sex —"

"You're very good at sex. The best." Claire interrupted. "But you suck at relationships. Yes, we need to work on our sex. You need to, what did you say, change your worthiness mindset, your self-esteem, and your belief about your equality in a healthy relationship."

"Tonight, we're here to look at our vulvas, not analyze our relationships," Amy dismissed Claire and refocused the group on the task. "Eleanor Roosevelt said, 'A woman is like a tea bag; you can't tell how strong she is until you put her in hot water.' Ladies, let's test the water."

Jeanette raised her chin. "I'm only doing the top half of my robe."

The other two women nodded in agreement. They lowered their robes with a jerky hesitation so their shoulders and breasts showed; the candlelight cast their bodies in a soft glow.

"This is surprisingly not weird." Claire sounded, what, relieved?

"Great job, ladies! Onto the main event." Amy nimbly uncrossed her legs, putting her heels on either side of the mirror and desk lamp, and let her knees fall to the side. Switching on the desk lamp, she readjusted the round mirror onto her vulva, with its well-groomed landing strip that led the way for her to take off.

"First impressions?" Amy asked as she looked away from her vulva and up to the in-awe faces leaning forward, inching in closer to get a proper look.

"This is a bit surreal." Isabella took a big gulp of wine.

"It's anticlimactic," Claire shrugged.

"Are we supposed to ask you questions?" Jeanette's eyes bounced from her wineglass to Amy's vulva.

"Ask away. I read up on vulva facts this afternoon to prepare." Amy said while admiring her piercing. "Hey, how about I show you my favorite masturbation technique? Or, wait, do you want to see my cervix? I still have my speculum somewhere in my back closet. I'll tell you about the night I picked up that little beauty in a strip poker game!"

"Masturbating and looking at your cervix was not part of tonight's program." Grinchy Claire reeled in Amy's fun. "How about you take us through the different parts of the vulva?"

"Your loss," Amy quipped, but smoothly shifted gears into professor mode. "As you can see, I have a beautiful vulva. These are my outer lips." Moving her fingers on the outermost part of her vulva, she drew an invisible line. "These are my inner lips. They are not symmetrical: my left inner labia hangs slightly lower than my right. Most women don't have symmetrical labia. Fun fact: as you become aroused, and this area engorges with blood, your labia opens up like a flower. Isn't that amazing?"

Amy's fingers parted her inner lips. "Here is my vaginal opening." Her pointer finger circled each area as she spoke. "There's my urethra. When I ejaculate, it comes out of here, and fun fact, the ejaculate isn't pee."

"Excuse me, what?" An addled Jeanette shook her head.

But Amy kept talking right past that teachable moment.

"Finally, my clitoris. Your clitoris has about 10,000 nerve fibers, and its only purpose is to give you pleasure. How wonderful is that?" Amy was pleased to see all eyes glued to her vulva.

"But isn't the clitoris the tip of the iceberg? What did Betty Dodson say in her video?" Claire, the astute student, asked.

"That's right! Attached to the outer structure are the internal clitoral bulbs that surround the vaginal canal and the internal 'legs' that wrap around the labia. When you're aroused, the leg's erectile tissue doubles in size. It's a female erection."

"How can I be thirty-nine years old and not know any of this?" Isabella whispered.

"Did you know you can feel your clitoral legs?" Amy said, eager to show the group something she had read that afternoon. "You press your ring finger on the glans like this. Your index finger rests on the shaft like this. When you press inward on your labia, you should feel the legs; they feel something like a round rubber cord." The group gave her a deer-in-the-headlights stare.

"That's me." Amy hurried, so the women didn't have time to think. "Who wants to go next?"

Amy was just about to suggest that Claire go when she heard.

"I will."

Everyone's heads spun in Jeanette's direction.

Jeanette

Betty Dodson Night

"I will."

Jeanette looked up from her lap to see the group gaping at her in disbelief. She was just as surprised as they were. The words jumped out of her mouth as if they had a mind of their own. Maybe they did. She'd given this Betty Dodson workshop to God, riding the wave of faith.

"Do you want me to guide you?" Amy asked as she laid out a new towel beside her.

"Yes." Jeanette rose and padded over to the empty towel before gracefully lowering her perfectly exfoliated, spray-tanned, long limbs onto it. Like a Moris code warning, the swivel mirror glinted in her eye, making her woozy, as if in a windy tunnel. She hardly heard Amy say something about doing the homework first and sharing what good sex meant to her.

Jeanette closed her eyes, took her hands off the steering wheel, and let Jesus drive. Her voice sounded foreign and far away.

"For me, sex equates to fighting, frustration, unhappiness, and being frigid. I have unresolved anger from years of fights about me not wanting sex. I've never experienced romantic love. Or what it's like to be sexy. I've never felt sexual. I might as well be dead down there."

Jeanette looked at each face, trying to cover up their appalled shock.

"What I want is to feel normal. To create a relationship with myself and work on my self-esteem and confidence. I've never had an orgasm and want to know what that is like. That's what good sex means to me." The room was silent as the women processed her confession.

"Have you thought about seeing a sex therapist?" Isabella asked.

"Yes and no. My husband wants me to see a therapist, but only to prove he's right that I'm sexually broken. He thinks I'm frigid. What if he's right? Plus, he believes he has no issues, and this is my fault." Jeanette ignored the collective intake of breath. "That's it."

"Respect, Jeanette. Really. Kudos to you," Claire looked at Jeanette with admiration.

"Thanks. It was good to say it out loud. Scary but good." Jeanette let the briefest of satisfied smiles cross her lips. "I want to get the next part over with."

Amy nodded and took the lead, turning on the desk lamp.

Jeanette attempted to open the bottom half of her robe, but her body remained immobile. Swiftly losing her nerve, she forced herself into her mind-over-body zone. While doing a grueling gym workout, she went into "the zone" to keep her mind from playing tricks on her. After some deep breaths, she let her legs fall open as if she were getting a gyno exam and stared straight ahead, concentrating hard on staying in the zone.

"You and your vulva are beautiful!" Amy adjusted the mirror so Jeanette could see her vulva.

"Thank you," Jeanette whispered. She was about to say it took time and effort to maintain her figure, but she lost the words, too busy staring at her vulva.

Amy followed Jeanette's gaze and softly asked, "What do you see?"

"I've never looked at it." Jeanette's hoarse voice found its way back. "I'm not sure why. It's not that scary."

"I can tell you've had kids." Amy's casual remark was Jeanette's worst nightmare, and she snapped her legs together.

"How can you tell? Is my vagina huge?" Jeanette wanted to grab her cell and book a vaginal tightening appointment.

"No, no, no. Your vagina is perfect." Amy soothed, putting her hand on Jeanette's knee and gently guiding her legs back down. "See here? Your inner labia are darker. A woman's labia skin flattens out and darkens after she has children. Another fun fact: If you have a vaginal birth, as the baby comes out, it roughens your vaginal walls. It makes intercourse feel better. It's Mother Nature's parting gift for your labor."

"Mother Nature must have had children," Claire joked, as a small "Huh" escaped Isabella's lips.

"Open those lovely inner lips. Can you see your vaginal opening and your urethra?" Amy asked, and Jeanette nodded. "Good. And there is your clitoris." Amy's pointer finger hovered and circled over Jeanette's clitoris without touching it. Then, unexpectedly, Amy leaned in for a closer look and whispered, "Oh my."

Again, Jeanette was in the middle of a nightmare.

"What? What's wrong with me?"

"There's nothing wrong with you," Amy spoke slowly, choosing her words carefully. "I'm not an expert, but it looks like your clitoris has its hood over it. No biggie. All you need to do is pull the hood back. Do you know how?"

Humiliated, Jeanette dumbly shook her head. "No, of course, I've never touched it." The wooziness came back, ready and wanting to shut this vulva party down. "I have so much shame," she heard herself say as she tumbled down an abyss.

From back in that windy tunnel, she heard Claire's faraway voice encourage her to make shame her bitch. Claire was right. Jeanette promised herself that she would get through this. Even though it took every ounce of her remaining strength and focus to return to the zone, she did it.

"What do you mean it has a hood?" Jeanette whispered, her eyebrows furrowed in concentration, staring at the tiny bulb in the mirror.

"Your clitoral hood is like the foreskin on an uncircumcised penis, and you can gently pull it back. Because it hasn't been, uh, tried out, it's never been pulled back. Why don't you try?"

Jeanette took a deep breath and did as Amy had instructed. Even though her clumsy fingers pulled her clitoral hood back, it didn't budge.

"Okay, if that didn't work, your clitoral hood must be stuck." Amy was all business. "It could be a buildup of debris, which is nothing to worry about. Take a shower and gently wash your vulva with warm water. Is that something you're willing to do?"

Jeanette nodded, mute at the thought of showing her dirty, uncared-for, ignored vulva to the group.

"Hey, perhaps you've never had an orgasm because of the clitoral hood." Isabella blurted helpfully, but it was Jeanette's tipping point, yanking her out of the zone.

She threw her robe over her legs, jumped up, and sat back in her spot. Adrenaline made her hands shake as she picked up her wine and drank deeply.

"Thank you, Amy." She finally managed, eyes downcast, her body riding big waves of emotion.

"You're so welcome. That wasn't so terrible." Amy was happy living in her la-la land, pleased with how this turned out.

Jeanette took another long sip of wine to regain her impeccable composure. Amy put down a fresh towel and pointed at Claire.

"Who wants to go next?"

Claire

Betty Dodson Night

CLAIRE SAW AMY POINT at her and went to uncross her long legs and get up. Her body refused to budge.

It must have seen the near-catatonic Jeanette alongside her confession, completely rattling Claire. How was it possible to be that old and never have an orgasm? Claire's orgasm issues slid into the "it's relative" category.

"Come on, Claire." Amy patted the fresh towel beside her.

Claire looked over at the petrified Isabella and back at Amy's ear-to-ear grin, willing her body to move and support her friend's kooky evening. Rising unsteadily, she tugged the robe tightly around her body and silently dared Amy to say otherwise.

"I know I'm your fantasy. Now you get to see the goods." Claire winced, her sharp tongue and sarcastic zings a nervous tell.

"Can't wait," Amy bantered back. Claire went to sit, but her legs refused to bend. "Claire-Bear? Let me help you."

Shaking her head no, not wanting to look weak, Claire lowered herself to the floor as Amy's protective arm went around her shoulders.

"Let's jump into the homework. What do you want from sex?"

Inspired by Jeanette, who, to everyone's surprise, had serious lady balls, Claire wanted to be open, honest, and authentic. If she really was about female empowerment, she needed to walk her talk.

Claire's logical brain reasoned that if this were easy, there wouldn't be billions of women worldwide spectatoring and faking orgasm. Women like Jeanette wouldn't have to make themselves small and insignificant. Too scared to stand up for their sexual happiness when they deserved so much more than a life full of regrets. It was her job to pay it forward and help Isabella become comfortable stepping into her sexual power. So, without looking back, she launched.

"I'm happy to announce that I did it. I stopped spectatoring and faking orgasm." Claire's words were a strange combination of breezy and clipped. Any sexual victory passed over, unacknowledged, in wanting to get the words out.

"You did what?" Isabella looked at Claire as if she had solved string theory. "Just like that, you stopped. Wasn't that, I don't know, awkward?"

"I'm not sure it's possible to wean yourself off faking slowly. You're faking, or you're not. So, yeah, it was awkward, and I didn't enjoy myself. At all. But it was equally awkward and unenjoyable when I faked it. So pick your poison. But while I was, uh, in the middle of things, I saw how much effort goes into faking, and it's a lot. Like, an unbelievable amount. I also got the sense that if I paid attention to my pleasure and then asked for what I wanted, it's more than possible that I could enjoy sex as much as Amy."

"What did Carlos do?" Amy asked.

"He said nothing." Claire stopped short, uncomfortable disclosing about Carlos without his permission, so she moved on. "What I want out of sex is to be present in my body. I've fallen into poor habits and want to fill the non-faking void with good habits. I don't know how to do this, but saying it out loud makes it seem possible."

"Have you considered meditation?" Amy asked.

"That was random. You know, I've never meditated." Claire wasn't in the mood for one of Amy's great ideas.

"Hear me out. I read an article about research from the Sexuality Laboratory at UBC. They found mindfulness significantly improves sexual desire, arousal, orgasms, satisfaction, and mood in women seeking treatment for low libido." Amy rattled off the data to persuade Claire. "If you know what you want but don't know how to get there, research shows this might be the way to create that path."

"Um, great. Will you send me the study? I'm unsure how to fit meditation into my packed schedule, but I will look at it." Claire already gave it a pass.

"I know that look. You've already given it a pass. Promise to at least read the article." Claire gave a noncommittal shrug, not wanting to get into it.

Isabella piped up, "Can you send it to me, too? That sounds interesting."

"You see, Claire, Isabella thinks it's a great idea." Amy tried, but then dropped it and shifted gears. "Alright, then, it's time for the main event. Are you ready to take off your robe?"

No, she was not ready to put her vulva on display or for Amy to discover fun facts about her vulva. Stalling, Claire asked Isabella to hand over her wine and took a big gulp. It didn't work. Out of self-preservation, she let her mind skitter to an addendum she needed to put in a legal brief. Leaning on her logical side allowed a tiny crack to open, which had a cascading effect. Her rational brain took over, pushing the reset button, taking her to a familiar place she could control and manage.

Her vulva wasn't unique, and she was being foolish to let her emotions get the best of her. This was a five-minute exercise, and then it would be over. The longer she prolonged it, the longer it would take, and she did not want it to take any longer than necessary. Pacified, Claire wordlessly untied the sash and dropped her robe, signaling she was ready.

Without hesitation, Amy snapped on the desk lamp and adjusted the mirror. It took a moment for Claire's eyes to refocus, and, as if outside her body, she made a logical assessment of her vulva.

"See how your inner lips are paler —"

Claire was only half listening to Amy's lecture, too busy chastising herself that the last few anxious days had been time wasted. There it was. Her vulva. So not a big deal. She came, she conquered, and now she had the vulva T-shirt.

She was already bored.

Amy encouraged Claire to open her inner lips to see her vaginal opening, urethra, and clitoris. Claire followed the instructions mechanically. It was interesting for all of five seconds, but Claire was done by the time Amy's little demo finished.

"Claire, are you even paying attention?" Amy snapped her fingers in front of Claire's face. "One day, Claire, you will need to let your walls down."

"Thanks, Amy. Now that you've seen the goods, are you still interested?" Claire eased back into the jokes and her robe. "What's the expression about the cow and the milk?" Claire raised her long body in one athletic motion, ignoring Amy's disappointment. She had done the exercise and refused to accept Amy's guilt.

Claire looked over at Isabella, curled in a tight ball, making herself invisible.

Claire hoped she had, in some small way, helped this poor woman know she would be okay.

Isabella

Betty Dodson Night

C‍laire crossed the tiny distance to Isabella and crouched, extending a hand to help her up.

"It's not that bad."

Easy for you to say. Isabella thought as she willed her body to stop shaking.

Claire had her *situation* under control, with her svelte, perfect body and self-confidence that oozed out of every pore.

Isabella had zero time to shower and shave, and her body was a hot mess. Her fleshy belly bloated from the pasta supper, her breasts saggy from nursing two babies, her generous legs and bum a cascade of dimpled cellulite. She had a dirty, smelly hoochie, and the state of her 1970s natural bush was the nail in the coffin.

Isabella had wanted nothing more than to take this leap, but her *situation* was too embarrassing.

"Let's take this one step at a time," Jeanette said carefully, her tone full-on momma-bear protection. "Isabella can do her homework where she is."

Claire gave a small, encouraging smile and squeezed Isabella's hand before standing up and returning to her spot.

That tiny act of kindness, the relief of not moving, triggered verbal diarrhea, and Isabella's words poured out in an incoherent rush.

"My husband and I used to have such a great sex life, and now I only look for ways to avoid sex." She tried pumping the brakes, but it was no use.

"I'm not sexy. And my body, I mean, look at my body. It betrayed me. And not only that, but it's impossible to create anything intimate with two small kids. I want Alex to touch me, but on my terms, if that makes any sense. I don't want to be on high alert, expecting him to pounce. It's not like we're having sex often, but even so, I'm constantly on guard, and it's exhausting."

"There's a lot to unpack here —" Amy interrupted.

"I used to be so sexy and love sex. I mean, nothing like you, Amy," Isabella pointed her way, "but we had some wild times. Now, we never talk about our sex life because it's too hard. And if we did, I'm afraid we would only complain about each other. My guilt of not wanting sex is a constant refrain. We're in a sex slump, but that's why I'm here, in this group, trying to make it work. What I want out of sex is to be an active participant in my own sexual experience. I want to tell my husband to nurture me." Winding down, her last words came out in a sad whisper.

"What I want is to know what it's like to run my fuck."

"What does running your fuck look like?" Claire chewed on her lip, also figuring it out.

"I don't know," Isabella admitted. "Before I started the course, I thought sex was straightforward. To run my fuck, I needed to grow a pair and explain, Samantha from *Sex and the City* style, how I wanted things done. But there's no way I could do that. It's way too scary."

"Here's an idea," Claire's inner lawyer took over. "Instead of asking how to run your fuck, which is vague, we need to be specific. To break it down into smaller steps. What's one small thing you can do?"

"I want to stop resenting sex," Isabella blurted, then immediately backtracked. "Forget I said that."

"No, that's good," Jeanette encouraged. "It starts with an awareness. Now that you are aware of resenting sex, you'll see it happen in real-time."

"How is that supposed to help me? What am I supposed to do, stop and discuss my feelings?" Isabella snapped.

"Oh my God, can you imagine?" Amy laughed as if Isabella's sex life were the funniest thing. "As Claire said, it's about replacing what you don't want with what you do want. When you catch yourself resenting, which you don't want, you replace it with something you want."

"That's not helpful. My situation is different from yours."

Isabella didn't have the energy to explain to a singleton what it meant to be in a full-time relationship, let alone one that included kids.

"Is it? Or is that an excuse?" Amy wasn't pulling any punches, and that one hurt. "If what you're doing now isn't working, you have nothing to lose and everything to gain by doing something you want."

"Can we move on?" Isabella pushed the confrontation away, forgetting what came next.

"I don't think we've discussed your situation enough, but if you're ready."

Amy shrugged and straightened the fresh towel beside her.

Isabella tried to lift herself, but it was as if a hundred-pound brick sat on her shoulders, and she landed back down hard. The flutter of a panic attack made its way up her back, and she was about to say she couldn't do it when Jeanette's voice floated her way.

"Isabella, you are a strong, powerful woman. You are beautiful inside and out. You are stronger than this exercise. We are behind you, supporting you. You have the tenacity and fortitude to do this. Now embrace your inner strength and boldly move forward."

Jeanette's fierce prayer drifted into her head, a warm hug for Isabella's heart.

There wasn't a grand aha. If she hadn't been paying attention, she might have missed it.

In a flash, Isabella saw herself as a powerful, sexy, and sexual woman. This exotic creature was already inside her, waiting for the right time to come out. The flash was gone, but it had shifted something inside Isabella. Equally bewildered and excited, she didn't know what to do or call it, but whatever it was, she would take it. And write about it.

Miraculously, Isabella's bravery came roaring out of nowhere, encouraging, "It's time to take off your big-girl panties and do this."

With shaky hands, she untied the sash of her grubby robe. She let it fall to the ground and ignored the tears running down her face. Being naked in all her imperfections in front of these dazzling women was frightening and liberating.

Liberating? A sliver of light made its way up from somewhere buried deep, where her most private fantasies lived.

Sitting beside Amy's naked body was new, yet oddly familiar. It felt like home. For the second time that evening, Isabella uttered, "Huh!" as she wiped the tears from her face.

Amy clicked on the desk lamp and adjusted the round swivel mirror. Isabella was about to apologize for her dirty vag and full-on bush when Amy chimed in.

"Isn't she stunning?" Amy's excitement was contagious.

"Uh, I guess?" Isabella kept her eyes downcast, unable to look.

"And you dressed her up for the occasion." Amy's grin almost split her face. "I'm so glad one of you took this Betty Dodson night seriously."

Isabella's eye flew to the little swivel mirror, and her focus took a moment to adjust.

Oh, no! Could this night get any worse?

In the frantic mayhem of getting out the door, Isabella only had time to do a quick vulva wipe. She must have used the same washcloth that cleaned her daughter's body after Rosa had a run-in with a glitter jar. Under the lamp's bright light, her vulva positively sparkled with its multi-colored glitter.

"Ms. Fancy. And you were worried about your robe." Jeanette giggled.

"I'm going to call you Sparkly from now on." Amy was besotted.

"I didn't mean to." Isabella stammered. "It looks —" She stared in wonder at her glittery vulva.

"It looks great."

"You're the cool kid at the vulva party," Claire quipped.

For once, Isabella was the cool kid with the cool vulva.

"Are you ready, Sparkly?"

"I am," Isabella spoke with a confidence she didn't know she possessed. Although she had an ordinary-looking vulva, Isabella saw it for what it was: the pure essence of female power.

"Wow!" Warm tears of happiness streamed down her face. She was in love with the beauty of her vulva as she eagerly asked Amy questions, never wanting this powerful high to end.

When Amy finally clicked off the desk lamp, the enchanting yoni-power-aura surrounding Isabella lingered.

"I'm so proud of you, Isabella." Amy gave her a full, skin-to-skin, naked hug that should have been weird, but wasn't.

Everything about this night should have been strange, but it was the opposite. Isabella learned so much about herself that she would never find in a textbook. She might even say it was life-changing.

There was her repressed life before this night versus what her life could become after. She was the master of her destiny. She was going to run her fuck.

"Amy, thank you so much. For everything," Isabella gushed.

"You're so welcome. I'm going to celebrate with my favorite vibe." Amy snapped her fingers and pointed at the group. "Hey, wouldn't it be cool if we coordinated a circle jerk? We set a time to get off at the same time tonight."

"That's a hard no. I need to get going." Claire gathered her clothes and rose. "Thanks, Amy. This will go into the record books as one of the wilder things you've made me do. And that's saying something."

"Okay, no circle jerk, but can we each say what our biggest learning from the evening was?" Amy asked. "I'll go first. I learned showing people their vulva is my calling."

"It is, Amy. You're so good at it. I learned that being naked with women is empowering, like in the Betty Dodson video." Isabella said, adding, "I'm going home to show my daughter Rosa her vulva."

"I learned it's not about showing your vulva; it's about the confidence you gain by doing it," Claire answered. "Taking the leap is the exercise. What about you, Jeanette?"

Everyone turned to Jeanette, whose face had regained its olive color.

"I'm going to go home and shower," Jeanette said quietly, but smiled faintly. "I'll report back."

"That would be awesome." Amy's eyes shone at the transformation. "Ladies, you're already mostly naked. You might as well change in the living room."

Isabella wanted to stay and discuss every minute detail, but the group looked tired and emotional from the experience.

"Why didn't anyone touch my appetizers?" Amy muttered.

Looking at the cold, gray nondescript lumps, Isabella averted her eyes to avoid Amy's bewildered face.

Jeanette Takes a Shower

March 1

KICKING OFF HER SHOES, Jeanette arrived home from the Betty Dodson night, wild and wired.

> *She had a clitoral hood.*
> *Her sexual satisfaction mattered.*
> *She was in the driver's seat and could change her sexual situation.*
> *She showed a group of women her naked body and vulva.*

And it was emancipating.

She needed a large glass of wine and a long moment to sort through all the exhausted but energizing thoughts racing through her head. With Max at her heels, she went to the kitchen and pulled a bottle of Bordeaux from the wine rack. As she went to open it, she heard the garage door open, and the corkscrew crashed on the white marble counter.

Andre was home after being out with his mistress. The big emotions swirling through her body surged up to her brain, shifting her perspective. With crystal clarity, she saw the reality of her sex life. Jeanette was no longer willing to take sole blame for *their* sex life.

It takes two people to have sex. So, yes, it was true that she didn't want sex. It was also true that Andre coerced her. And the only way to deal with bullies was to stand up to them.

Sitting primly on the edge of the breakfast stool with Max on her lap, she waited as the side door opened. If Andre wanted her to improve their sex life, he was about to get an education on female anatomy.

"Oh, hey, I didn't think you'd be up this late. You're usually in bed," Andre fake-acted, being contrite while keeping his distance.

His clothes were rumpled and smelled of tacky perfume. Had he always been such a lousy liar? Why had she put up with his lies for so long?

"I was at a group night where we looked at our vulvas." She said matter-of-factly, deeply satisfied to see Andre do a baffled double-take. "I'm so glad you signed me up for this sex course. It turns out I have a clitoris."

"Every woman has that." His handsome mouth, swollen from kissing another woman, sputtered defensively as if he were an expert on women's bodies.

"Yes, well, this is the first I've heard of it. It's what gives me pleasure."

For the first time in her marriage, talking about sex did not make her deeply ashamed. Jeanette felt vindicated. Everything she'd ever wanted to say during their countless fights sat on the tip of her tongue. But if there was one thing twenty-eight years of marriage had taught Jeanette, it was to choose her battles. First, she needed to sort this clitoral hood thing out.

Standing her ground, she looked Andre square in the eye.

"I'm going upstairs to find it."

"You're what?" He was incredulous, and she was delighted to see him so rattled at her audacity. He also must have sensed their power dynamic shift and declared in his I'm-in-charge-of-this-relationship tone, "It's my job to find it."

"You've had twenty-eight years to figure it out. I'm good on my own." Jeanette said over her shoulder, walking away before he could see her body shake.

Climbing the stairs, she heard him talking after her, something about how it was her fault and how he would have found it if she hadn't shut him down constantly. His words became muffled as her bedroom door clicked shut. They were the exact words he had used many times, but they didn't sting as much tonight. It was as if she wore a shame-proof vest that bounced his words right off her.

"Here's a great tip: Fighting about sex never once got me in the mood," Jeanette muttered, the truth a salve on her jangled nerves.

Leaning against the door, her heart palpitating in her throat, she looked around her bedroom. When she and Andre quietly moved to separate bedrooms, it was because *she* was in perimenopause and *her* sleep patterns were erratic. But it wasn't just her. Andre had also become a restless sleeper. Together, they kept each other awake at night, and there was no way he could do his job properly on two hours of sleep.

Not once had she questioned the part he played. She took on the burden of their problems while he pointed the finger of blame. Allowing their sexual troubles to be her fault. Never once pushing back. Never once believing her sexual needs could matter as much as Andre's. An intense rage that started at her toes and worked its way up her body formed big drops of angry tears.

She'd been a fool to have kept her mouth shut, but it would never happen again.

Andre's muffled steps climbed the stairs and stopped momentarily by her door. His presence turned her guilt and shame meter to high. The unacknowledged, deep-seated anger and dread about bedtime obligations, when he would come to bed and, regardless of her sleep state, expect a goodnight quickie to help *him* fall asleep.

She blew out a long, shaky exhalation as he shuffled to his room. Plunking down on the edge of her bed, she stared listlessly at the cream walls as the years of fighting over sex ran like a well-worn movie reel. But this time, she cut the movie short.

I'm not taking the blame.

Her thoughts flitted to Amy, encouraging her to wash her clitoral hood with warm water gently. Mechanically, she undressed. As she padded to the bathroom, she caught her tear-stained face and naked reflection in the full-length mirror. Instead of looking away, she forced herself to stop and look. She saw a wise woman looking back with a new perspective.

Turning on the multiple shower heads of her custom-built shower, guilt wrestled with Jeanette for what she was about to do. She let her body experience the hot water as it streamed down her body, between her legs. Her hand, heavy as cement, clumsily touched her breasts, and her nipples grew hard in response. She forced the other tentative hand to slide down her flat stomach, but it stopped at her pubic hair. Inching her fingers downwards, the water cascaded from her arm to her fingertips and onto her clit. The sensation scared her, and she snatched her hand back.

She didn't want to believe. Scratch that. She couldn't believe her body could give her pleasure.

I need to do this.

Her hand slid back down to her vulva, and her fingers fumbled around but failed to find her clitoral hood. Shame swooped in, taunting her that she'd forgotten and making sure to sprinkle humiliation in with the shower spray. Jeanette pulled her hand away, telling herself she could try again tomorrow. But then she saw Andre's smug face, telling her she was frigid and, of course, she couldn't find her clitoris.

Never again.

Jeanette remembered Amy showing her how to open her outer lips, and her fingers tried again. But the cascading water off her fingertips made the maneuver difficult, and she reasoned it would be simpler to use the shower head. Jeanette took it off its hook, the spray descending on her body. When the hot water met her vulva, her entire body woke up, and a ripple of sensation went from her stomach to her breasts to her neck. Not knowing how to clean the clitoral debris, she guided the shower head closer to her clitoris.

Her knees buckled as an involuntary gasp escaped her mouth, and she had to steady herself with her free hand. She pulled the shower head away, but her body demanded that she put it back. She put the stream of water back on her vulva and, this time, quickly found the spot.

Her pleasure spot. The sensation mesmerized her, and she kept her eyes tightly shut so she didn't have to see what she was doing. A moan broke free from her lips as the hot jets pulsated on her vulva and clit.

Emboldened, she let out a louder groan. She liked hearing herself make that noise and did it again. She could feel an intensity rising in her body and intuitively widened her legs to let the jet stream flow. She stood there drinking in this wonderful new sensation until her vulva and clit became too sensitive. Reluctantly, she pulled the showerhead away, immediately wanting to put it back on herself.

Did I have an orgasm?

She didn't think so, but ...

Stepping out of the shower and wrapping herself in a big fluffy towel, it was guilt's turn to swoop in with a vengeance, and she had nothing left to fight it off. Somewhere in the back of her mind, she heard Dr. Gwen and Amy fighting for her right to pleasure, but shame joined forces with guilt and pushed those two strong women to the ground and ordered them to be silent.

Still wet from the shower, Jeanette slid beneath her soft sheets, completely drained. The weight of all the big and conflicting emotions she'd experienced in only five short hours pulled her into a fretful sleep. Something quiet worked its way up from her subconscious. One little thought.

Amy will help me.

Isabella Looks In The Mirror

March 2

ISABELLA OPENED HER SLEEPY eyes as the dreams and wonderful memories from the night before slipped away into the ether. She turned her head to see the other side of the bed empty. Alex was already up. The ultimate luxury was not having to get up and take care of the kids; instead, she got to snuggle under the duvet and treat herself to a lazy stretch.

I did that. I freakin' did that! Isabella glowed.

Everything about last night was life-affirming.

Only a week ago, the idea of running her fuck was ridiculous. Then she stumbled upon and discovered this sacred part of herself. This morning, her world opened up, and she was a strong, capable, and bold woman in control of her sexuality. It was nothing short of a miracle that her self-image changed in the blink of an eye.

I'm that woman who would fly to New York and take Betty Dodson's workshop.

An effervescent giddiness bubbled up as Isabella remembered Amy's naked body, so beautiful and sexy, twirling in her "It's all about ME" panties. The profound impact it had on her to see another woman's unphotoshopped body, loud and proud. Then, she witnessed the transformation of Jeanette and Claire after they got naked and showed their vulvas. Among everyone's vulnerabilities was a brief moment where Isabella accepted her body.

I accepted my body!?

Sitting naked beside naked Amy, Isabella had a glimpse of herself without her body-hate filters. She saw her body as it was. It wasn't perfect and never would be, and that was fine. Without the body-hate filters, she discovered how she'd blown her body flaws way out of proportion.

That moment of clarity, the transformative change of perception, completely blew her mind. And frankly, it seemed too good to be true. Surely, body love couldn't be that straightforward. She simply had to throw herself into being incredibly uncomfortable to see a decisive, life-affirming shift.

That's the power of Yoni. The new, fierce Isabella reasoned.

One moment she hated her body, and the next, she loved it just as it was. She wanted her readers to have this liberation. She wanted every woman worldwide to have this body confidence and to feel as empowered as Amy twirling in her blue panties.

It's up to me to share and raise women up.

The inspiration hit, and Isabella sprang from her bed like Tigger from *Winnie the Pooh*, bouncing to her laptop and booting it up. She typed the keywords into Google, and hundreds of articles popped up. She perused the top ten articles with hyper-focus before finding a step-by-step tutorial on body love.

"When the student is ready, the teacher will come," Isabella whispered, acknowledging the epiphany.

Her long, fraught struggle with body hate melted away, and the path to body acceptance opened effortlessly before her.

According to the article, every day she had to stand in front of a mirror naked or as close to naked as she could tolerate. It wasn't pleasant, but doable.

Last night, she dropped her robe and let her group see her naked, so surely she could get naked in front of herself. The article then said she needed to find something about her body that she liked: the look in her eye, her smile, her wrists, or her hair.

There must be one thing on my body that I can like.

The article's writer urged Isabella to expect a gradual change. First, she needed to appreciate how her body helped her function. Next, she needed to shift her focus from looking for what was "wrong" and objectifying her body to accepting it as it was.

As Isabella sat in a haze of awe and discovery, she looked down at her mom-jammies with disdain.

These make me feel frumpy. I don't like what I see every time I look at myself. Why do I keep wearing them if I hate how I look?

Buying new PJs to boost her confidence was an easy fix.

Each wondrous epiphany fell like gentle rain on her parched skin.

Fueled with purpose, she strode back to her bedroom and pitched the despised pajamas. She looked down at her hairy bush calmly, but then shifted her focus, and her gut clenched, seeing the cellulite-pocked stomach.

Mind over matter, she encouraged herself.

She thought about how powerful she felt sitting next to naked Amy and tossed the gut clench in the garbage. Where it belonged. Being naked was the most natural thing. Her thing. She may have been a nudist her entire life and was only discovering it now.

Caught up in the thrill of her newfound sexual confidence, she stepped in front of the full-length mirror, looking for something to like about herself. Her almond-colored eyes scanned her body and blinked. She then blinked again, looking down at the floor as bile ran up her throat. The stomach acid burned her tongue as she swallowed it back down.

Function over objectification, she tried, but it was of no use.

Isabella shut her eyes tight, repelled by what she saw.

The disheveled woman staring back at her was fat and ugly. Her breasts and tummy were stretched marked, and saggy. She carried weight on her bum and thighs, which were totally out of proportion with the rest of her body. The hint of pre-baby cellulite had multiplied and taken over her tummy and the backs of her legs. The flaps under her upper arm waved back at her as she raised them. The first wisps of fine wrinkles on her face and spiderweb veins on her legs had already marked her body.

You have the opposite of a sexy body. A cruel, jeering voice mocked her, taking stiff jabs at her absurd body-loving journey. *You have the sad, loathsome body of a woman* careening *toward middle age. You'll find nothing to love in this body.*

Her fragile confidence collapsed like a straw house, a punishment for getting too confident.

As she turned away from the mirror, body hate forced her to zone in to see the cellulite jiggle on her enormous bum. Body hate reminded her of how she had to spend her life camouflaging herself because it was so ugly. Body hate taunted her that if only she were more motivated to exercise and eat better, her bum might fit into pants.

There was a bump in the next room, and, hearing the kids stir, Isabella didn't have time to wallow. She quickly threw on her frumpy mom-jammies and headed to their bedrooms. There was nothing she could do but push down the mental image of her horrible naked body.

For the rest of the day, the kids picked up on her fragile, broken energy and acted out in a big way. The image of her ripply, fat, repulsive bum looped in her head like a terrible earworm.

She had less than nothing left to give and wanted to retreat, never to feel this acutely bad again.

Jeanette

Class Four, March 3

JEANETTE FALTERED WALKING INTO the university's foyer. A young lady with light-green bangs poking out from a cheap black-and-turquoise striped toque sat in the atrium, looking effortlessly cute, hip, and young.

Jeanette's delicate hand, with its large, square diamond wedding ring, trembled as she reached into her perfectly organized Prada bag for a zero-calorie mint. She popped the tiny mint into her mouth and didn't notice the intense flavor. Even though she looked like a runway model in her camel-colored Tom Ford shearling winter coat, she felt old and invisible.

Then again, she'd been agitated and out of sorts for the entire day. She wasn't afraid of change, even significant life changes. But this change had her firmly wedged between knowing there was something different and not knowing how to get there. She wanted to do the right thing, but had no guide or compass to tell her what that right thing was.

She was running on a thin strand of faith.

During that afternoon's frenzied closet cleaning, she looked up from polishing her salt-licked winter boots and realized she was excited about tonight's class. Perhaps it was the novelty of a new class, environment, or ideas. She was sharp and focused despite her perimenopausal brain wanting her to believe otherwise, and enjoying the well-earned sliver of pride for being the first to go at the Betty Dodson evening. The life-changing shower afterward. Then, doing the soul-searching homework and, most impressively, submitting it online like a lady boss. Jeanette was happier than she'd been in a long time.

Age is just a number. She thought as she walked past the young lady to the empty classroom.

Students she knew by face entered the drab, gray-lit room. Five minutes before class, Isabella was the first of the group to show up, looking frayed, with the buttons on her winter coat askew. Amy strolled in, wearing another one of her strange outfits. Right behind her was Claire, her face scrunched in total concentration while speaking on her phone. As different as they were, they had come together as a cohesive group at the Betty Dodson night and were now invested in each other's success. Silently, the women took their seats, not ready to discuss the evening.

Dr. Gwen arrived last, walking briskly to the front, putting her attaché down on a table adorned with round coffee-mug marks, and taking only a minute to set up. She wore her standard navy blue business suit with a crisp white button-down. Finishing her setup, the professor surveyed the class from behind chunky square glasses and smiled. Her low, authoritative voice broke through the crowd. "Good evening. Please bring your attention to the front."

Jeanette noticed an energy shift in the class, a burgeoning reverence. Everyone was now a big Dr. Gwen fan.

"Let us review what we have learned." Dr. Gwen didn't mince words as usual, and Jeanette appreciated her directness. "Women put her sexual needs a distant second, but are expected to orgasm first. Although orgasm is nice, many women need something more, yet society dictates it is selfish to expect and take her pleasure. That women worldwide do not believe she is worthy enough to be sexually equal is a systemic problem no one is willing to talk about or tackle."

Dr. Gwen paused. "Yet, her inability to communicate even her basic wants creates deep resentment, guilt, and shame. These negative emotions distort her perception of sex, which manifests into a nasty cycle that millions, probably billions, of couples get trapped in. Never able to resolve. This is why, once women get bored and stuck in an orgasm-focused sex rut, it seems impossible to change the dynamic. Ultimately, she never gets to experience her full sexual potential."

Dr. Gwen tugged on her jacket. "All of this simply because the average woman isn't comfortable asking for what she wants." She paused again.

"Does that sound fair?"

It doesn't sound fair, but how can women change this?

Jeanette sat back and contemplated Dr. Gwen's words. A long-term relationship wasn't black-and-white. Somehow, women had to ask while navigating the nuanced layers of a couple's complicated communication.

"That stops here." Dr. Gwen slapped her large hand on the desk, and the class jumped. "Women need to take action and ask for what she wants sexually. Let us be clear: this is not a big ask. This is the bare minimum of what a woman should expect."

I don't know what I'm supposed to be asking for.

The agitation and feeling out of sorts from earlier that day returned. Jeanette had the same shaky pull of her feet solidly in two different camps. One foot was in her upbringing as a faithful Christian wife, the other in the knowledge that she deserved something better.

"One woman might feel powerless to change her sexual dynamic, but millions of women make this the norm. The solution is for women to join forces and raise each other up. Like women did with the Me Too movement." Dr. Gwen opened her arms. "Each woman here is breaking this cycle and changing the way sexuality looks for women globally."

And there it was. The epiphany finally arrived! The reason God wanted Jeanette in this class. She was meant to raise her church community up. The tiny seed of purpose grew hope inside her.

"I give you this speech because knowing your truth and walking your truth are two different things. The majority of women are not confident or comfortable asking for her sexual needs to be met. Asking is so scary that she prefers to stay stuck in an orgasm-focused sex rut that makes her miserable on the inside for the rest of her life. Or until she moves on to a new relationship."

A new relationship? What would that look like?

It was the first time Jeanette dared to think about a relationship beyond Andre.

"Tonight, you will learn how to ask for your sexual needs to be met." Dr. Gwen let the words sink in. "It is a radical notion for a woman to want something different from what society says should sexually satisfy her. It is okay to demand sensuality, communication, relaxation, trust, and relating to each other. To ask for something that does not mesh with her partner's needs. To set high standards for *her* sexual happiness."

Jeanette heard a "Hell, yeah!" from the back.

"Imagine if we flipped the script where your sexual needs came first, and you only ever wanted to give each other massages." Dr. Gwen adjusted her stance, waiting for the laughter and eye-rolling to die down. "It satisfies your partner at first, but after a year of only ever giving and getting massages, your partner is unhappy and wants to have an orgasm. But you are in a massage rut, and they do not know how to ask for something different."

That wouldn't stop Andre from asking for what he wanted. Jeanette thought. *So why can't I?*

"Would you want a relationship with a constant undercurrent of resentment that sex is about meeting your needs, not theirs?" Dr. Gwen shrugged. "Do you want your partner to tell you they need something different? If yes, it should make sense that your partner also wants to know. They want you to tell them."

Women need to speak up for herself and I need to be the woman who lifts her up.

Jeanette looked over at Amy, who pulled her into a new sexual reality. She would do the same for her church group.

Isabella

Class Four

ISABELLA SNORTED SOFTLY WHEN Dr. Gwen declared, "It makes sense that your partner wants to know. They want you to tell them."

Do they really?

Isabella pictured herself telling Alex over their morning coffee, "Hey, I'm not happy with the way we have sex. From now on, instead of having an orgasm, I want 'sensuality, communication, relaxation, trust, and'" What else did Dr. Gwen say? "'relating to each other.'"

And for Alex's reaction to be a delighted "I'm so glad you told me this. I also don't want to focus on your orgasm. I want us to be equals so we can create a better sexual experience together."

Hardee-har-har, like that would ever happen. It sounded good in theory, but not for a busy mom.

Why are you resisting? Her friend Allison made a guest appearance in her head. *Don't moms deserve this, too?*

Of course, moms deserved this. But the reality was her marriage was barely skimming by, and just the idea of having that conversation with Alex overwhelmed Isabella. She wasn't resisting. It was self-preservation.

Dr. Gwen held up her hand to signal a stop.

"Not asking for what you want is a barricade that blocks you from tapping into your pleasure spectrum." The professor paused and scanned the class. "What is the worst thing that could happen if you opened up and explained to your partner that you want something different?"

My husband will reject me. Isabella's answer came out of nowhere.

Alex would never reject her, especially if she wanted to do something different. She jotted down her reaction as the professor continued.

"Chances are, saying you want more and deserve better will produce a visceral reaction. Society has convinced you that you are a second-class citizen, so simply saying you are sexually equal will not fool your smart brain."

Dr. Gwen posted a quote on the whiteboard and read it aloud.

"Each of us has an inner thermostat setting that determines how much love, success, and creativity we allow ourselves to enjoy. When we exceed our inner thermostat setting, we will often do something to sabotage ourselves, causing us to drop back into the old, familiar zone where we feel secure. Gay Hendricks."

Isabella read the quote a second time to let it sink in.

A jolt of shock rushed through her so fast that it was like Dr. Gwen walked up to Isabella and pushed a trigger on her body. She sat back hard in her chair and, with a fresh set of eyes, analyzed the looking-at-herself-naked disaster. She had "exceeded her inner thermostat setting." The acutely painful triggering and sabotaging afterward forced her to dive headfirst back into her comfort zone.

It was seriously messed up that her comfort zone was to be so ashamed of her body. She desperately wanted a new thermostat setting but was afraid that moving forward would mean more failure. Filled with equal parts of hope and hopelessness, Isabella listened to Dr. Gwen's explanation.

"The good news is, you can outwit your smart brain by gradually making consistent and small changes over time." Dr. Gwen put a new slide on the whiteboard. "It is a straightforward three-step process."

Isabella braced for another step-by-step on body love. Déjà vu swooped in, playing the horrible naked body memories, making a persuasive argument for staying put in her body's comfort zone.

That's the rejection and fear of failure talking to you. Allison's voice came again. *Don't let it get you down. Open up to what Dr. Gwen is telling you.*

Anxious but determined, Isabella lifted her chin and listened.

"Step one is to make a tiny change. Think teeny." Dr. Gwen put her thumb and pointer finger together. "Your ego will want you to do something bigger, but keep the stakes low to limit relationship waves, triggers, and self-talk sabotage. A tiny change means less drama, less fighting, and less fear of failure. They will still be there, but it will be something you can deal with."

That made sense, and Isabella could manage tiny changes. Still, a weariness tugged at her. If it sounded too good to be true, then it probably was.

It's okay to be a little lost. Allison cheered her on. *Say yes and see what happens.*

"The second step is to put yourself into motion and make it happen. The smaller the change, the simpler it is to follow through, set boundaries, and acclimate to it being your new normal."

Isabella saw Claire lean in, listening intently. She tapped Claire's forearm, and they exchanged a knowing look, promising to support and help each other. Isabella was grateful for the company.

"The third step is to celebrate and acknowledge what you have done. Please, under no circumstances, skip celebrating, even though it may seem frivolous. Celebrating recalibrates your mindset and confidence. Once you go through this process, return to step one with the next tiny change."

That was it? Isabella could do that. She turned her head to look at Amy and remembered her beautiful body twirling in the "It's all about ME" panties. She yearned for a world where women embraced their bodies.

"Can you give an example?" The young lady with a halo of curls asked.

"Sure. For step one, you can compliment your partner." Dr. Gwen paused. "Good, I see the eye rolls. If you think this is not a valid change and is unrelated to your sex life, that's your ego talking. It is important to tell your partner you want them and find them attractive."

Is it? Isabella wasn't sure she'd ever told Alex she wanted him or found him attractive.

"Step two, you follow through and compliment your partner. It was not difficult, awkward, or embarrassing. By making this small choice, acting on it, and then following through, you have changed the trajectory of your sex life, so celebrate as if it is a big step. Because it is.

"Each time you loop through this process, your smart brain shifts from a negative mindset to a positive mindset. Then, one day in the not-so-distant future, confidently telling your partner what you want and need will be your norm." Dr. Gwen smiled benignly, not knowing she had set off a million different emotions inside Isabella.

Maybe it wasn't so outrageous to tell Alex over morning coffee that their sex life needed to change.

"If your internal thermostat setting is low, start by nurturing and building trust and confidence in yourself." Dr. Gwen put a new slide on the whiteboard. "For example, create initiation rituals with your favorite sense. Listen to relaxing music—light scented candles. Put on silky lingerie that is luxurious on your body. Perhaps read erotica. Do whatever helps you tap into your sensuality."

Isabella remembered how good the hot-water bath felt. She would like to have that TLC at least once per month.

"Or, if there has been a long break in sex, or it has been sporadic," Dr. Gwen continued. "Make small changes so scheduling sex becomes a consistent habit."

The TLC's warm fuzzies disappeared, and Isabella cringed at the idea of scheduling sex. As if reading her mind, Dr. Gwen went on.

"There is a big social stigma around scheduling sex, but research shows couples who schedule sex have better sex more often. Which makes sense. Scheduling allows you to proactively make space for your pleasure. You are in charge of when and how sex happens."

Isabella's hand went up.

"I'm already scheduled up to the wazoo. Saying I'll have sex on Tuesday at two o'clock sounds mechanical. The opposite of sexy. Isn't sex more fun when it's a spontaneous surprise?"

"Scheduling does not have to mean a specific time." Dr. Gwen was unfazed by the outburst. "Rather, if you know Tuesday is a flexible workday, sex can happen sometime during the day. Look at it this way: Sex is a team sport, and scheduling helps you and your partner work together to create a mutually beneficial space."

The insight caught Isabella off guard, so she scrambled to write it down before it slipped away. *Spontaneous sex has women waiting to be pounced on. Scheduling sex is so much easier than constantly having your guard up.*

I deserve that freedom, said a small, shy voice.

Did she deserve this? Isabella had never uttered those words, and she wanted to repeat them. The next time, more boldly. At the Betty Dodson night, she got a glimpse of the strong, sexual woman inside her. She was in there, somewhere, and Isabella would coax her out. One teeny step at a time.

"Dr. Gwen." Claire's hand shot up, her butt fidgeting on the hard seat like she had to pee.

Claire

Class Four

CLAIRE WAS TERRIFIED, BUT that was the point.

"Can I share a quick story?" Claire interrupted Dr. Gwen, who turned and looked at her watch, her lips forming a "no," but Claire pressed, "It's about starting small and going slow."

"Yes, of course." The professor nodded. "Please keep it short."

What Claire wanted out of her sexual experience was to abolish this shame, create a healthier mindset, and move into a better sexual experience. The Betty Dodson night taught Claire that taking a leap opened a new world of possibilities. So she girded her loins and leaped.

"Before I took this course, I wanted to surprise my boyfriend with a special night. I called it *Project Up My Sex Game*."

A few mean-girl titters peppered the room, tripping Claire and turning her leap into a free-fall. Dr. Gwen shut the haters down with a swift, stern look, but it was too late. Wordlessly, Claire shook her head. She couldn't go through with it.

"Claire, please look at me." When Claire looked up, Dr. Gwen gave her a beguiling smile and a wink. "You can do this."

Amy grabbed Claire's hand, but her mouth went sandpaper-dry when she tried to speak. Her cool, logical brain vanished, and she felt like a shaken champagne bottle, not wanting to explode under the pressure.

"Claire, you need to make shame your bitch," Jeanette, in full-on momma-bear mode, announced, loud enough for the class to hear. The class titters turned to gasps. Dr. Gwen's bewildered expression helped to loosen the grip of shame as Claire snorted. She took a deep breath and a second leap.

"Amy and I planned the *Project Up My Sex Game* carefully, but I knew going in I was out of my depth." Claire's hand shook, but Amy held her steady. "I thought pushing myself out of my comfort zone would help me, but it did the opposite. I exceeded my thermostat setting and forced something I wasn't ready for. It makes sense now why it was a complete disaster. It did a number on my head, and I'm scared to initiate anything now."

"This is an important and on-point example, Claire. Thank you." Dr. Gwen gave Claire a look of concern. "If you were listening to this as a friend, what advice would you give to yourself?"

Claire had the answer before Dr. Gwen even finished speaking. Like it was jostling to be set free, breaking its way through her many aloof layers.

"You are the opposite of a failure," Claire said with shaky conviction. "You went out on a limb to make an amazing night. Next time, don't be so ambitious and don't overcomplicate things. Take Dr. Gwen's advice: start small, go slow. Do one idea at a time instead of everything at once."

"Well done, Claire. Now is the time to forgive and then celebrate. Do you promise to do that?" Claire nodded, and Dr. Gwen gave her a pleased and proud smile.

Claire's shoulders relaxed as the adrenaline rush caught up to the confession. Another piece of the jigsaw puzzle clicked into place, and Claire experienced a change in her mindset in real time.

If Amy were the queen of masturbating, then Claire was the queen of habits. She could build tiny, daily habits and schedule sex like a boss. For the first time since she started dating Carlos, Claire sensed it would be okay. She could figure this out.

Dr. Gwen turned from Claire and addressed the class.

"Let us return to our three-step formula and get specific. You decide to initiate sex. You think of the smallest thing possible and are aware of any triggers, sabotaging self-talk, or sex speed bumps. You go to follow through and initiate, but you find you cannot. Why?"

Claire remembered how her body froze in the Wonder Woman pose when Carlos walked through the door. Even though she willed it to move, her body wouldn't budge.

"Most women do not initiate sex and need to build up that skill set. Traditionally, men get a lot of practice initiating sex." Amy booed, and Dr. Gwen gave her a warning look. "Numerous studies show men initiate sex over three times as often as women. The more one partner initiates sex, the less their partner will, creating what is called 'the seesaw phenomenon.'"

Isabella lurched forward, her body vibrating.

"Each time you let your partner be in charge of when and what happens during sex, you are defaulting to your partner's wants and rhythms. In doing so, you hold the power."

"I don't hold the power!" Isabella spat out.

"The gatekeeper controls the outcome of sex and therefore holds the power." Dr. Gwen replied calmly. "With seesaw-initiation, both men and women believe they are victims. Men for enduring rejection; women for carrying the burden of rejection. Both have unspoken frustrations about their selfish partner repeatedly getting their way. It's easy to imagine how many sex speed bumps that creates. Conversely, it is just as selfish for you not to initiate."

"Hold on. I'm selfish for not initiating?" Isabella's eyes bugged out. Her pen was hovering, waiting to write down Dr. Gwen's next words.

"So you expect your partner to carry the load, take the brunt of rejection, while you never once consider the toll on their self-esteem?" Dr. Gwen asked mildly, perfectly at peace with pushing everyone's buttons. "For those who do not initiate, put yourself in your partner's shoes. In good faith, they initiate sex and must wait for you to say yes or no. Perhaps you give an unenthusiastic yes out of guilt, making your partner assume you do not find them attractive. Or if you say no enough times, they tire of the repeated rejections and shut down, giving up. Or they get triggered and start a fight—which helps you be a seesaw victim."

Claire studied Isabella, who looked as if she'd been turned inside out. There was so much to talk about at the next group meeting.

"If you resent when your partner initiates, ask yourself why you do not initiate more. Research shows that initiating sex makes men feel desired above all else."

Claire wanted Carlos to know she desired him. Completely and utterly. The first habit on her sex to-do list was to initiate sex.

This time, she would be wiser, start small, and go slow.

Amy

Class Four

"Who initiates sex regularly?" Dr. Gwen's hopeful eyes scanned the class as a look of disappointment passed over her face. Curious, Amy looked around. Hers was the only hand that went up.

That's not right! Betty Dodson dictated to Amy in her no-nonsense way. *Every woman here needs to be in charge of her sex.*

Don't worry, I'm on it. Amy assured Betty and put on her professor's hat.

"Can you tell the class about your experience?" Dr. Gwen nodded to Amy.

"Initiating is a rush. It gives me a sense of power and control. And I like to be in control. It's like taking a drug that makes you feel so good about yourself without the hangover. I'm in charge, and we are doing things my way. I don't understand why more women wouldn't want to feel powerful in her relationship —"

"Did any of your partners not like it when you initiated? I'm asking because the class needs to understand rejection and pushback."

Paul, with his goofy grin, popped into her head. He also brought along the big feelings of angst and the unspoken question that nagged at her. Did she come on too strong? Is that why he ghosted her?

Dr. Gwen softly cleared her throat. The class didn't need to know about Paul, and Amy shoved the painful memory back down.

"Yes, of course." Amy waved off rejection as if it wasn't a big deal. She didn't like talking about the bad parts of sex and didn't understand why Dr. Gwen did. "I had a few partners who weren't used to a woman taking charge and felt threatened, but eventually that weirdness went away —"

"Excellent, thank you," Dr. Gwen cut Amy off again as she sat on the table's edge. "Initiating sex does not come naturally. It is a learned skill. When you learn any new skill, sex or otherwise, there is a learning curve. For example, if you have never baked a cake, you could not walk into a kitchen and spontaneously bake it. You would, at the very least, need a recipe." Dr. Gwen put a photo of baking ingredients in separate bowls on the whiteboard. "There is a cooking term, 'mise en place,' which means everything is prepped and in place before you start. This helps to make the cooking process seamless."

What does that have to do with sex? Amy thought, irritated at being cut off twice.

"Cueing your partner takes practice and patience. To confidently initiate when you don't know how means ensuring everything is mise en place. That translates to mindfully pausing, getting yourself into the right headspace, and doing self-care to get your body in sync. Some women are comfortable with planning, while others prefer things to be spontaneous." Dr. Gwen clicked to the next slide with an "X" over the word spontaneous.

"If you are new to initiating, this is not the time to wing it. You need to plan and come in prepared." There was a chorus of groans from the class. "You can think of planning as either a chore or a foolproof way to build your anticipation and confidence. It's entirely your choice, but planning will get you where you want to go faster." The confused murmurs persisted.

"Okay, let us put this into a three-step process. Step one: You decide sex will happen on Tuesday." Dr. Gwen looked over at Isabella and winked. "Step two: You have your initiation rituals mise en place. You reframe your thoughts and purposefully put yourself in a healthy mindset. You cue your partner and initiate the sex you want to have. Step three: You celebrate running your fuck."

There was a gap of silence at the exact moment, as Claire said to Amy, "It makes me wonder why feminists fought to have equal orgasms and not equal initiation." Making the class laugh.

A shy voice interrupted Dr. Gwen's chuckle. "My boyfriend never initiates sex. It's always up to me."

"Is it Lucy?" It was the first time the young lady with long brown hair shared with the class. "Would you mind telling us what that is like?"

"Mostly, I don't mind. I like having sex on my terms. But sometimes, knowing he's into me would be nice. I don't understand why he doesn't initiate. Like, ever." Lucy hesitated, and Dr. Gwen gave her an encouraging nod. "It bugs me when he complains we should have more sex. I'm like, dude, if you initiated once in a while, we would have sex more often. If you don't like the number of times I initiate while you do nothing, you can't complain. But he still complains." She crossed her arms as if she were hugging herself.

A memory of Amy's ex-husband constantly rejecting her and then complaining about their sex life bubbled to the surface. She didn't want or need that negative energy in her life, thank you very much, and she pushed it right back down with Paul's goofy grin.

"What you are experiencing is not uncommon." Dr. Gwen was about to launch into a discussion when she glanced at her watch, and her eyebrows shot up. She gave Lucy an apologetic look. "Unfortunately, we do not have time to work through this. Please see me after class so we can chat about solutions. Excellent share, thank you." The professor turned back to the class. "My apologies. I ran over our time and need to wrap this up."

"Your sexual equality means tapping into your unique pleasure spectrum and doing what pleases you. But that means you need to ask for what you want. This is easy to accomplish when you implement the three-step process. Step one is to decide on a tiny change. Step two: follow through. Step three, celebrate your achievement."

"Your sex'cess happens in the follow-through." Dr. Gwen tugged on her jacket. "Your sexual equality hangs in the balance of taking your first step. Planning and mise en place are your biggest assets. Suddenly, running your fuck is relatively simple to achieve." The professor nodded to the class and turned off the PowerPoint. "Everything we discussed tonight is in your homework notes. I will be here for the next fifteen minutes to answer your questions. You are free to go."

The rest of the class huddled in their groups and then drifted out of the room.

Amy stood up and stretched, glancing over at Isabella, who looked agitated and stressed. The same look she had before taking off her robe at the Betty Dodson night. But then she fell in love with her sparkly vulva. It was a life-changing moment. For both of them.

She's struggling. I should call her. Amy made a mental note.

Speaking of the Betty Dodson night, Amy turned to the group, eager to discuss her great idea of attending The Taboo Sex Show the following month. Going to the everything-to-do-with-sex trade show was a great excuse to keep their group going. But the three women looked drained and ready to leave. She would bring it up at the next group meeting.

"I'll email to coordinate the next meeting," Jeanette said as Claire and Isabella said their goodbyes and left.

Amy picked up her things, ready to leave, but Jeanette moved in close. Her head was down, her long fingers fidgeted, and she shuffled from foot to foot. "Can I ask a favor?"

When she looked up, Amy saw the post-Betty-Dodson-night Jeanette. Her Teflon veneer was gone, and her face was an open book of insecurity. Amy recognized that look. Jeanette was in the middle of a significant life change.

But Amy was reluctant to help Jeanette.

She looked over at Dr. Gwen, who was in a deep conversation with Lucy, being a good sexual steward and helping any woman who asked. As different as Amy and Jeanette were, the great equalizer was that they were both women. As Dr. Gwen said, women needed to support and raise other women up.

Amy took Jeanette's hand and said, "Sure, what is it?"

Amy Calls Isabella
March 4

I DESERVE THAT FREEDOM. The small, shy voice from class turned out to be patiently persistent.

Isabella put her hand on the nearest wall for support, her tired head resting on her arm. It was the day after class, and every emotion in her body whirled like a tornado, giving her the spins. The shy voice bumped up against all of her insecurities. She wanted to become the strong, sexual woman inside her.

But at what cost? Her vision filled with a flash of her naked breasts sagging over a stretch-marked stomach.

It had been like that since she woke up. Just as she was getting on with things, SHAZAM, a new, awful naked image, flashed before her eyes. She was trapped in a house of mirrors, with her dumpy, naked reflections staring back at her.

Mercifully, both kids went down for their naps without a fuss, and she had twenty minutes to wrap herself in a tight ball and decompress. Climbing into her unmade bed, she stared at a stain on the comforter when the cell in her back pocket pinged. She pulled it out to put it on her nightstand and noticed Amy had sent a group photo from the Betty Dodson night with a brief text.

"U were so brave. Be proud of yourself!! <3"

With dull eyes, Isabella looked at the photo of herself, Jeanette, and Claire. Her fingers gripped a wineglass tightly, her face terrified, her wan smile masking the panic in her eyes. When she expanded the photo to full screen, she saw her dirty flannel robe, a few sizes too small, stretched over her lumps and bumps. She was the ugly duckling between two swans.

You went above your thermostat, she reminded herself in a bid for self-compassion.

But it made no difference. Shame was driving this bus.

And then that robe came off, and I was naked.

She closed her eyes tight as a wave of humiliation rolled over her, and her body wrapped itself into an even tighter ball. She must have been a sight: the frumpy woman with her untamed bush, glittery vulva, hairy legs, and massive cellulite ass. How could she ever believe, even for a second, that sitting beside naked Amy was the most natural thing? Her thing.

Her cell phone pinged with another photo from Amy. Even though it was irrational, she didn't want to look at the picture. It might be a selfie of her sitting beside Amy, spread-eagle, her naked glittery vulva on full display. She closed her eyes as the spins returned.

How does Amy love her body? She'd do anything to uncover that secret.

I deserve that freedom.

She looked at the first photo again, and her fingers texted Amy before she had time to think.

> "I looked at my naked body. It wasn't good."

Within seconds, her cell rang, and Isabella let it go to voicemail. Immediately after came a text.

> "Can we talk? Please! Will call until U answer."

The course, this group, Amy — it was too much. She couldn't face the group meeting or attend the remaining class. She crossed a line. End of story. Feeling this bad wasn't worth it. She would give her editor, Jessica, an excuse like her child was in the hospital. Even Jessica couldn't get mad at that. She'd send a group text and explain she was quitting. Anything to make the spins stop.

Quitting was the right decision.

Amy called again. Isabella drew a sharp breath in through her nose and out through her mouth, then answered, her voice dull and defeated, "Hey."

"Hey, yourself. Everything okay?" Amy's voice sounded light, but Isabella heard the overriding concern.

"Yeah, I'm good. Thanks. So, I decided to quit the course. Long story. Sorry, but I'm in the middle of something and must go." Isabella lied to get off the phone and have the ten remaining minutes of uninterrupted me-time. "Okay, bye."

"Then I'll get straight to it." Amy put a metaphorical foot in the door. "Can you explain what happened between the Betty Dodson night and today?"

There was a long silence as Isabella contemplated hanging up and ghosting her group. She wanted the relief of closing this chapter in her life and moving on.

"What are you afraid of?"

What was she afraid of? Everything. And that was when the penny dropped.

"I don't want this BS anymore," she murmured. The spins stopped as she bolted up in bed and told Amy all about it. She forced out every word of the heart-wrenching experience of looking at herself naked. Amy listened until Isabella stopped talking, then asked.

"What did you expect to see in the mirror?"

Isabella's unfocused eyes stared at the ceiling. "I thought I'd see one thing I liked." She gave a brittle, bitter laugh. "I'll never do that again."

"Never is a long time. If I tell you something, will you listen?"

Isabella nodded but remained silent.

"Shame is controlling this conversation."

"Yeah, I get that. Please don't patronize me." Isabella's mouth spat the words out before she could take them back. Lately, unexpected angry outbursts were coming out of nowhere. "Sorry, Amy. I understand, but it's one thing to know the theory. The reality is more complicated."

"Exactly. I want you to smash this shame to smithereens." Amy said with the ferocity of a big girl who knew the plight and wanted no more body shaming.

"Me too." Isabella softened. "But I don't know where to begin."

They both took a moment to think. Amy broke the silence.

"When was the last time you looked at yourself naked? On purpose?"

"Over ten years, at least. I'm not sure I ever looked at my naked body on purpose. It's always been by accident."

"Okay, good. So it's fair to say you're not used to looking at yourself. The last time you looked was, what, in your late twenties? Is it possible you expected to have a twenty-year-old body? Instead, you saw a mature, curvy body that created and housed two babies."

"My body has changed so much since having kids." Isabella's voice broke. "I didn't recognize myself."

"It's time for tough love," Amy said with a gentle fierceness. "Shame will not be in control of your body from this moment on. You must get back on that horse and look at yourself naked again."

Isabella didn't answer because she didn't have the heart to tell Amy her pep talk was a non-starter. Amy didn't notice her silence and kept talking.

"But don't look at yourself with your eyes. Look at your body with my eyes as if I were appraising your body. Could you please do that for me?"

"No, I'm sorry, but that's impossible," Isabella whispered, tears running down her cheeks.

"Remember when Dr. Gwen said you need to choose yourself? You must take a small, tiny, even minuscule step. That's it. But you have to do this for yourself."

Isabella had to choose herself.

"Just because I want to do this doesn't make it easy," Isabella confided.

"You're worth it, and you deserve this —" Amy started, but Isabella didn't want another pep talk.

"My kids are up. I've got to go. Bye," Isabella hung up, hearing the bumps of someone getting out of bed.

She pulled her heavy body out from under the covers, annoyed that she'd used her precious me-time to talk to Amy.

I deserve that freedom. The shy, patiently persistent voice returned, adding.

I choose me.

Isabella's Column

My Needs Versus The Hockey Game

IN A PERFECT WORLD, two people equally share sexual pleasure.

The reality for fifty percent of the population is that during sex, most women have one chance to orgasm. It's at the start of sex when her brain is transitioning from her busy day to her body. Because of her delayed response, chances are she can't orgasm in that time frame. Once that window of opportunity is closed, her part of the pleasure ride is over. It's on to the main event—her partner's pleasure.

Is it any wonder women are angry and resentful when sex is initiated? Because we can't communicate this, eventually, we become apathetic. Apathy is where your "I don't care if I ever have sex again" lives.

We certainly don't deserve that. Your sexuality needs to flourish.

The logical solution is to start sex differently. Yes, it's intimidating and scary. It is also straightforward.

Asking for your needs to be met starts with making the time and space to have sex. Some might call that scheduling. If the word scheduling makes you feel asexual, call it something you prefer. Like unicorn.

The point is that good sex won't magically or effortlessly happen by itself. You have to make it happen.

I get it. It's challenging and inconvenient.

Ultimately, this is a crossroads where you choose which sex path you want to take: apathy or flourishing.

On This Week's Sex Menu

Class #4: I need to ask for something I want.

Answer: I want a full-body massage. But I will settle for a foot massage. Or half a foot massage. My standards are low.

Problem: I don't have any practice asking for what I want. I don't know how to put my sexual needs first. I don't feel like I deserve it. This is the most challenging thing I've ever done sexually.

Let's put my answer to the real-life test.

What Could Go Wrong?

For months, I've fantasized about a hot rock massage with warm stones on my back. I thought asking my husband for a foot massage would be fast, easy, and uncomplicated.

But, of course, it wasn't. There are so many complicated layers to trying to "unicorn" couple time.

We had a friend visiting. Granted, he's the kind of friend we can say, "We're going off for a while. Potato chips are in the cupboard. You know where the remote is."

However, my husband needed the male-bonding time. I didn't have the heart to pull him away from the nightly hockey match. With two toddlers, I can no longer count on weekend naps to fit in sex. I wasn't willing to wait until after 11:00. And the list went on.

Dithering all week, I bolted up in bed on Thursday night, realizing the next day was Friday. Our weekend was full of activities, so the foot massage had to happen on Friday night. Friday morning, I handed my husband a tube of foot lotion and, as flirty as I could muster before my second cup of coffee, asked, "Can you massage my feet tonight?"

He gave me a pained look and whined, "But we're watching the hockey game."

I glared at him belligerently. Seeing that I would not relent, he gave me a you're-inconveniencing-me sigh and said, "Sure."

His lackluster response brought up a lot of guilt, which flatlined my libido. Wouldn't you know my husband dodged my "unicorn?"

I confronted him Friday night at 9:00.

"I thought you were giving me a foot massage."

"I have to clean the fish tank."

"Isn't having a couple of times more important than cleaning your fish tank?"

(Dear reader, I couldn't make this up if I tried.)

At that moment, I wanted to put my tail between my legs and retreat. It was humiliating to beg for something I wanted. I didn't feel worthy to ask for my sensual needs to be met. When I had a sudden realization. When the roles are reversed, and my husband initiates sex, does he have the same guilt, expecting his orgasm needs to be met?

Even with the swell of negative emotions coursing through my body, it was hard to put my foot down. Truthfully, the only reason I followed through was because of this column.

I handed my husband the tube of massage lotion. At that moment, our two-year-old daughter woke up. Sigh. The three of us trudged to the bedroom. As an act of goodwill, I massaged his feet first. He held our daughter, and I saw both of us relaxing as his foot massage progressed.

Then it was my turn. Hooray! Finally, the highly anticipated and much-needed pampering.

As soon as my husband handed our daughter to me, she started to wail. My husband half-heartedly got on with it. I didn't notice the first (mediocre) foot massage while calming my daughter down.

Frustrated tears formed on my lower eyelids. I had asked for my needs to be met, and my husband was indifferent. Frustration quickly turned into resentment, and I was about to call the whole thing off when my toddler settled down. Salvaging the second foot, I did my best to relax and calm my frazzled nerves.

Then it happened.

My husband and I started chatting and giggling. We then — gasp! — shared a bona fide couple connection. My husband joked, and I laughed while he gave me some TLC. Then, my daughter smiled at me, and the world felt more than perfect.

This is where mindset is so important. I have a choice. (1) To complain that everything leading up to those meager five minutes of couple connection was a bust. (2) Focus on finally getting what I wanted.

I'm so glad I chose option number two.

I asked for my needs to be met. How we got there wasn't what I wanted or expected, but in the end, I got what I needed. The prized couple's intimacy I crave. Those five minutes changed how I felt about us for the rest of the week.

With the foot massage done, my husband jumped off the bed and kissed my daughter and me on the forehead. He bee-lined out of the bedroom to watch the remainder of the hockey game.

Back to Amy's Hook-Up

At the Pub, February 27

Jackpot!

Amy was looking for trouble when she arrived to meet her Tinder hookup. She found it when she walked into the bland neighborhood pub with its bright lighting, sports pendants, and the smell of fish and chips. Only a few men were watching the hockey game, so Adesh stuck out like an exotic creature with his good looks and stylish clothes.

Walking over to him, she saw he was way cuter in person than on his Tinder profile. With his movie-star-thick head of black hair, dark skin, and brooding bedroom eyes.

Amy stood at the table, waiting for him to acknowledge her. He didn't.

"Hi, you must be Adesh."

"Hey," he replied without looking at her, his eyes on the game.

His young, cocky swagger with no real-life experience was an instant turnoff. Foolishly, Amy ignored the red flag, telling herself his machismo wasn't a deal-breaker; she could put up with it for a couple of hours.

"Can I buy you a drink?" She swallowed her impatience.

"So, look, let's cut the crap. We're both here for one thing."

He finally turned her way and slowly let his dark eyes travel the length of her like he was buying a used car. He pursed his lips and looked resigned.

"I'm not feeling your outfit, but I can let it slide. How about we go back to mine?"

What was he talking about? Amy looked great in her outfit. She wore a purple flowery blouse to match her hair's purple streaks. Paired with a long skirt with a diagonal stripe, the purple-and-blue leopard boots tied the blouse and skirt together.

She wanted sex, but she didn't need this shit.

"Well, you look like a complete asswipe, and I'm sorry to have wasted my time."

Picking up her bag, Amy turned to leave when she heard a deep, belly laugh, making her stumble mentally.

"Whoa, wait a minute. I like a strong woman with spunk." The admiration in his voice disarmed her. "Please sit down. Let me buy you a drink."

Mollified to hear his manliness deflating, Amy sat down.

"Even though we're here for the same thing, you can drop your shitty attitude," she warned.

He raised his hands in mock defense and gave her a dazzling smile. Adesh was gorgeous, and only someone this good-looking could help her get her mojo back. But they spent the next fifteen minutes in silence, sipping their drinks, with nothing to say.

More red flags frantically waved in her face, but Amy didn't care if she connected with Adesh on an intellectual level. Finishing their drinks was simply the countdown to sex.

"So." Adesh looked at her like he had fulfilled his part, and now she needed to put out. Someone would teach this guy a lesson one day, but it wouldn't be Amy.

"Let's go to my place." Amy texted her address, and he left the cheery pub without waiting for her.

"What's the rush? You can't get in without me," she said to his back.

It was a short drive, and as she pulled up to her townhouse, she heard a loud thump, thump, thump of a bass. There was Adesh, leaning against his car, the doors flung open, blasting music. It was ten freakin' thirty, and her neighbors were looking out their windows.

Scrambling out of her car, already regretting this decision.

"Hey, Adesh, do you mind turning off the music?"

"Why so uptight?" he mocked, turning off the engine. The street fell silent.

"Did it ever occur to you that my neighbors might not like your music?"

She heard how old she sounded and didn't like it one bit. He twirled his keys noisily as they walked up to her townhouse.

"Sorry." He put on his best shamefaced look, but he wasn't sorry. His cuteness factor was sliding downhill fast.

Everything inside her screamed to abort. That this would not turn out well. Amy looked over her shoulder at Adesh, inadvertently glancing at the street where Paul had said she looked beautiful in the moonlight. She couldn't unlock her door fast enough.

The moment Amy closed her front door, Adesh had her pinned to the wall. He pulled his body into hers and kissed her deeply as his hands traveled the length of her body. He parted her legs, moved up her skirt, pulled her panties to the side, and found her clit.

Relieved, Amy braced herself on the door frame, eager to have her first orgasm. Her brain switched off as her body's urge to scratch her sexual itch took over.

Both were too preoccupied to notice the watchful eyes of her cat, Orgasm.

Jeanette & Amy Go Shopping

March 4

"Okay, I'm on the website you suggested," Jeanette told Amy on speakerphone while sitting on her white couch.

Her inexperienced eyes scanned the web page as she leaned closer to the laptop screen, her morals queasy at what she was looking at.

"Bingo, I found one," Amy replied excitedly. "Go to page two, second line down, third in. It's called the Touch X by We-vibe. Do you see it?"

Jeanette scrambled to follow Amy's instructions. A long gap of silence followed before she located it.

"I see it." Jeanette's brow furrowed as she sat back, baffled, before clicking on the pointy-figure-eight-shaped blue device. "But —?"

"I know, right?" Amy giggled in delight. "Women engineers now design products that better work with women's bodies. Fun fact: Men design most vibrators, which is why they look like penises. Products designed by women will best fit your vulva. Trust me."

"Okay."

Embarrassed to talk about a vibe fitting her vulva, Jeanette only half listened. She read the Touch X's product description, which was identical to every other description on the site.

"Wait, cancel that. If this is your first vibe, let's look at something that will stimulate your clit, like a small but powerful bullet. Once you get used to that, you can move to internal, dual stimulation."

Jeanette didn't know what internal dual stimulation meant, but trusted Amy to steer her in the right direction.

"Hey, here's a good idea: let's Google the best first vibrator."

"I can do that." Jeanette typed the keywords into Google. She scrolled through the endless list of articles, each with a unique spin on the "best first vibe." Closing her eyes, her determination waned at how complicated and exhausting it was to buy a vibrator. "I'm sorry, Amy. I thought I was ready for this, but I'm not."

"This would be easier if we went to a store. You can pick up the vibrators and see how they work." Amy coaxed. "It just so happens that I'm free now."

"Now?" Jeanette wasn't good with spontaneity, but something inside pushed her to ask Amy for help. "Okay. How did you want to do this?"

"I'll text you a map to a store I like," Amy said, distracted.

Seconds later, Jeanette's cell pinged with the directions.

"See you in twenty," Amy said, and disconnected.

Jeanette stared, not seeing, as she closed her laptop. She'd just agreed to go to a sex shop. A flash of her standing in the middle of the store, surrounded by hundreds of vibrators, had her stomach in hysterics. Even saying the word vibrator made her chest tighten as waves of nausea threatened her throat.

Everything was happening way too fast. She didn't want the vibrator anymore and picked up her cell to cancel.

Calm down. Dr. Gwen's voice came to her. *This is your internal thermostat, uncomfortable with change. However, you are jumping into a big pool of your upper limits. Are you sure you want to take this big a step?*

Reflexively, she shifted her gaze to a framed photo of her and Andre, looking beautiful and happy. But their marriage had always been a sham.

Outrage swooped in, righteously spewing that she'd believed she was frigid for almost thirty years. She didn't know her sexual needs could matter. But they did matter. She mattered. In one small step, she could walk away from this horrible reality. And one more small step to move into a pleasure she'd been denied her entire adult life.

Without thinking, she thrust the laptop aside and jumped off the couch. Grabbing her keys, bag, and houndstooth coat, she said goodbye to Max before frog-marching herself to the garage. Her body buzzed with adrenaline for the entire ten-minute drive, and she parked on the far side of the lot. Looking around, she tapped her French-manicured nails on the steering wheel.

Where was Amy?

Her head was churning, her body restless, and she needed to move. There were zero people in the empty parking lot, so Jeanette put on her sunglasses, flipped her hood up, and hopped out of the Range Rover. A soft buzz welcomed her as she opened the opaque glass door.

A young lady with ear gauges and a large neck tattoo looked up from her phone.

"Hi there. Let me know if you need any help."

"I'm waiting for my friend," Jeanette's timid voice made her nerves stand on edge. She removed her sunglasses to see better the tiny, organized shop, packed floor to ceiling with products.

"No worries. Take your time looking around." The girl went back to scrolling on her phone.

Inspecting the store, it was like an online sex shop with too many choices, and dread settled back in Jeanette's stomach. She forced her feet to walk three steps over to a display of vibrators along one wall, noticing the Touch X she'd seen online. She picked up the surprisingly hefty and cushiony-soft vibe with tentative, trembling fingers and turned it around, not knowing what to do next. Humiliated, she threw the vibe back onto the shelf.

I can't do this.

She turned to make a beeline for the door, but the clerk had silently appeared beside her.

"My name is Lana." She gave a big, youthful smile. "I see you found our Touch X, which is an excellent first vibe. Let me show you how it works."

She picked it up and offered it back to Jeanette.

"Uh —" Jeanette took it as words gushed out of her mouth. "My friend recommended it while we were shopping online. I couldn't figure out how it worked."

"Are you okay? Oh my goodness, I'm sorry you're frustrated." Lana replied as she reached over and turned it on. "Right here. The controls can be tricky if you don't know where to look."

Everything Jeanette believed about being a promiscuous woman wrapped itself around the dread in her stomach, clenching until it hurt. Jeanette recognized the signs of a panic attack and had to get out fast.

She flung the Touch X back at Lana.

"Thank you for showing me this," she said, squeezing around the tiny space between Lana and the shelves to leave.

A gust of cold air and a soft buzz welcomed Amy into the store.

Isabella

Class Five, March 10

ISABELLA AGGRESSIVELY PULLED HER car into the university parking stall and turned off the ignition, trapped in a big black cloud of resentment.

The course opened a Pandora's box of anger she didn't know existed. It was like starting a skincare regimen, expecting your skin to get better. Instead, the shit comes to the surface, your skin red and rashy, and it takes a while to clear away. The last week had been a constant onslaught of anger and moodiness as her shit came spewing out.

Alex avoided her, ducking out of any room where she appeared. (At least she didn't have to worry about having sex.) But that's why she'd taken this course, to get her sex life back on track. Here she was, in the last class, worse off than when she started.

She and Alex were busy with their lives, completely disconnected, acting like roommates, staying together for the kids.

When her editor, Jessica, called this morning, the kids were out of control. Isabella had to lock herself in the bedroom closet while they ran wild and unsupervised. She couldn't concentrate as Jessica begrudgingly congratulated Isabella on her columns, which brought in significant numbers. Women loved how Isabella was vulnerable and authentic about her sex life. *Femme's* editor-in-chief wanted more of this and gave Isabella a budget and a pay bump. It was everything Isabella had ever wanted, but she couldn't enjoy the moment. She was much too stressed that her kids might be running after each other with the big knife found on the kitchen counter.

Jessica's clipped voice asked how Isabella would wrap up this series. Isabella wanted to tell Jessica that she quit. Her personal life was in shambles. She didn't know if she had the mental fortitude to withstand the onslaught of more shit being thrown her way. No column was worth this.

She wanted to go back to the way things were. To accept her fate, have mercy sex once a month or avoid sex altogether until Alex was too old and couldn't get an erection.

Jessica would be posting for a new sex writer before the call finished.

The only reason Isabella showed up tonight was because of the washing machine. That morning, when she went to do a load of laundry, it made strange noises. Isabella realized that without her job, they couldn't afford a new washer. She came tonight for the *Femme* paycheck.

Isabella climbed out of her car, wanting to get this over with. A dull pain wrapped around her neck, like a scarf pulled tight. As usual, Jeanette was the first person in the class, and for an instant, Isabella saw Jeanette for who she was — a lonely woman without a purpose. When Claire and Amy walked in, Isabella's stomach knotted, dreading the body-love update. Fortunately, no one spoke as they sat staring at the front.

This right here. This was why women put up with the BS.

If this is what women's sexual empowerment looked like, then Isabella took a hard pass. She was so caught up in her thoughts that she barely registered that Dr. Gwen, in her crisp navy professor's uniform, had started.

"Tonight, we will discuss receiving pleasure." Dr. Gwen's deep voice rose in the silent, sullen classroom. "The ultimate irony is that many women crave more intimacy from sex, but when she's presented with too much intimacy, she shuts down. It's assumed that receiving pleasure is instinctive and biological. Once your body is properly aroused, you can naturally lean back and receive pleasure. But that's simply not true."

Receiving pleasure? That was pretty weak for their last class. Isabella crossed her arms, unwilling to let Dr. Gwen disrupt her life anymore.

"There is no way to teach someone how to receive pleasure because your pleasure journey is unique." Dr. Gwen gave a sympathetic smile. "By the looks on your faces, it has not been an easy journey."

Were the volatile emotions part of her process? Isabella wondered. Why would Dr. Gwen want her class to feel this bad? It didn't make sense.

"To help you keep the faith in your pleasure journey, I have a short video of other women who went through this course. If any of you want to give a video testimonial, let me know."

Isabella wanted to give Dr. Gwen's class an F-minus and forget any video testimonials.

The lights dimmed, and an amateur video appeared on the whiteboard. A lady in her forties, with straight brown hair, sat in a chair in abysmal, shadowy lighting, looking into the camera as her hands fidgeted. She had a determined look in her tired, scared eyes.

"I want to speak openly about my journey without feeling shame." She took a breath. "Before taking this class, I was in denial. My shame made sexual decision-making confusing, and sometimes, I put myself into unsafe situations. I didn't have the self-esteem to stand up for myself."

After a second unsteady breath, she spoke. "I now understand what self-care is and why taking care of myself and my needs is important. Sexual and otherwise. Going through this experience was difficult, but now I'm making progress, which gives me hope and confidence. I make healthy decisions that bring me happiness. I've learned it's only as hard as I choose to make it." The video skipped forward, and she added, "If I could share one piece of advice, it's that writing things in my journal was the best way to work through my issues."

It's only as complicated as you make it.

Despite her mood, Isabella knew a quality sound bite when she heard it.

The screen went fuzzy, and a new woman in her twenties with short, spiky black hair appeared.

"I almost quit the course because we had to do group work. I've never enjoyed being in groups and didn't want to tell a group of strangers my secrets. Sharing my sexual insecurities and what I wanted from sex was one of the hardest things I've ever done."

She gave a small smile. "I lucked out and had a great group. The group meetings turned out to be the best part of the course. With the support of my group, I felt safe to face the shadowy corners that I could never go to by myself. I now believe groups hold a space for women's sexual empowerment."

Isabella longed to relive those magical feelings from the Betty Dodson night, wishing they weren't so fleeting.

The young lady continued, "If I could give one piece of advice, it would be to dive into your group work. Push way outside of your comfort zone. It's a safe place to discover yourself and have your blind spots called out by women who support your success." The screen went blank for a few seconds.

The next woman appeared on the screen in her early thirties with a round, dark face and kind eyes.

"I saw cracks in my marriage long before taking this course. The struggles of motherhood and working full-time made me feel asexual.

My marriage was hanging on by a thread, and I took the course because I was desperate to fix our sex life. When I started working on myself, I discovered pent-up anger that led to more fighting. It was so frustrating because I was going backward. My sex life was getting worse instead of better."

Isabella sat forward in her seat, relating to every word.

"I love my husband and wanted our marriage to thrive. Plus, I trusted Dr. Gwen's process. Ultimately, I had to choose myself, which helped me stay determined and put in the work. What I thought I wanted out of the sexual experience going in wasn't what I needed. It took a while, like months, long after the course was over, before I could say out loud what I wanted. Getting there wasn't for the faint of heart, but it was worth it. My work and effort planted a seed for play, pleasure, and desire for my husband and me. We're having better sex now than at the start of our marriage."

A big, infectious smile spread over her face as Dr. Gwen cheered off-camera.

Isabella needed to track this woman down to do a then-and-now interview. She wanted to know if her sex life was still satisfying. Or if the course was a blip and their sex life was back to what it had been.

"My advice is: if you are in a long-term relationship, and especially those with kids, there is light at the end of that long, dark tunnel. It will get much harder, and you will want to call it quits. It will mean you must work twice as hard to get what you want, but the rewards will be twice as sweet. You are worth it. Your spouse is worth it. And it's worth it to your children for them to have happy parents and role models of what healthy sexuality looks like."

The video ended abruptly, and Dr. Gwen turned the classroom lights back on.

Isabella exhaled the breath she didn't know she'd been holding. Like a flower after a long winter, poking its delicate stem from the cold ground was the first bloom of hope that things were okay.

She didn't know how, but she could change her situation and stop putting up with the BS.

I deserve that freedom, and I choose me.

She pulled her spaghetti-sauce-stained yoga jacket tighter around her ample breasts — an unseen stray spaghetti noodle stuck hanging off the back of her arm — as the cloud of anger slowly drifted away.

Claire

Class Five

THE AMATEUR VIDEO ENDED abruptly, and the women's testimonials were relatable but irrelevant.

Claire hoped they had a point as she rubbed her tired eyes, glad this was the last class. In the blur of the previous five weeks, she completed the course, the required reading, homework, and her usual minimum 60-hour-a-week workload—pulling all-nighters to get it done. To say she was stretched thin and super cranky was an understatement. On top of everything, Carlos complained she had no time for him.

Dr. Gwen's micro-braids swayed as she turned to face the class.

"I showed you these women's experiences to say that by doing the work, receiving your pleasure is waiting for you on the other side."

On the other side of what? Claire thought.

To experience in real-time, she was not equal. That she, a modern woman, could not say what she wanted and automatically put Carlos' sexual needs first. How she felt a deep feminist resentment of the sexual inequality and injustice, where she was once content and ignorant. A few years back, a university professor asked whether it was better to know or to be blissfully unaware. Before this class, Claire's choice would have been blissfully unaware.

Would you really? You were so unhappy before you did bizarre shit like Project Up My Sex Game.

Claire closed her hazel eyes, underlined with purple shadows, as she pressed her thumb to her temple. She stopped faking, and now the infrequent sex with Carlos — because she was so busy with this sex course — was silent and weird. Her sex life was worse now than at the start of the course.

And yet, Claire trusted Dr. Gwen's process and knew this was part of her change journey. She shifted on the uncomfortable, hard plastic chair and crossed her arms, ready to hear what Dr. Gwen had to say about receiving pleasure.

"Can anyone guess what the women in the video had in common?" Dr. Gwen waited for a beat and frowned at the lack of response. "They bravely worked through their issues, which changed their mindset. Their shift in mindset naturally segued into them asking for the sex they wanted. The confidence they gained from turning their situation around created a space for them to receive pleasure. So whatever situation you are in, as you work through it, your mindset will gradually change and open your ability to receive pleasure."

Claire thought about the last five weeks and how far she'd come, but she couldn't tell if her mindset had shifted.

"If you go to Google and type in the keywords, 'women receiving sexual pleasure,' over 160 million hits about intercourse and orgasms will fill your screen. If you dig further and type other keywords like 'women receiving sensual pleasure,' it will produce over 25 million hits. Among the millions of articles, it's virtually impossible to find anything teaching women how to receive pleasure outside of intercourse and orgasm." Dr. Gwen adjusted her square glasses.

That can't be true. Claire's fingers itched to go onto her cell phone and fact-check this astonishing claim.

"Receiving pleasure does not come naturally. Rather, it is a learned skill that needs to be practiced and mastered." Dr. Gwen tugged at her jacket. "Unfortunately, many women get into the habit of rushing through sex. While there is nothing wrong with a quickie, repeatedly rushing to the finish line never allows your body to relax and sink into your arousal fully. When you do allow yourself to relax, you will discover a uniquely sensual experience with a fully aroused body."

Claire snapped to attention, wide awake and alert.

I've never received pleasure. She was dumbfounded. *I'm not sure my body has ever been properly aroused.*

"Receiving pleasure is being aware and focusing on what is happening to your body at that moment." Dr. Gwen stopped pacing. "Teaching your body to relax and receive does not have to be hard. It will, however, take time for your body to adjust to feeling pleasurable sensations. To allow yourself to let go and sink into the experience fully. There is a path of least resistance, but too many women are frightened by her powerful, true sexual selves and resist."

Claire thought about letting go of her self-control, and her vagina closed up. Control was her thing. She had built a life and a career around being in control, disciplined, and focused. How was she supposed to let go?

"Sex is not something from a rom-com movie where a consultant choreographs sex scenes. You will never have a perfect sexual encounter. Sex is messy and supposed to have awkward moments, funny moments, and sensual moments. There will be silly noises, awkward leg cramps, and head bumps, which are part of the ride. Vulnerability helps you laugh at those awkward moments, creating deeper intimacy."

Claire only ever had serious jackrabbit sex. She couldn't imagine having a chuckle with Carlos over a leg cramp. Was that Amy's secret? She didn't try to control the outcome but went with the flow.

"Receiving pleasure is your birthright. It takes a leap of faith to get there. You trust that because you have done the work to set yourself up for sex'cess, everything will happen with impeccable timing. And, for the record, it is liberating not to be in constant and complete control of your sexuality." Dr. Gwen uncrossed her arms and opened them wide. "It is time to take your hands off the steering wheel with the belief that you deserve to lean back and take in your pleasure."

The high-achiever in Claire wanted to cross the finish line and experience pleasure. She needed to communicate with Carlos to do that because he wanted this for her. Even though communicating was awkward, it couldn't be any worse than the not-faking. Claire had nothing to lose and everything to gain, so why not go for broke?

The thought of letting go of her tightly held control and receive pleasure sent a thrill down her spine. She was ready to do whatever it took to get there.

Jeanette

Class Five

This is almost over.

The countdown was on. In under an hour, this would be over, and Jeanette could tell Andre to shove it. Vindicated, the course had done nothing for her.

Jeanette's eye twitched, a giveaway that she wasn't telling the truth.

Her perspective *had* changed, but it wasn't the results Andre wanted or expected. Jeanette saw their sex life for what it was: satisfying his desires with no concern for her happiness. She broke free from the shackles of believing she hated sex. She was a reformed woman with a new outlook on what her sex life could be.

And it didn't include Andre.

For years, she stayed silent and let him get away with so many lies. Because of this course and her group, she drew a line and would never put up with his lies again or go back to the way things were. Her body braced for another wave of anger as her brain learned to set boundaries.

She and Andre managed not to speak for the entire week. Even though their standoffs were becoming more commonplace, Andre must have sensed this standoff was different. He had thrown out his usual barbs, but she reacted differently. He didn't know how to react ... so he left.

Jeanette looked to the front and tuned back into Dr. Gwen.

"It's time to take your hands off the steering wheel with the belief that you deserve to lean back and take in your pleasure."

Dr. Gwen opened her arms wide, as if welcoming pleasure.

I experienced pleasure, came a whispered knowing. *One day, I'll welcome it in.*

She knew in her heart that this was true. Jeanette's body awakened to new, intoxicating feelings, while her insecurities begged her not to get her hopes up. Her shame and pride mixed in a bittersweet cocktail. Pride in knowing that Andre was wrong. She wasn't frigid. Shame because she did that thing in the shower, and it felt so good. She had no self-control and wanted more.

Dr. Gwen continued. "Less than ten years ago, it was difficult to find any information about women masturbating. As we learned in the first class, although most women still cannot openly admit to masturbating,"

Dr. Gwen looked down and let out a big, frustrated sigh while Jeanette squirmed in her seat.

"Women masturbating is now an accepted societal norm. Enter the next sex hurdle: Women relaxing into and receiving her sexual pleasure."

I masturbated.

The admission disgusted Jeanette as a hard lurch in her stomach made her bend forward. She wanted to have sex with herself, but not with her husband.

Sex with yourself was cheating.

"If you ask someone who enjoys sex why they do, they will tell you it's because they expect their sexual needs to be met and, without hesitation, receive the pleasure they asked for. But fully sinking into your pleasure will probably be an unfamiliar experience for many of you." Dr. Gwen put a new slide on the whiteboard.

"The first time you are vulnerable, experience full-on intimacy, or receive the pleasure you asked for, it will feel awkward. You have spent your life being guarded, pushing pleasure away, and being the gatekeeper: not getting pregnant, not getting an STI, not being labeled a whore."

"If your fear of intimacy or rejection is strong, it will awaken many triggers and shut down your ability to be vulnerable. Sabotaging self-talk is normal and centers on fear of abandonment or fear of failure." Dr. Gwen continued, "Some people cheat, pick fights, or become too controlling, while others become too needy and clingy."

Some people cheat. Dr. Gwen's words swirled in Jeanette's head.

Her husband cheats. More to the point, she let him cheat because she wasn't able to see a life beyond her marriage. She'd never been alone and didn't know how to be alone. Being alone was just too scary.

"Your self-sabotages will be sneaky. There will never be a neon sign hanging over your head to tell you." Dr. Gwen pointed her fingers above her head. "Instead, sabotages are rapid and fleeting, show up as brief images or symbols, occurring in seconds, and then leave. So, they are easy to disregard unless you pay attention or know what they are. Their repetition wreaks havoc, leading you to respond unconsciously or indirectly. Suddenly, out of the blue, you have a full-blown headache. The headache is real. Meaning, your self-sabotaging thoughts are powerful enough to make that headache happen."

Jeanette noticed Isabella wrap her arms around her body, hugging herself. Perhaps she was also replaying the whirlwind of the past five weeks.

Jeanette thought about her chain of events: the Betty Dodson night. Then the shower. The shopping trip with Amy, where she bought the Touch X. Her fingers curled around the hard plastic chair, bracing her core to stay still while feeling pulled inside out. No wonder Isabella was hugging herself.

"It's also common to have impostor syndrome, unable to trust that you deserve to feel this amount of satisfaction." Dr. Gwen pressed on. "Fortunately, there is no instant gratification. Rather, you're playing the long game. Learning to receive pleasure is like turning an enormous cruise ship around. It will happen slowly, and this is a good thing. Going slow means you can work through the sabotaging self-talk and your triggers while simultaneously learning the skill of how your body feels sensuality and pleasure."

I deserve sensuality and pleasure, came the whispered voice.

But at what cost?

Jeanette had never taken responsibility for her sex life. To be fair, she didn't know she was supposed to. This wasn't about Andre. It was about Jeanette letting it happen to her. What she was experiencing in her life was solely of her own making. Which was a very hard pill to swallow.

Which meant she had to return to the start of this course and work through the negative emotions getting in her way.

Jeanette glanced at her watch. Forty-five minutes until the class was done. She crossed one shaky black cashmere leg over the other, unsure she could handle her transformation alone. Her navy-blue eyes moved to her group, who, five weeks ago, had been strangers. Now, she worried about Isabella, who looked defeated. Claire wanted to force a conclusion on her sex timeline. And against all odds, she and Amy had formed a fragile bond.

She had come to trust these women, and they would be gone after today. Sitting back in the hard plastic chair, she shook her head no.

Jeanette needed the group's help to figure out what to do next.

Amy

Class Five

AMY WANTED TO SWAY her cell phone over her head with the light on, like at a rock concert.

"Receiving pleasure only happens when you accept deep intimacy." Dr. Gwen's commanding presence made the tired class drink in every word.

"Being vulnerable and showing up as your authentic self is a learned skill set. It will take time and be a bumpy journey. Each time you can show up a little more authentically and a little bit more vulnerable, you have a deeper connection. It's in these pockets that you get to experience tender, exquisite, and joyful moments. Which is what good sex and a life well lived are all about."

Everything about Dr. Gwen's curriculum was spot-on. She was changing the world one student at a time. Amy glanced around at the youthful faces who would grow old with a sexual self-confidence her generation did not have. Her brown eyes then landed on her group.

I already miss them.

In true Claire fashion, she stopped faking orgasm. Full stop. Then she looked at her vulva?! The pièce de résistance was when Claire would ask for what she wanted in the bedroom. Amy understood there was a fallout from Claire being a bull in a china shop. But, come on! Claire changed her sexual experience in under five weeks. That was freakin' amazing.

The dark horse and Amy's biggest surprise was prickly, elusive Jeanette. From out of nowhere, she went into a sex shop and bought a vibrator. That was huge. They lived on opposite ends of the sexual belief spectrum, yet somehow formed a friendship based on trust and mutual respect. Once Jeanette committed to the course, she showed serious lady balls, and her transition was nothing short of a miracle.

Amy's gaze then settled on Isabella, whose shift was subtle, and given her busy life, it would take more time, which was okay. Not everyone could or should be Claire. When Isabella sat naked with Amy at the Betty Dodson night, Amy caught a vibe. But when she looked at herself naked, like an armadillo, she rolled into a ball and retreated. It would take time and patience before Isabella had a shift in how she saw her body. Still, her body perception would never have changed without this course.

The three women had come so far. Amy smiled, invested in their happy ending, and gave herself a pat on the back for a job well done.

Dr. Gwen tapped her long finger on the table to emphasize her point.

"Vulnerability is the difference between good sex and great sex. To know that someone sees and loves you exactly as you are is a life-changing experience. Hopefully, it also makes sense that accessing your vulnerability can push triggers. Under the layers of self-preservation, at the core, is a fundamental fear that your partner will find out who you are and reject you." Dr. Gwen stopped and looked around. "Let us assume your partner will not reject you. Instead, go in with the mindset that they will be thrilled and accept you as you are."

Amy took a sharp breath as Dr. Gwen's words touched a deep nerve she didn't know existed. A painful memory from her marriage struck with the force of a thunderclap. Loud, rattling, and charged with electricity.

"To have intimacy, you must accept that you deserve to be loved and supported. For most of us, appreciating that we deserve intimacy is a lifelong journey. That said, you are guiding your intimacy narrative. So please ask yourself: Ten years from now, how does your future self look living with a deep, intimate connection? What is the freedom you and your partner have because you can easily communicate about sex with each other?"

That's what I want. What I've always wanted.

The memory flickered in Amy's eyes, and she felt a strange, intense, tender pain: delicate but fierce, like a long, thin needle piercing her skin. She looked down and plucked at her orange-and-pink floral cotton skirt, her discomfort radiating from every pore. She shut her eyes as her face closed, and her decision was made.

That's not for me.

"Receiving pleasure takes courage." Amy shook her head and focused on Dr. Gwen's conclusion. "During sex, go out of your way to seek out and understand what feels good to your body. Notice things you like and make a mental note: a brush of the skin, a kiss on the neck, how your partner's body felt. It will only take a few seconds, and you can skip it if you're not paying attention. When you mark these moments, it reinforces that sex is a rewarding experience."

Amy blinked, tossing away the exquisite pain of her vulnerability and intimacy being smashed to smithereens. It was why she helped other people, because she couldn't trust herself to have a happy, stable relationship. Her walls up, the old Amy was back, in fine form, ready to help her group receive their bliss.

"A pleasurable moment equals a victory." Dr. Gwen clasped her hands and waved them over her head as if she'd won something. "When you are present in your pleasure, please appreciate how far you have come.

You opened a door and welcomed satisfaction in. I cannot overstate how massive this is. That fleeting moment is life-changing. You have normalized leaning into and receiving your much-deserved pleasure."

Dr. Gwen's brows furrowed as she looked at her watch.

Twenty minutes left. Amy glanced at her cell.

Her brain scrambled on how she could set up an impromptu group meeting after class to convince the ladies to go to The Taboo Sex show.

Anything to forget the disastrous Adesh hook-up.

Dr. Gwen

Class Five

Dr. Gwen's intelligent brown eyes narrowed, looking for "the ones." With her search came the usual ache, the acute disappointment settling in her throat that at least 75 percent of this class would never use any of this information.

A fresh, painful reminder of why women's sexuality stayed stuck.

You can lead a horse to water, but you cannot make it drink.

Her therapist used the old cliché to coax Dr. Gwen out of her moral funk. As if changing her headstrong ways would ever be possible.

For the record, she would never understand why women did not want to drink. Why would women choose a life of mediocre sex? Of course, many people were not ready to face their demons, did not want the conflict, or were too young with no relationship experience. Her therapist often reminded Dr. Gwen that her job was to plant seeds, and with any luck, those seeds would bloom when these students matured.

All Dr. Gwen ever wanted was for women to get it.

Women's sexuality was so much bigger and more powerful than having sex. It was her power center, and once women got this, she would rule the world. And that was a world Dr. Gwen wanted to live in.

She spent her career making it happen, but she was getting too old to push water uphill. Her disheartened gaze landed on Amy's group — her gut deciding they were her best prospect. Dr. Gwen silently prayed that these four mismatched ladies were up for the challenge.

A dry, impatient cough snapped her out of the brain fog.

It was time to send this class off into the world. Dr. Gwen needed to motivate this class to respect their bodies as if they were their most precious commodity. Because it was. The agitation at the base of her throat stirred.

Most of these women would never have true body love. She hoped it would not take a lifetime of neglect before they figured it out.

"A life of sexual fulfillment is not a sprint. It is a marathon." Dr. Gwen tugged on her snug jacket. "Your sexual mindset has changed, but your life has not. Sexuality is so much more than stimulating genitals. Your ability to be sexual will forever bump up against what is going on in your life.

"Sex will never be perfect, and you and your partner will not always be in sync. Sex will be messy. You will have good days, bad days, horny days, apathetic days." Her back was acting up again, so she sat on the table's edge.

"Your ability to receive pleasure won't be consistent. One time, you will be completely open to receiving pleasure, and the next time, you will not. There will be no rhyme or reason to it, so please don't make it mean anything other than you are human."

Dr. Gwen glanced at her watch. There were only five minutes left. She had spent too much time in triggers and sabotaging self-talk. Balancing her time was never a strong point.

"When, not if, you hit a sex rut, you now have the self-awareness and maturity to flex your choice muscle. To focus on what you want and how you want to feel. You now have the power to believe you are worthy. To set new boundaries and expect the best for yourself."

Dr. Gwen caught herself rushing. If she were five minutes over, so be it, and put her last list on the whiteboard.

"First, write about where you feel shame. Bring that shame out, acknowledge it, forgive, and move on. Next, determine what you want out of the sexual experience. Set your change in motion by going slow and taking small steps. And celebrate each small step as if you climbed Mount Everest because, in a way, you have."

Dr. Gwen looked at each student to connect and make a lasting impression.

"My wish is that you walk away from this class feeling confident, in control, and powerful. For your sexual happiness to grow and evolve as your life changes. To be agile and brave enough to pivot is surprisingly simple when you pay attention."

Through their homework, Dr. Gwen had gotten to know each one of these people in such an intimate way. Probably more than their partners. Everyone was starting from a different place. Their challenges were tricky but manageable, and they had what it took to work through to the other side.

This was their journey, and she could not force them to drink. She swallowed hard.

"Emotional and sexual intimacy cannot survive if ignored. It is like putting a houseplant in a shadowy corner and forgetting to water it. Eventually, it will die from neglect." Dr. Gwen paused, exhaled, and let go of her expectations. "Ask yourself: how will you keep your sexual health a priority throughout your lifetime?"

"My parting advice is to look back and connect the dots."

Dr. Gwen stood straight and threw the last seeds of change at this group.

"See where you started and how far you've brought your sexuality. How it feels to speak openly about your sexual wants and needs. What vulnerability and intimacy do for the quality of your partnership. How, by stepping up and positively changing your sexual experience, you helped women worldwide."

She put the last quote on the whiteboard.

"A journey of a thousand miles begins with a single step."
Lao Tzu.

"It's time to take your first step." The professor looked at the class with affection. "That is it for this class. Now go forth and make me proud."

The click of the PowerPoint turning off echoed in the deafening silence. Her stomach clenched.

Did the class not like me? Or worse, my curriculum.

It started with a soft clap and ended with the class giving a standing ovation. For a moment, Dr. Gwen allowed herself to relax. She had learned how to be gracious with this show of affection. But accolades were never her thing.

She would much rather these women go off and create a fantastic, abundant sex life.

Dr. Gwen gave a grateful smile and raised her hands in thanks as the applause died down. Within seconds, the groups huddled together; once strangers, now knowing the innermost details of each other's sex lives.

A chill ran down Dr. Gwen's body from the now chilled, depressing room, which was only ever stifling hot or arctic cold. The next day, she met with the dean to review this class and discuss doing a 201 sex course. For whatever reason, she liked it here. Enough to settle down for a couple of years and meet someone who would put up with her activism.

Unlike the other stops.

As each group got up, reluctant to leave and say their goodbyes, she looked at Amy's group.

They would drink.

Dr. Gwen made a mental note to visit Amy's office and invite her group to the 201 course.

She saw students move forward, queuing to ask questions, and her brain switched back to professor mode.

Claire's Big Ask

March 11

CLAIRE FROWNED AT THE noticeable stubble on her long legs, which were acrobatically raised over her head.

She was "fully present" in the sexual experience and "receptive" to Carlos rhythmically thrusting his penis deep inside her. Not that it was doing much good. She sneaked a glance at her bedside clock. They'd been at this for seven minutes, and she was bored, on the verge of irritation.

Swallowing a sigh, determined not to fake her pleasure, she moved her gaze up to look at Carlos' intense sex face. His dark eyes were closed in concentration, deep in a fantasy world, no doubt enjoying the build-up to his orgasm.

Must be nice.

She was able to focus on her pleasure for about thirty seconds when Carlos's fingers were skimming her lower back, making her skin tingle. To be fair, they were a good thirty seconds, but then, poof, it was gone. For the last six and a half minutes, she was aware of everything not happening to her body in the bleak silence.

Not spectatoring, it turned out, was more exhausting than faking. And awkward. Not to mention cringe-worthy. Lying there in the dreadful silence, waiting for it to be over or for Carlos to notice, was excruciating. At least with spectatoring, she had something to do.

It would be so much easier to give a little moan. It took every ounce of her willpower to remain silent.

Carlos deftly moved his hips to swirl as he thrust. Believing that by changing his rhythm, it would suddenly wake up her vagina and kick-start it into an orgasm. It didn't. Glancing back at the clock, her body gave a start.

She had two tasks to achieve, and procrastinating had cost her eight minutes.

Say it as you practiced, she told herself and went to speak, move, or do anything.

But her mouth and body refused to cooperate. So she tried again. Nothing.

This shouldn't be difficult.

Claire's fists balled up and punched the bed.

If I'm truly equal, telling my partner what I want should be easy. Carlos wants me to tell him. What patriarchal belief system is stopping me now?

Claire caught her righteous rant in the nick of time and frog-marched herself back to focusing on and completing Step One.

She forced her timid eyes to his focused face and whispered.

"Carlos."

His dark eyes opened, widening in surprise to see her looking at him. He gave a wicked smile without losing his twirling rhythm, and the effect was intoxicating. Claire's stomach gave a happy, shy flutter as a new feeling enveloped her.

It was nice to see him and to let him see her.

That Step One worked without a hitch was so unexpected that she almost laughed out loud. Mentally going through Dr. Gwen's checklist, she now needed to celebrate. She imagined doing a happy dance with her legs dangling over her head and put the celebration away for later to share with Amy.

Carlos gave a deep grunt, signaling he was close to orgasm. His thrusting became less about satisfying her and more about his needs. Claire's brain snapped to attention, needing to get Step Two done. Buoyant after her last victory, she opened her mouth, but again, nothing came out.

What the hell?

"Is this good?" Carlos panted. "I'm close. Are you close? Come on, baby, cum with me."

"Mmm" was the extent of Claire's sex vocabulary.

With the clock ticking down and desperation being the mother of ingenuity, she moved to Plan B.

Show him.

Snaking her shaky hand down toward her clit, she touched it lightly, surprised at how ready and willing it was to lead her to an orgasm. In one swift motion, Carlos shifted her legs and entered her from the side, knocking her hand away.

"Is that better?" He teased her with tiny thrusts of the tip of his penis.

Had he seen her hand and then shifted her body? He wouldn't do that, would he?

"Tell me how you want it," he said, his breath ragged, his body tensing.

Okay, it's go time. He asked what you want. He wants to know. So tell him.

"Carlos," Claire hated how meek her voice sounded.

He stopped thrusting.

"Is everything okay? You aren't, uh, you know, enthusiastic."

She heard the agitated edge and wanted to apologize. For what? Inconveniencing him? Not making this entirely about him and his needs?

Claire squashed the feminist righteousness and got back to task. She looked him straight in the eye and opened her parched mouth.

Again, nothing came out.

Claire thought she was ready to take this step, but her nerve ebbed away as Carlos stared. Amy's voice swooped in, preaching female sexual emancipation. This was Claire's chance to prove her needs mattered.

She's right, Claire thought as her brain scrambled to put Amy's Plan C into action. As if Amy were there helping, Claire took Carlos's hand and guided it to her clit, clumsily attempting to show him how she wanted to be touched.

I need you to do this. She willed her eyes to say, unsure what to do with his hand.

She felt his body stiffen as his softening penis slipped out of her.

"Do you not like how I make love to you?" A flash of Latin anger and hurt filled his confused eyes.

Her first instinct was to appease him and smooth things over, but she held her ground.

She no longer wanted to pretend that she enjoyed the fifteen minutes of thrusting. She needed her clit stimulated to reach an orgasm. Before the sex course, she didn't know what she didn't know. That she had faked was on her. But now, she needed to tell him what she wanted if they were to make it as a couple. Telling him what she wanted was only fair to Carlos.

"So, you won't talk to me?" His face was blank, but his words were spoiling for a fight.

"I want us to do something new." Defeat pummeled each pathetic and apologetic word.

Pursing his lips, he climbed out of bed and slipped on his imported French-cut underwear. Claire watched his superbly sculpted bum stomp into the bathroom.

This wasn't how asking this was supposed to go.

According to Dr. Gwen, Carlos would be open to the idea. Together, they would build a better sex life. This was the exact opposite of how things were supposed to turn out. This was her worst nightmare.

How did I get this so wrong?

Claire pulled the warm duvet around her naked and vulnerable body.

Communicating shouldn't be this difficult, but neither had the skill set. How was it possible to complete a sex course without it teaching something so basic as communicating?

Carlos reappeared in the bathroom door frame, and Claire braced for him to tell her it was over. As if reading her thoughts, he held out his hand as an olive branch.

"We need to talk."

Taking his hand, Claire resolutely vowed that she would figure this out.

And so *Project Up My Sex Communication* was born.

Jeanette at the Sex Shop

March 4

THE COLD GUST OF air followed Amy as she entered the small sex store, rubbing her hands together, now red from the cold.

Trapped, Jeanette needed to get out. Her navy-blue eyes darted left and right, looking for a second exit, but there was only one door. Oblivious, Amy undid the buttons on her blue furry jacket, then shook the cold from a floaty skirt paired with a ripped Sex Pistols t-shirt.

"You made it," Lana, the store clerk, greeted Amy as she smiled at the two women.

"Look, I'm sorry, but I've got to go." Jeanette's heart was beating out of her chest. She put her hands into her jacket pockets, fortifying herself for battle as she shouldered past Amy.

"What's going on?" Amy put a gentle but firm hand on Jeanette's shoulder to stop her. Her alert eyes were assessing how this had gone from a fun gal's shopping trip to dealing with a situation.

Good manners drilled into Jeanette from birth forced her to explain the sudden change in plan. She opened her mouth to speak, but nothing came out. Instead, a traitorous tear escaped, no doubt, smudging her mascara.

"Can you give us a moment?" Amy asked Lana, who stood there, taking in Jeanette's humiliating spiral. Amy turned to face Jeanette.

"Please. Look at me."

Jeanette dragged her gaze from the carpeted floor to look into Amy's deep brown eyes, where she saw a safety net. If Jeanette were going to jump, Amy would be there, holding steady to catch her. Not ready to let go, Jeanette hesitated, unsure whether to put her faith and trust in a person like Amy.

"What happened between our phone call and now?" Amy asked.

"I can't do this."

"Okay," Amy's voice was steady. "Why can't you?"

"Christian women don't come to stores like this." Jeanette waved a frantic hand at the cramped shelves full of sex toys. "I'm not allowed to do this."

As the words left her lips, she saw the appalled look pass over Amy's face. A month ago, Jeanette would have delivered those words with conviction, but today, she heard them from Amy's perspective.

The stars fell from Jeanette's eyes. Naïvely, for fifty-three years, she believed her pleasure was wrong and a sin. Her sexual happiness meant nothing. She was simply a vessel for her husband's sexual satisfaction.

The realization hit her hard, and every inch of Jeanette's body hurt. Her knees buckled. She felt two strong arms as Amy drew her in for a motherly hug. Jeanette's body was rigid, her mind a whirl as she leaned heavily against Amy's soft, soothing curves — an oasis for her touch-starved body.

The single tear became a tsunami of tears, and she broke down in the tiny aisle, surrounded by sex toys. Coming up for air, she saw Lana looking on discreetly, witnessing the scene.

Mortified, she jerked out of Amy's embrace.

"Jeanette, I'm so sorry I made you come here," Amy said too kindly.

Her pity felt like a slap in the face.

"I'm good," Jeanette said disdainfully, pulling a tissue out of her purse to fix her tear-stained face. "Excuse me, Lana?"

Jeanette stepped past Amy and went the short distance to the display wall.

"You were showing me this."

"Uh, okay, right." Lana faltered while pulling the toy off the shelf. "So, this is We-vibes Touch X." Lana pushed an invisible button.

She handed the vibe to Jeanette, who didn't want to put this anywhere near her private parts. She placed it back on the shelf, where it went around in loud, noisy circles.

"There are vibrations, and there are rumbles." Lana picked up a different vibrator from the shelf. "Can I put this on your forearm?"

Jeanette reluctantly pulled up her jacket sleeve.

"Vibrations feel like this." Lana placed the vibrator on Jeanette's arm, then switched to the Touch X. "Chances are, if you prefer the rumbly feeling on your arm, the Touch X is a better choice. Then you need to create a wank-bank."

"A what?" Jeanette asked, unaware that Amy had signaled for Lana to stop.

"You know, a wank-bank. A collection of fantasies you think about when you're using the Touch X —"

"Great. Thanks." Amy cut in, grabbing Jeanette's hand.

"I'll take the Touch X." Jeanette wrenched her hand free, leaving the two women as she headed to the cash register.

The transaction was swift. Jeanette winced at the bag with the store's logo blazed across it and threw the Touch X into her purse.

"Thank you, Lana," Jeanette flung open the door and left the wake of her drama back in the store for Lana to clean up.

"I'm proud of you, Jeanette." Amy said breathlessly as her short legs worked hard to keep pace.

Arriving at her Range Rover, the hairs on the back of Jeanette's neck stood up. Brusquely, she turned, eyes narrowed, never wanting to hear Amy's patronizing wisdom again.

But when she looked at Amy's stunned face, a warm, glimmering mist enveloped Jeanette. Never questioning why God would intervene in this moment of grace, she let her guard down. What Jeanette saw was a woman trying her best.

Even though Amy was going through her own struggles, she was there supporting Jeanette. Humbled, the fight in her faded.

"Thank you, Amy. For helping me through this." She wanted to say so much more, but didn't have the words.

"I'm a phone call away if you need to talk about ... any of this." Amy looked like she wanted to say more, but left it at that.

"I will," Jeanette said, knowing Amy was absolutely a person in whom to put her faith and trust.

She watched Amy cross the parking lot, struggle to open her driver's door, and wave goodbye. Climbing into her Range Rover, Jeanette put her purse on the passenger seat, and the Touch X glowed inside like a blob of nuclear waste. Jeanette looked around the parking lot for a garbage can but didn't see one. She was unsure what to do with this thing.

You've been through enough today. Put this thing in the back of your closet and figure this out tomorrow.

Driving back to her lonely house, Jeanette needed a cup of tea and a Max cuddle.

Back at Amy's Hook-Up

February 27

AMY PUT HER HAND on the bulge, straining to get out of Adesh's jeans. That he was of reasonable size and girth and knew where her clit was checked off two things on her list of what she needed from a hook-up. But there wasn't much room inside Amy's tiny foyer.

"Let's go into the living room," she breathed.

They kicked off their boots and abandoned their coats on the floor.

They moved into the living room while carelessly ripping each other's clothes off. Amy accidentally popped a button on Adesh's shirt. He unintentionally ripped the hem of her skirt while negotiating the two of them onto the sofa.

With him lying on top, Amy fumbled with the button on his jeans. Unzipping his fly, she pulled the elastic band of his underwear and grabbed hold of his penis, relieved. Big cocks weren't her thing. Average-sized cocks suited her just fine.

"Take off your jeans," Amy panted, nuzzling her lips against his neck, inhaling his spicy cologne.

"What?" a flushed Adesh asked as if he'd just noticed her.

Amy ignored the red flag.

"Take off your jeans," she ordered. "I can't do anything when you're lying on top of me." She gave him a slight push off the couch.

Adesh stood and suggestively pulled down his jeans and underwear for the "big reveal." He did not disappoint. Young men guarantee a rock-hard, standing-at-attention erection. But then he ruined it by flapping his dick in Amy's face like he was starring in a porno.

At least she knew where he got his moves from.

He gave a devilish smile and raked his hand through his thick head of hair to show off his bulging biceps. He then attempted to remove his jeans in one sweeping motion. Except they got caught up at his ankles.

"Sit down." Amy smothered a laugh.

He sat on the couch, preening like a peacock, flexing his muscles while Amy tugged the pants free.

"Let me show you how to do it." She gave her own wicked smile and did a proper striptease, satisfied to see his tongue hanging out.

"Your body is incredible." He gave a throaty whistle as she did a slow pirouette.

"Yes, I know. So is yours," she replied, stating what they both already knew.

After her clothes came off, Adesh's hands were all over her.

Neither noticed her cat, Orgasm, maliciously glaring at Adesh from under the coffee table.

"I like this." She took his right hand, licked his fingertips with her tongue, and put them on her right breast. He massaged her nipple in a circular motion for a few seconds, but lost interest.

"Well, I like this." He took her hand and put it on his penis.

"Of course you do," she said under her breath.

He let out another belly laugh, but Amy didn't find it as charming this time. Still, he showed good moves in her foyer and held out hope that there would be a sexual quid pro quo. She reached over to her side table and opened the ornate box filled with condoms.

"Whoa, you have a box of condoms? You must get around," Adesh half-teased, but was half serious.

"Are you intimidated to be with an experienced woman?" She asked, pleased to ruffle his feathers.

He watched her open the package and put the condom in her mouth.

"What are you doing?" His erection deflated slightly as his hand went on her shoulder.

Taking the condom out of her mouth, she sighed, "I'm putting the condom on before blowing you."

"Why would you do that? I'm clean," he said defensively.

Has no one ever had 'The Talk' with him?

This boy was so wet behind the ears.

"This way, you'll stay clean. Do you want me to do this or not?" Amy held her ground.

When he took his hand away from her shoulder and put it behind his head instead, she took that as a yes.

She popped the condom back into her mouth and bent over his penis, rolling the condom over his shaft. Her purple-highlighted, spiky hair brushed his taut stomach. Moments later, a deep groan let Amy know she was teaching this young'un a thing or two he wouldn't find in a porno. Loving the power, she started getting into a blow job rhythm, licking and sucking, lightly squeezing and tugging at his balls.

After only a few minutes, Adesh gently pushed Amy's head away from his penis.

"I'm close," he said, moving his body around to mount her.

"Hey, wait, it's my turn." She couldn't believe he was serious.

"You got me so close, and I need to finish," he said soothingly. "You understand ..."

"No, I don't understand."

But he was probably shit at giving head, and it would make her more frustrated, so she acquiesced. He climbed on top of her without saying a word and started thrusting.

Within a minute, less than sixty seconds, she felt his body arch, heard the orgasm groan, and his soft penis slip out of her.

"That was great. You really know how to suck a guy off." He slumped over her. "Kudos, dude."

With no pretense of wanting to stay or return the favor, he was up, throwing the used condom on her coffee table, searching for his underwear. Since this hook-up was a complete bust, Amy also wanted it over and for him to get out of her townhouse.

As he bent over to reach for his underwear, Orgasm shot out of nowhere and launched at the "dangly toys" between Adesh's legs.

He let out a screeching howl of pain while Amy watched everything unfold as if in slow motion. Adesh swatted the cat away, but Orgasm took a stealthy second jump and clung to Adesh's right leg with his claws.

"Get your fucking cat off me!" Adesh hopped up and down, his eyes popping out of his head as he screamed in pain.

Amy dodged and parried, trying to grab Orgasm, but every time she got her hands on him, Adesh jerked his body, and she lost her grip. It was only a matter of seconds, but it felt like hours.

Mortified, Amy watched drops of blood trickle down Adesh's leg. Finally, she got a solid grip on the calico and pulled hard, leaving scratch marks around Adesh's leg.

"What the fuck?" He looked at his bleeding, clawed leg and screamed into her face, "I mean, what the actual fuck?!"

"You should probably go to the emergency room to get that checked out."

Feeling equal parts terrible and not wanting to spend any more time with this jerk.

"Cats can carry sepsis. Sorry ... dude."

Jeanette Opens the Box

April 2

I'M NOT READY.

Later that morning, Jeanette sat on the edge of the bed, looking at the box. Her body shivered with the now familiar deep bone chill in her lower back. As she wrapped her arms around herself, finding comfort in the soft, warm cashmere from head to toe, her angel gave her a gentle push.

Just get this over with.

Opening the sturdy box with tentative fingers, she recalled everything the inside of this box had put her through for the last month. The angst, worry, and stress hives. All of it was for nothing. Inside the box, the tasteful packaging encased the green Touch X.

Jeanette blinked at the anticlimactic letdown. She tugged the figure-eight-shaped device out of its molded insert. Turning it around, its soft texture was a comfort in her hand.

Now what?

She wasn't ready to undress or use it.

Jeanette lifted the molded insert to find a white silk bag, an instruction booklet, and a charging device. She picked up her reading glasses from her bedside table and read the booklet.

She was supposed to nestle the Touch X between her legs while lying down. She studied the diagram, showing a tasteful drawing of how to place it on her vulva. The pointy end went on her clitoris, the figure-eight part on her outer and inner lips.

Jeanette pulled the oversized collar of her tunic sweater around her neck, steeling herself from the negative waves, and kept reading. "Take your time. If you prefer less intense stimulation, hold the Touch X horizontally to feel vibrations across a broader area. You can also flip onto your stomach and use the toy hands-free."

Suddenly, Jeanette's head was heavy, her body bone-tired, and she wanted to lie on her soft Egyptian cotton sheets and sleep for the next week. She pushed herself to keep reading, but felt her resolve waning.

"After you orgasm, press the Touch X closer to your vulva at the lowest speed. Breathe deeply, soak up the sensations, and orgasm again if it feels right."

Jeanette didn't know whether she could have one orgasm, let alone a second. Her tired head morphed into a nasty headache. She barely read the bottom of the information booklet, which recommended she use a water-based lubricant. She put the booklet down. With a strength she didn't know she possessed, she grabbed her cell from the bedside table and texted Amy.

> Can you recommend a water-based lubricant?

With the stress headache pounding, there was no sense in trying the Touch X. She put everything back in the box, put it in the drawer of her bedside table, and went downstairs to get an Advil.

About an hour later, Amy texted back.

> Is this what I think it is?!

Amy texted GIFs of a champagne bottle popping, hands clapping, and a toothy smiley face alongside her suggestion for a water-based lube.

Opening her laptop, Jeanette logged onto the website to purchase the lubricant. The notification in her inbox said it would take 3 days to ship. Jeanette prayed to God to give her strength and be ready to use the Touch X when the water-based lubricant arrived.

Claire And Amy Forgive

April 3

CLAIRE SAT ON AMY'S university couch, which had seen better days, sipping tea from a big mug that read, "Woke up sexy as hell again."

A nondescript shoebox sat on the coffee table, but neither woman acknowledged it. Amy's cat, Orgasm, waited on Amy's bed, conspiring about his revenge for being locked up.

"So admit it, I was right." Amy sipped the delicious herbal tea she bought from the swishy cafe. "You loved the sex course."

"Love is a strong word." Claire dismissed but then looked down, gave her head a slight shake, and looked back up at Amy, her hazel eyes full of sincerity. "On my jog this morning, I thought about where I would be if I hadn't taken the course."

She closed her eyes as a grimace passed over her lovely oval face, looking like she dodged the bullet of a life filled with terrible sex.

"It was disruptive and turned my world upside down. Even though my sex life is still recovering, it was worth it."

"What was your biggest takeaway?" Amy smelled the warm, spicy tea as she sipped it.

"It's funny. Our sex hasn't changed much, but I've changed. It's like I'm looking at our sex with a new set of eyes. That would be my mindset, right? It's opened up. Instead of focusing on what's wrong, I see what is possible, even though I'm not there yet. It's a subtle shift I would never have paid attention to before this course."

"Once your perspective changes, everything around you changes."

"I'm now working on our communication." A cloud passed over Claire's face, and it didn't look like she was ready to talk about it.

"Are you never satisfied?" Amy teased. "Give poor Carlos a break."

"It is all about me," Claire zinged back.

"I'll drink to that," Amy toasted her large mug that read, "Lick it till ice scream."

Claire put her feet on the coffee table, and her eyes moved to the shoebox.

"Are you sure you want to be celibate for a year?"

"Yes," Amy said firmly. "I've deleted the Tinder app."

Something clicked after the hook-up with Adesh, the course, Paul ghosting her, and Dr. Gwen's last class. She never wanted her ex-husband, Li, to get in the way of her having a great relationship again. She woke up from a restless dream, wanting to forgive Li and herself and move on with her life.

Earlier that day, Amy stood in front of her bedroom closet, her heart heavy, feeling the push-pull of being ready but not ready. From the back of the overflowing closet, she pulled out the shoebox filled with memories of Li. Perched on top was a photo of both of them, young faces full of joy, hope, and promise.

Amy looked at Li's handsome face, wondering how he could do that to her. Or whether he had done that to someone else. Why, she never saw the signs. She would probably never know and had to be okay with that. But holding on tight to the pain Li inflicted on her was not worth her future happiness. She wanted to break free and move on.

"Let's do this?" Claire grabbed the shoe box and got up from the couch, offering Amy her hand. Amy nodded and lifted herself off the spot that had her butt prints.

Putting on their jackets, they went to the tiny back patio with interlocking bricks, where a small fire pit sat with two beach chairs. It was a gloomy April day, matching the somber occasion. Amy placed the box in the fire pit, and Claire put balled paper around it. Amy struck a wooden match, and immediately the wind caught it and put it out. She crouched closer to the firepit as a gust of wind blew the box top off, exposing the memories inside.

Li's handsome face stared at Amy as she lit him on fire. Her fingers trembled, holding the match. Big emotions rolled through her body, and she had to stand up. Her teary eyes looked at the dreary sky, and her face felt the cool spring day.

You're a lot wiser, kid. She took a deep breath, and her nose picked up the musky spring smell of the moist ground. *It's time to forgive and move on.*

Amy crouched, lit the match, and put the tiny flame under a ball of paper. It immediately caught fire, igniting the corner of the thin cardboard box.

"I deserve better," Amy said softly. It felt good to say it . "What was that thing Jeanette said about forgiving?"

Amy looked at Claire, who was doing her best not to be impatient while she waited in the uncomfortable silence.

"Let me look it up." Claire was glad to be tasked with something and found it on her phone.

"I Love You. I'm sorry. Forgive Me. Thank You."

Amy wanted to believe she could find a happy relationship, but had failed too many times at dating.

"I'm not ready. Can you go first?"

"Sure," Claire looked back at the mantra on her phone."Okay. I love you, Claire. I'm sorry that I have such high expectations that make you feel you must be perfect. Forgive me for being so judgmental when you needed compassion. Thank you for persevering through this rocky transition time."

Claire moved around the firepit and put her arm around Amy's shoulder, kissing her cheek.

"Thanks for dragging me into the sex course. I never would have done this without you. Because of you, Carlos and I will have a stronger, healthier, and happier relationship. I'm grateful, and yes, I loved it."

The two women watched silently as something inside the box caught fire and melted, creating a plume of black smoke.

"Li, I love you. I'm sorry that I didn't set boundaries. Forgive me for giving myself away. Thank you for leaving and letting me have my life back. I forgive you, Li. I forgive myself for getting lost in you. I am moving forward without your baggage."

They watched the things that caused Amy so much stress, self-doubt, and angst go up in flames, joining the atmosphere.

At that moment, the sun peeked from behind the clouds to shine on Amy's teary face.

Isabella Makes Her Deadline

April 4

"Jessica, can you hold for one moment?" Isabella said in her most professional voice, then put her editor on mute.

She looked around her quiet, messy dining room office, strewn with toys, and exhaled.

Isabella had yet to write a happy ending for the sex course series. Jessica was "helping" brainstorm ideas with gems like, "Isabella could send her husband a thrilling sext at work." Have a secret sex code in front of the kids. Wear provocative lingerie under her mommy uniform and reveal it Superman-style. Or, Isabella could throw Alex on the bed and give him an expert hand job.

"A his and hers happy ending. Get it?" Jessica laughed at her joke.

Fed up, Isabella put Jessica on mute.

The old Isabella would have grimaced, but put on a brave face and pushed through. Earnestly telling herself it was better to have mediocre sex than no sex at all. She needed to try harder and force herself to insert play and fun. Her column's title: *Some Sex Is Better Than No Sex*.

Now that her column was the most read by *Femme* readers, she felt more confident about — as Jeanette advised — setting boundaries. The new Isabella bristled at Jessica's ideas because they were about Alex's pleasure, not hers.

But her overdue deadline didn't care that she was still processing, unsure of what her pleasure spectrum was. But she couldn't admit to Jessica that she had yet to write a single word of her happy ending column.

"Let me get back to you," Isabella said, disconnecting.

The following day, while folding clothes from the never-ending pile of clean laundry, Isabella was in full resentment mode. She loathed the daily grind of coming up with a nutritious and delicious supper idea. Then it hit her.

Planning my supper!

Dr. Gwen's advice about mise en place. Creativity waved its magic wand, and Isabella's head filled with funny quips and quotable points she would make in her happy-ending column.

This time, she was well aware — after the looking at herself naked disaster, the unused lingerie, and the mixed-signals foot massage — to start small and go slow.

Isabella's plan was to initiate sex when the kids were down for their naps. She ignored the chatter that she could do more. Dr. Gwen held her fragile ego steady and assured her that initiating sex on Isabella's terms was more than enough.

Bright and early Saturday morning, she found Alex at the kitchen table, reading the news while drinking his morning coffee. She must have had a goofy grin because he laughed when he looked up and saw Isabella staring.

"What?" he asked.

You're having sex today, that's what. She thought.

Was she flirting with her husband? And did it feel fun?

Between making snacks and ending fights over Mr. Wigglebottom, Isabella somehow managed to get herself ready. She showered, brushed her teeth, and put on the newly bought, never-worn set of black, lacy underwear.

In the flurry of getting ready, she noticed an excited, nervous flutter in her stomach, like when they were dating.

When it was finally nap time, Isabella made a beeline for Alex and hesitated when she saw him working on his laptop. His office was dealing with an emergency, and she didn't want to interrupt him. Losing her nerve, she started to turn around, but the column deadline forced her feet to move forward.

Taking a deep breath, telling herself this was a slam dunk, that Alex would never reject her, she walked over to him and put her hand on his shoulder.

"Hey."

He didn't look up from his laptop, barely mumbling a "Hey" back.

She stood there for a beat, hoping they shared a telepathic power, willing him to understand her invitation.

He didn't.

Rejection swooped in, telling her she was stupid for even trying, and she should throw in the towel.

She did.

Backing away, she went upstairs to her bedroom to sit on her bed and let the ripples of rejection flow through her tired body. But then Claire was in her head, kicking rejection to the curb. In her no-nonsense lawyer voice, she demanded that Isabella not get tripped up because it didn't work out on the first attempt. She needed to pick herself up, get a backbone.

Just do it.

Fortifying herself, Isabella took off the uncomfortable underwear and watched for a second opportunity.

It showed up the next afternoon. Both kids were napping while Alex watched hockey. Isabella saw the small window of opportunity and launched. She ran to the bathroom and washed her vag with a baby wipe, gave her teeth a quick brush, and put on her nice but comfortable underwear.

After yesterday's rejection, she hesitated, but Jeanette pushed her forward, saying this was important for her marital happiness. Approaching Alex on the couch, Isabella said the lamest thing possible.

"Do you have some time?"

He slowly turned, as if he had imagined the words, and then stared in confusion at her oversized t-shirt and the nice but comfortable panties.

She held herself in place, feeling the sharp edge of vulnerability, as she waited for him to accept or reject her. Looking into his soulful brown eyes, she saw a man who had waited a long time for this. He wiggled his eyebrows and responded with an equally corny one.

"If you've got the money, honey, I've got the time."

He got up and put his hands on her waist, then massaged her lower back. Isabella's body suddenly awakened to feeling things, and his touch was lovely.

Sensing something different about this time, about Isabella, Alex pulled her in and kissed her with tenderness and passion. And she kissed him back, feeling her desire stir below as she welcomed her arousal back.

They silently went upstairs to the bedroom and took off their clothes. Isabella touched Alex's chest, breathed in his smell, and enjoyed the warmth of his skin.

I want more of this. Said the voice that had been talking to her since the end of the course. *More touching.*

Their sex was the same as the sex they'd always had. With one big difference. Isabella experienced sex with a new awareness. She was sort of running her fuck and marveled at how powerful it felt. Suddenly, a memory swooped in of Alex, interrupting her me-time bath, and that precious connection vanished. There was nothing she could do but press on and put her body into motion to awaken her responsive desire.

She saw Alex going in, making his play. He reached down for her clit while he thrust, but her clit was extra sensitive, and his enthusiastic touch made her clit want to retreat. She braced herself; her pleasure shutting down as she waited for the sex to be over.

But then Amy tagged in, saying, "Oh hell no. You deserve better. Tell him."

Isabella was beyond scared, didn't want to start a fight, wanted to please Jessica, and give her readers a happy ending.

But she needed to do this for herself.

With every ounce of courage she possessed, she mumbled.

"Uh, could you take it down a notch?"

Her body tensed, expecting the fallout, waiting for Alex to get upset.

But Alex shrugged it off, putting less pressure on her clit.

And it felt good.

With his thrusting, she felt her body move back into arousal and start the climb to orgasm. And even though there was a constant chatter in her head, she let herself go there and felt the sweet release as Alex came, too.

Afterward, they kissed like lovers and moved into their happy couple cuddling position.

Dozing off, Isabella's mommy's ears heard a bump of someone getting up. She jumped out of bed, kissed Alex, threw on her oversized t-shirt, nice but comfortable panties, and a stray pair of sweats with Play-Doh on the bum.

Later that evening, when the kids were in bed, Isabella sat at her desk and wrote her happy-ending column.

Isabella's Femme Column

What's In It For Me?

As HINDSIGHT IS 20/20, it was shockingly easy to let my sex life and relationship slide.

Like bystanders, my husband and I watched as we tumbled head-first into poor relationship habits. We then found ourselves wedged in a sex rut that we didn't know how to get unstuck from.

If I had known then what I know now, I would have thrown myself in front of that fast-moving, bad-sex-habits freight train. I would have made a million different choices. But I didn't. I'm here now, having to learn who I am and what I want from sex. This journey isn't for the faint of heart.

Yet, I discovered a bravery I never knew I had, thanks to the sex course and my supportive group.

Your burning question might be: With my hectic life, is sex worth the time and effort?

I learned the better question to ask is: Am I worth it?

That answer is more complicated and a work in progress. Most days, creating new sex habits means I try, fall, get back up, have to brush myself off, and try again. I'm working twice as hard to return my relationship to neutral, which is discouraging and energizing.

I'm doing this for me.

Little by little, I recognize that, yes, I'm worth feeling sexy and sexual. As I become more confident, I experience why it's worth putting in the time to help my relationship grow happier and healthier.

> It simplifies my life. When I'm content with myself and my relationship, everything else effortlessly falls into place.

I'm also leaning into the idea that my sex, my relationship, and my life will always be a little messy. Messy is where intimacy, vulnerability, and authenticity live. So bring on the mess!

On that fateful Betty Dodson night, I met a woman who was a seriously badass sexual goddess. All this effort is about coaxing her out and letting her freak flag fly.

> Can you imagine what my husband will say when I introduce her to him?! (Insert a wicked giggle.)

To help me with that, I'm going to the Taboo Sex Show and then taking the next 201 sex course.

Stay tuned, dear reader. Things are about to get interesting.

On This Week's Sex Menu

Class #5: I need to receive the pleasure I asked for.

Answer: Taking charge means I need to create a space and plan out sex. Counterintuitively, scheduling opens the door to my sexual freedom.

Problem: I can't force the outcome I want and expect. I need to respect my mind and body's slow pace.

Let's put my answer to the real-life test.

Sexual Power is in The Planning

I recently had sex. Instead of letting it be sex-on-repeat, I took charge, and it was equal parts scary and powerful. I used the dynamic duo of mindset and mise en place, and they're a game-changer ....

The Last Group Meeting ... Or Is It?

April 1

"Welcome."

The smell of expensive coffee filled Isabella's nose as she stood at the posh counter, and the good-looking, blonde, toothy barista asked for her order.

It had been two weeks since the sex course ended, and this time, *Femme* magazine wasn't paying. Her meager writer's wage, with the added pay bump, just bought a new washing machine, so she ordered a small black coffee.

Amy had called this meeting, and Jeanette secured seats on the tiny outdoor patio. Zipping up her cheap black puffer jacket, Isabella pushed her dark, curly hair out of her face and took the coffee outside.

It was a gorgeous April day, and she welcomed the freedom to be outside after a long, cold winter. The group, huddled in their winter jackets under a space heater, was deep in conversation and barely noticed Isabella sit down.

"Hey," Claire smiled up at Isabella. "It's good to see you."

She sipped her coffee and felt a cool air current fighting with the bright, warm sunshine. As much as Isabella didn't have the money for a babysitter, she had processed so much, had a lot to say, and no one to say it to. The only people who could understand her journey were the three women sitting there. Each of them helped Isabella on her journey. She admired Claire's just-do-it approach. Wild, colorful, and eclectic, Amy was everything Isabella could wish for in a sex-positive friend. Sophisticated Jeanette wasn't afraid to do the hard emotional work on herself.

"Exciting news!" Amy let her words hang in the air.

"Yes, that's why you called this meeting," Jeanette said, looking disheveled. Yes, she was still perfectly coiffed, but fuzzy around the edges. There were tiny frizzies on top of her hair, a scuff on her boot, and a scarf hanging limply around a classic, perfectly cut black wool jacket.

"Dr. Gwen came to my office," Amy went on excitedly. "I almost had a heart attack when she knocked on my door."

"Well, you are a professor." Claire reminded Amy.

Isabella would never understand why Amy was insecure, but she supposed everyone was insecure about something.

"Associate professor, anyway, she's teaching a level 201 in September and requested our group be guinea pigs." Amy made a giddy ta-da motion.

Isabella looked up at the cloudless, sunny blue sky, coming up with a polite but firm way to say no. The sex course had turned her life upside down, and she was still getting over a turbulent five weeks. Meeting deadlines. Meeting momlines. Meeting wifelines. There were so many lines that she never crossed. Although it had been exciting and she had learned a lot, it had also been a roller coaster ride of big highs and big lows. Her busy life needed stability. She couldn't think of any reason to get back on that roller coaster.

This doesn't have to be complicated. You and Alex want the same thing.

Isabella ignored the voice that had spoken to her since the last class.

"I don't want to be someone's guinea pig," Jeanette frowned.

"I thought you might say that," Amy said cheerfully. "We can agree that Dr. Gwen is amazing. Plus, we have five months to process the first class. And ..." A laugh burst out of her throat.

"Oh no, Amy, not one of your 'great ideas.'" Claire's lips thinned as she held her coffee mug to warm her long fingers. "Look, I enjoyed the class. I got a few nuggets. The looking at our vulva thing was interesting. But I'm trying to make partner. Partner, Amy. I cannot justify taking a second course."

"I thought you might say that too," Amy replied, looking slightly smug. "We only scratched the surface. Aren't you a little curious about the 201 course?"

Isabella knew the next course would write her columns for her, but she didn't have the emotional bandwidth to take it to the next level. She saw her sex life with a new mindset and a fresh set of eyes, which created a subtle shift in how she interacted with Alex. That was more than enough for now. She needed to wait and let everything sink in.

"Okay." All heads snapped in Jeanette's direction.

"Okay, what? Okay, you'll do it?" Amy asked.

"Yes, I will do it," Jeanette sniffed, sipping her mint tea.

"Excellent, that's one. Now, Claire, you're a master of scheduling." Amy leaned in and nudged Claire's shoulder. A dark cloud passed over Claire's face as Amy put the screws to her friend. "Come on. It will be fun."

"Maybe," Claire blew out a sigh, already caving. "You know I'll have to turn my life upside down to make this happen."

"Easy-peasy for you." Amy dodged the guilt Claire threw at her. "Okay, that's two. Isabella?"

All eyes turned to Isabella, and she didn't like the peer pressure, so she took her time.

"I enjoyed the first class, but I don't have the time. Sorry." She gave a what-can-you-do shrug. "I'm not like Claire. I'm not a master of scheduling, and it's tough with little kids to commit to something like this."

"I thought you might say that —" Amy started, but Jeanette interrupted.

"It is hard with little kids, but I need you to listen." Jeanette turned her body to Isabella, her intense gaze going straight into Isabella's soul. "Looking back, I wish I had taken this course. Everything in my life now would be less, um, complicated. Less ..." she searched for a word, put her head down, brought it back up, looked Isabella square in the eye, and said, "... dysfunctional."

Her soft words hit Isabella hard in the stomach. Jeanette and Isabella opened up about their marriages during the last group meeting. They both knew Isabella was hurtling down a sexless marriage path, and the further she went, the more complicated it would be to fix.

Isabella was stuck and cornered, and to get unstuck was a massive, uncomfortable inconvenience. But she was also clear that she never wanted to put up with the BS again. She didn't know how she would manage or endure another course, but she also never wanted to be where Jeanette sat now.

Her gut forced her to answer, "Okay."

Jeanette put her slender, manicured hand over Isabella's.

"For what it's worth, when you look back ten years from now, you'll be happy with this decision."

Isabella already regretted it, stressed out, and emailing the group that she had changed her mind.

"Good, then it's settled." Amy enthused. "I've already signed us up."

"Of course you did," Claire shook her head in mirth.

"To keep up the good momentum, let's meet bi-weekly." Amy jumped to the next topic. "There are two things I want to talk about at this meeting. First, I've decided to be celibate for a year. Second, the Taboo Sex Show is next month."

Isabella felt the pressure headache work up along the back of her neck. She didn't enjoy being pressured into taking the course, and she didn't like having to take it. *Femme* would happily pay for the tuition and babysitting; at least, that was one thing she didn't have to worry about.

As she looked at her group, she got a flash of what her sex life could look like ten years from now and felt an existential push to let go and take the plunge.

"What could go wrong?" Claire deadpanned, but with a shift in her seat and, perhaps, perspective, made plans for the Taboo Sex Show.

Isabella lifted her chin, tuning out Claire's words, letting the sun's warmth hit her face, and willed the spring air to help her feel like there could be new beginnings.

Discussion Questions

The Sex Course

About the Book

1. At the beginning of the story, each woman arrives at The Sex Course for different reasons. What initially motivates them to attend, and how do their expectations compare with what they experience?

2. The course quickly pushes the women outside their comfort zones. Why do you think the author uses discomfort and vulnerability as a central part of their growth?

3. Friendship becomes an unexpected outcome of the course. How does the group dynamic influence each woman's willingness to confront her beliefs about sex, intimacy, and relationships?

4. The novel explores the gap between what society says about female sexuality and what women actually experience. Which moments in the book highlight this disconnect most strongly?

5. Several scenes explore how performance — rather than authentic pleasure — shapes women's sexual experiences. Why do you think so many women in the story feel pressure to "perform" sexually?

6. The Betty Dodson evening is a pivotal moment in the book. Why do you think the group went along with this idea?

7. During the Betty Dodson workshop video and discussion, the women react very differently. Which reactions stood out to you the most, and why?

8. The scene raises the topic of masturbation and self-knowledge. Why is this portrayed as such a powerful turning point for the characters?

9. How does the Betty Dodson discussion challenge the women's previous ideas about orgasm, pleasure, and honesty in relationships?

10. Throughout the book, the women confront not only sexual issues but also emotional and relational ones. In your opinion, is The Sex Course more about sex or about self-discovery?

11. By the end of the novel, how has each woman's understanding of intimacy changed? Which transformation felt the most surprising or meaningful?

Character Questions

12. Isabella often reflects on her past confidence and how it shifted over time. What do you think caused her to lose that earlier sense of sexual empowerment, and what helps her begin to reclaim it?

13. Claire's storyline touches deeply on performance and honesty in relationships. What do you think holds her back the most, and what moment signals the beginning of her change?

14. Amy often brings humor and openness to group discussions. Do you see her as the most liberated character, or is there more complexity beneath the surface?

15. Jeanette's storyline quietly builds as she wrestles with whether to stay in an unhappy marriage or choose herself. What moment in the book best captures her turning point?

16. Dr. Gwen challenges the women in uncomfortable ways. Do you see her methods as empowering, confrontational, or both? Would you take a course like hers?

The Sex Homework

Find out what the women wrote in their homework

Want to peek inside the women's Sex Homework?

Download your **FREE copy of** *The Sex Homework* at **TrinaRead.com** and read the private assignments each woman writes after every class.

Follow the story even deeper and discover more freebies and **Dr. Trina's MasterClass** while you're there.

Unfiltered

Isabella's Sex Columns

Loved Isabella's sharp tongue and zero-filter takes in **The Taboo Show**? Now imagine her off the leash.

Grab your free copy of **Unfiltered: Isabella's Sex Columns** at here at **TrinaRead.com** and dive into twelve scandalously smart, laugh-out-loud columns straight from the pages of *Femme*. They're bold. They're brash. They'll make you text your best friend immediately.

While you're there, snag the groovy handouts and explore the free **You. Me. Bed. NOW!** masterclass. Because let's be honest—your bookshelf deserves a little more sexy.

Sex ed was never this fun. And Isabella? Well, she's just getting started.

*W*ish arousal felt easier and orgasms *felt stronger?*

Say goodbye to lackluster sensation and hello to cult-favorite stimulating products blended with premium hemp seed oil!

*H*igh On Love is an award-winning line of luxurious, botanical-based sexual wellness products designed to enhance pleasure and comfort for women.

Their bestselling Stimulating O Gel and Sensual Stimulating Oil are blended with premium hemp seed oil to heighten sensitivity, intensify orgasms, and reduce discomfort or dryness.

> Really beautiful packaging, high quality product, with a yummy scent. Perfect for an anniversary, Valentine's Day or special occasion. Worth the extra $. — *Courtney*

*R*eady to elevate your pleasure?

Shop High On Love and use coupon code **DRTRINAREAD** for *15%* off your entire order.

Scan the QR code or visit *trinaread.com/taboo*

SCAN & EXPLORE

If you purchase through this link or QR code, Dr. Trina receives a small commission at no extra cost to you. Thank you for accepting cookies, so the commission can be tracked.

Ready to turn *"same old"* into *"wait ... that was really hot. Let's do it again!"*

Stop guessing, make it easy with guided exploration that brings you closer!

Melba is a voice-guided intimacy app that turns connection into play.

Choose from dozens of immersive 15–30 minute experiences tailored to your mood, no scripts, no pressure, just you and your partner exploring together.

Best of all, try it for **FREE** for thirty days.

Over 1 million couples trust Melba to help them break the routine, deepen their bond, and unlock new pleasure.

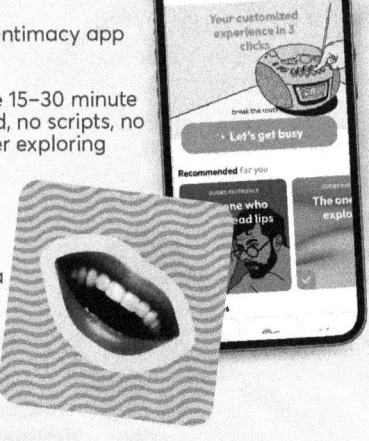

> After years together, we needed something to help us talk about what we actually wanted. Being guided freed us up in ways we didn't expect—it brought back the excitement and took the pressure off.
> — *Alex, 38*

Ready to explore?

Enjoy Melba free for **30 days** with code **DRREAD30**

Scan the QR code or visit ***trinaread.com/taboo***

SCAN & EXPLORE

If you purchase through this link or QR code, Dr. Trina receives a small commission at no extra cost to you. Thank you for accepting cookies, so the commission can be tracked.

*T*ired of your busy brain *killing the mood* *B*efore it even starts?

Say goodbye to feeling disconnected and hello to luxurious sensual products that bring you back to your body!

*E*xSens' line of body-safe, vegan line is designed by women, for women.

From their bestselling Hot Kiss Arousal Lip Gel and aromatherapy massage oils infused with real crystals, to warming oils, lubricants, and arousal gels, every product helps you move from your overthinking mind into being present in your body.

These aren't just products; they're tools for creating *"erotic threads"* which makes sex better, easier, and more frequent.

> " I wanted a sampler pack. Tried the strawberry warming oil and it was super flavorful and slippery—warmed up like a space heater! We had so much fun that we just laughed like crazy. All in all, it's great and I can't wait to try the rest of the flavors! — *Sarah Marie* "

*R*eady to bring sensuality back?

Explore the full ExSens line and use coupon code: **SENSUALITY** for *20%* off.

Scan the QR code or visit *trinaread.com/taboo*

If you purchase through this link or QR code, Dr. Trina receives a small commission at no extra cost to you. Thank you for accepting cookies, so the commission can be tracked.

*L*adies, do you struggle to communicate what feels good or discover what actually works *for your body?*

Say goodbye to guessing and hello to research-backed techniques from **20,000** women that's transforming **sex for over 1 million people!**

OMGYES is an

online research-based platform that reveals findings from the largest-ever study into women's pleasure (20,000+ women).

Through honest videos, clarifying animations, and interactive touchscreen simulations, **OMGYES** teaches specific techniques that help women discover new kinds of pleasure and help partners understand what actually feels good.

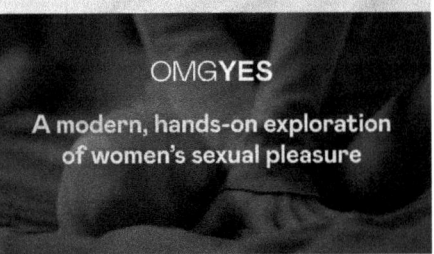

OMGYES

A modern, hands-on exploration of women's sexual pleasure

With over 1 million users worldwide, **OMGYES** explains:
- how female pleasure works
- how to communicate about it
- how to experience more satisfying, connected sex

> After watching the videos on Rhythm I just discovered an amazing sensitive spot that I had no clue existed. For the last 20 years I've only been able to cum with toys. Until today. I used OMGYES to figure out what I liked alone, and then how to ask for it. — *Rosa*

*R*eady to discover what 1 million people already know?

Explore **OMGYES** and transform your pleasure and intimacy.

Scan the QR code or visit *trinaread.com/taboo*

SCAN & EXPLORE

If you purchase through this link or QR code, Dr. Trina receives a small commission at no extra cost to you. Thank you for accepting cookies, so the commission can be tracked.

Ready to add some naughty adventure to *your love life?*

Say no to boring and yes to **blindfolds**, and **soft cuffs** that make experimenting sexy, simple, and seriously hot!

Sportsheets is the original beginner-friendly S&M gear.

Including their iconic Under the Bed® Restraint System and The Original Sportsheet®. Sportsheets is perfect for S&M-curious – it's safe and fun for couples at any experience level.

From soft blindfolds and adjustable cuffs to complete restraint systems that set up in minutes, every product is designed with one promise: *you're only as tied up as you want to be.*

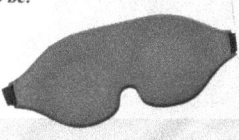

> " We started with the beginner's kit and haven't looked back. Everything is well-made, body-safe, and thoughtfully designed. It's clear this company understands what couples actually need. — *Alex, 44* "

Ready to explore?

Shop **Sportsheets** and use coupon code: **DrTrina2026** for *20%* off (excluding sale and promotional items).

Scan the QR code or visit *trinaread.com/taboo*

SCAN & EXPLORE

If you purchase through this link or QR code, Dr. Trina receives a small commission at no extra cost to you. Thank you for accepting cookies, so the commission can be tracked.

Just Because *It's Common*... *D*oesn't Mean *It's Normal*.

Leaking when you sneeze. Pain during sex. Feeling disconnected **"down there." "You were told it's normal"**. It's not.

Women have been taught the wrong solution. For decades, we've been told to squeeze harder with Kegels. But here's the truth most women never hear:

Tension is not strength. And most pelvic floors aren't weak, they're overworked, tight, and stuck.

That's where the *Cooch Ball* comes in.

The Cooch Ball is a simple, science-inspired pelvic floor fitness tool designed to help women release first, restoring circulation, nerve communication, and awareness to muscles that have simply forgotten how to do their job.

In just 3 minutes a day, fully clothed, women create the environment their pelvic floor needs to function again before rebuilding strength the right way with Pilates-based, pelvic-floor-centric movement.

> " Thank you Cooch Ball! The pressure I was feeling 'down there' is gone! I have noticed that I am able to feel more complete elimination when I do go so way less constipation and bloating. The best part - sex is enjoyable again for ME. I have the pelvic floor awareness to participate positively again! — *Tara M Jana* "

*T*he Cooch Ball has helped 100,000+ women reclaim their bodies without shame or suffering.

Explore Cooch Ball bundles for Intimacy, Perimenopause, Menopause, or whole-body pelvic health.

Scan the QR code or visit *trinaread.com/taboo*

SCAN & EXPLORE

If you purchase through this link or QR code, Dr. Trina receives a small commission at no extra cost to you. Thank you for accepting cookies, so the commission can be tracked.

Suffering from vaginal dryness, painful sex or recurring odor that even *your doctor can't fix?*
Say goodbye to band-aid drugs and hello to **NeuEve**—
the nutrient-based solution backed by science and safety!

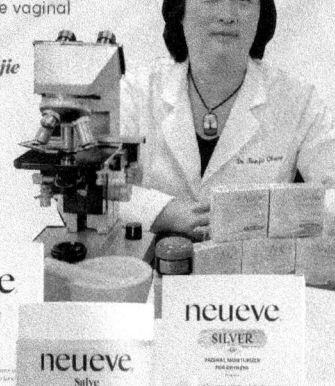

NeuEve is a line of all-natural, hormone-free vaginal health products.

Created by scientist and gynecologist **Dr. Renjie Chang** to address vaginal dryness, painful sex, and odor without the cancer risks of estrogen or the recurrence problems of antibiotics.

NeuEve has helped over 250,000 women, including those with severe vaginal atrophy. With products for dryness, BV, yeast infections, and more complex conditions like vulvodynia and vaginismus.

NeuEve offers the safest and most effective solutions for women's intimate health concerns.

Started at age 60. Before NeuEve we went through years of menopause unable to have sex. Not an easy time. Now we are happy. Dryness gone, the feeling is back. Worth the cost. — *Coleen M., 63*

Ready for real relief?

Visit **NeuEve** using
https://www.neueve.com/TRINA and receive
15% off your first purchase.

Scan the QR code or visit *trinaread.com/taboo*

SCAN & EXPLORE

If you purchase through this link or QR code, Dr. Trina receives a small commission at no extra cost to you. Thank you for accepting cookies, so the commission can be tracked.

*T*ired of feeling like you're missing the secret *playbook to great sex?*

Say goodbye to trial-and-error fumbling and hello to **Caitlin V's** proven system that teaches men how to truly satisfy their partners—and themselves!

*C*aitlin V is a sex expert for men who want to become confident, skilled, connected lovers.

Caitlin's programs teach skills most men never learn.

With courses like *Legendary Lover, Come When You Want, Make Her Squirt,* and *Epic Relationship*, men gain practical, step-by-step training that builds both technique and sexual confidence.

Give her the kind of pleasure she craves while deepening intimacy and connection

" Thanks to your guidance, I have been able to raise the bar and truly amaze my wife! I thought that the early days of our relationship was as good as it was going to get. Then your videos caught my attention and I couldn't help but watch, listen, and learn. Thank you so much! — *Verified User* "

*R*eady to level up?

Explore **Caitlin V's** courses and become the confident, skilled lover you've always wanted to be.

Scan the QR code or visit *trinaread.com/taboo*

SCAN & EXPLORE

If you purchase through this link or QR code, Dr. Trina receives a small commission at no extra cost to you. Thank you for accepting cookies, so the commission can be tracked.

Your Next Chapter

IF THIS BOOK STIRRED something in you — curiosity, courage, discomfort, longing — pause for a moment. That stirring matters.

> Desire doesn't expand all at once. It grows through reflection, conversation, and small brave choices.

Explore

This book is part of a larger world. Each offers education without pressure. Take what resonates. Leave what doesn't.
- The Pursuit of Pleasure Podcast
- The Sensational Sex Podcast
- Sex'Cess Substack
- YouTube channel discussions
- Free handouts like *5 Pleasure Secrets of Satisfied Couples*

You can discover more fiction, essays, podcasts, and free intimacy resources at TrinaRead.com.

Talk

Bring this book to your book club. Ask your partner what surprised them. Say one thing out loud that you've been keeping quiet.

Reflect

Revisit the passages that made you feel seen.
- *Unfiltered* — Isabella's 12 sex columns
- *The Sex Homework* — the actual exercises written by the four women
- The audiobook editions for a different, more intimate experience. Sometimes hearing the words lands differently than reading them.

Go Deeper

If you're ready for structured support, explore You. Me. Bed. NOW! — a guided program designed for couples who want more than "fine."
- *You. Me. Bed. NOW!* free masterclass
- The *You. Me. Bed. NOW!* free workbook

Stay Connected

Join Dr. Trina's Sex'Cess Newsletter and community for ongoing conversations and resources. Find out more at TrinaRead.com and on social @DrTrinaRead.

You don't need to become someone else to live a first-class, intimate life. You only need permission to become more honest.

This is the beginning of your story.

Acknowledgments

If you like this book, please thank my husband, Dennis. The only way I could spend three-plus years writing (mainly during the COVID pandemic) was by him supporting me and this project. Which is the true test of love. Thank you, Dennis, for always believing in me, showing up, having my back, and hanging on during the tough times. If I had to choose again, every time, it would always be you.

I was on the fence about being a mom, and it was a roller coaster ride going from completely self-absorbed to (mostly) selfless. Andrew and Evan, you are my heart, my everything. You are the soft, mushy spot on my thick coat of armor. You are hands down the best thing I've ever done, and I am so proud to be your mom.

Melanie McKay, I was on the verge of leaving this career when you asked me to speak at your Camp Hoo-Ha. I was reminded that women crave and need this knowledge. This book is because of Camp Hoo-Ha.

Serendipitously, when I did the Camp Hoo-Ha events, I listened to Denise Duffield-Thomas's book *Get Rich, Lucky Bitch*. I was leaving this career because I could not make money even though I did everything right. Denise, you gave me a new money mindset and then said, "This formula works for everything." *You. Me. Bed. NOW!* formula was born.

During the same time, at my lowest, I went for breakfast with my girlfriends, dreading the "What are you up to?" question because I was spinning on no axis. When the question came up, I blurted, "I'm writing a book." I knew it was the truth but was too scared to admit it. Thank you, Jenny Holicza and Andrina Tweit, for being a safe space.

Steve Cooper, you are the best kind of human. When I decided to contribute to a new website, HitchedMag.com, it gave me a cheerleader in my corner every step of the way. Thanks for being the first editor on this project. Danielle Leclair, I needed someone to believe in this book as much as me, and you showed up. You did the heavy-lifting editing and helped wrestle it into shape. For my editorial team, Bobbi Beatty, Aimee Walker, and Sophia Dembling, thank you for working hard to make this a great book.

Oprah has been a guiding light and a significant influence on this book. It made perfect sense that the seasoned, no-nonsense sex professor, Dr Gwen, is actually Oprah.

My hero, Marian Keyes, whose writing taught me the importance of finding the funny in our darkest moments. I learned (and borrowed) so much from Liane Moriarty's writing style.

My family would never forgive me if I didn't thank our dog, Max. Thank you, Mr. Moo, for forcing me out in -30-degree weather for walks. You've brought this family so much love and joy.

> Dr. Trina is your best, funniest friend telling a story that's bracingly honest, sexy, heartbreaking, fearless, and provocative. It's the conversations you're too afraid to have, but need to hear.

The Sex Course
Award-Winning Upmarket & Book Club Fiction

Four very different women take a sex course ... curious, cautious, and completely unprepared for how it upends their worlds.

The Sex Course helps women understand her sexuality in a cheeky, irreverent, non-self-help'y way. It's sex ed mixed with hilarious fiction.

The Taboo Show
The highly anticipated sequel

The four women walk into the *Taboo Sex Show* ... and walk out forever changed.

"Yes, *The Taboo Show* is hilarious, but each character's sexual challenges are real, serious, and complex. Dr. Trina brings big depth to her writing, and I was rooting for the four characters."

You. Me. Bed. NOW!
The award-winning workbook that turns "we should talk about this" into actual, satisfying sex.

This is a playful, no-fluff, five-step program designed to help women stop circling the problem — and start enjoying sex!

*F*ind out more about these books and check out the **FREE** resources, handouts and masterclasses at **TrinaRead.com**

Dr. Trina Read

Canadian Sexologist, award-winning and best-selling author Dr. Trina Read has a big life mission: To help women in long-term relationships thrive ... after the honeymoon stage is over.

She lives in Calgary, Alberta, Canada, with her long-suffering husband, who never wanted his sex life discussed with millions of strangers. She is the proud mama of two brilliant but stinky teenage boys. The only guy in the house who listens to her is (good boy) Max, the dog.

Dr. Trina does her best to walk her talk. She's been (mostly) happily married and sexually engaged to her patient husband of over twenty-three years.

Find out more and join the Sex'cess Newsletter at TrinaRead.com.

www.ingramcontent.com/pod-product-compliance
Lightning Source LLC
Chambersburg PA
CBHW070958160426
43193CB00012B/1832